454

Oaten Reeds and Trumpets

Oaten Reeds
and Trumpets

Pastoral and Epic in Virgil, Spenser, and Milton

D.M. Rosenberg

Lewisburg
Bucknell University Press

London and Toronto: Associated University Presses

© 1981 by Associated University Presses, Inc.

Associated University Presses, Inc.
4 Cornwall Drive
East Brunswick, New Jersey 08816

Associated University Presses Ltd.
69 Fleet Street
London EC4Y 1EU, England

Associated University Presses
Toronto, Ontario, Canada M5E 1A7

Library of Congress Cataloging in Publication Data

Rosenberg, Donald M 1934—
    Oaten reeds and trumpets.

    Bibliography: p.
    Includes index.
    1. English poetry——Early modern, 1500-1700——History
and criticism. 2. Pastoral poetry——History and criticism. 3. Epic poetry——History and criticism. 4. Milton, John, 1608-1674——Criticism and interpretation.
5. Spenser, Edmund, 1552?——1599——Criticism and interpretation. 6. Vergilius Maro, Publius——Criticism and
interpretation. I. Title.
PR408.P3R67 1980   809.1′3   80-17974
ISBN 0-8387-5002-8

Printed in the United States of America

for Grush

Lo! I the man, whose Muse whylome did maske,
As time her taught, in lowly shepards weeds.
Am now enforst, a farre unfitter taske,
For trumpets sterne to chaunge mine oaten reeds.

The Faerie Queene, Book I

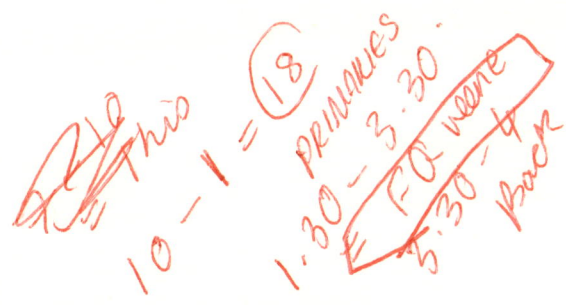

Contents

Acknowledgments

I am grateful to Michigan State University for the sabbatical leave and research grant that made it possible to write this book.

I should like to express my appreciation to William Madsen, who first introduced me to the study of Milton's poetry.

I am also indebted to the students, friends, and colleagues who have offered valuable suggestions, criticism, and encouragement: Alan DiPerna and Michael Wilson, James Epperson, James Hill, Jay Ludwig, Douglas Peterson, Jack Yunck, and Alan Hollingsworth. Finally, I wish to thank Mrs. Betty Uphaus for her patience in typing the manuscript.

East Lansing, Michigan
March 1979

D. M. Rosenberg

Introduction

The purpose of this book is to examine the generic and thematic development of the pastoral and epic as expressed in the works of Virgil, Spenser, and Milton. Although there have been several studies, notably by Smith, Hamilton, Cheney, and Knott, that consider the relationship between the two genres, this work provides a thorough study of their essential interdependence, and traces the evolution of the heroic toward increasing accommodation of the pastoral.

The book begins with Virgil and proceeds historically, examining the pastoral poems and then the epic for each poet in turn. The Virgil chapter defines the nature of the reciprocity between pastoral and heroic ideals, demonstrating that Virgil's pastoral fiction operates as a measure for the experiential world, that the pastoral world cannot be self-sufficient because it is always vulnerable to destruction from without and within, and finally, that epic action depends upon pastoral ideals to give it meaning and direction. The discussion of the *Eclogues* emphasizes the ways in which Virgil's thematic preoccupations with various challenges to the Arcadian ideal broaden the range of the pastoral, taking the genre through several permutations, and ultimately requiring that it be abandoned for a more complex form. The *Georgics* is included because it functions as the bridge between Virgil's pastoral and epic, providing him the opportunity to experiment with heroic themes and conventions, and to cope more fully with the contingencies of mutability and history. The *Aeneid* discussion introduces ideas that are developed throughout the book: the redefinition of heroism and the use of pastoral enclaves within the heroic poem to illuminate and guide the hero's actions. The analysis gives emphasis to the inwardness of the quest of Aeneas, who is not a purely Homeric military hero, but a contemplative man sustained by pastoral ideals.

The Spenser chapters take into account the Christianization of both genres, with the consequent outward movement of the pastoral toward the moral world, and the movement of the epic toward greater inwardness. *The Shepheardes Calender* is seen as the English manifestation of the change in the pastoral from a predominantly lyrical mode to one that also encompasses complex social and religious issues through satire, didacticism, and allegory. *The Faerie Queene* chapter focuses on pastoral episodes in each book, because it is through the pastoral that Spenser clarifies the meaning of the virtue that each Christian knight represents in the allegory and protects by his heroic deeds.

The Milton section, which constitutes the second half of the book, demonstrates that the mutual inclusion of the genres reaches its culmination in Milton, in that he writes pastoral poems that are more heroic than those of his predecessors, and produces an epic in which the pastoral becomes the central setting, theme, and ideal. The purpose of the chapter dealing with Milton's pastoral poetry is to describe the ways in which Milton exposes the illusions inherent in pastoral conventions in order to undermine pagan assumptions and introduce moral heroism, thus creating Christian pastoral values. Essential to the interpretation of *Paradise Lost* is the argument that Milton condemns military heroism, as represented by Satan, and replaces it with the heroism of pastoral humility and meekness, as represented by Christ and the regenerate Adam. For Adam the pastoral becomes a spiritual paradise within, continually renewing his power to act as a just man in the fallen world; in the figure of Christ, the Good Shepherd and Hero-Redeemer, pastoral and epic ideals finally merge. Although there are visions of celestial paradise in the heroic poems of Virgil and Spenser, in Milton's epic the vision of an eternal and perfect pastoral operates as the defining value of the whole poem.

This study not only provides a new basis for understanding the poetry of Virgil, Spenser, and Milton, and the reciprocal development of pastoral and epic, but also establishes principles for interpreting the works of other major poets who set out to resolve the tensions between imagination and reality, contemplation and action, poetry and prophecy.

1

Virgil

BECAUSE Virgil progressed in his poetic career from the pastoral *Eclogues* and *Georgics* to the epic *Aeneid,* he created a model for aspiring poets of the Renaissance. This Virgilian paradigm provided a generic scale for the poet to ascend, challenging him to imitate a literary kind at each step. He could advance in a logical way from youthful apprenticeship in the pastoral toward the heroic poem in his maturity, and discover through the Virgilian model a kind of plot for his own literary career that imposed upon his life the formal design of art. Such a formal and heuristic pattern enabled the poet to be more conscious and deliberate in discovering his individual talent through the growth of his mind as he followed the steps of a well-established tradition.

Virgil himself deliberately imitated Theocritus's *Idylls.* By serving as a kind of humble apprentice to his precursor, the youthful Virgil could learn his craft through imitation. When he based his *Eclogues* on the *Idylls* he followed the parent-form with care. There are obvious borrowings and echoes throughout the *Eclogues*; indeed, Virgil calls the reader's attention to his imitation by acknowledging it in the poems. But he demonstrates that he is also capable of innovative transformations of Theocritean conventions and themes. Although he retained the same thematic emphases, on love, death, and poetry, Virgil created a different kind of artistic unity by integrating several idylls into each eclogue. Something new and singular emerged from these original combinations. Creatively imitating the *Idylls,* Virgil showed respect to his predecessor, placed himself in the stream of world poetry by confronting a traditional model, and tested his own abilities. The Theocritean pastoral provided for Virgil's initiation and self-discovery as a poet. When Virgil in turn became the model for others, particularly Spenser and Milton, they began with the *Eclogues,* and the tradition that grew out of them, and by incorporating and converting elements within the form, contributed to both pastoral poetry and the collective poetic imagination.

Pastoral gains the imaginative power that it attracts. It enables the beginning poet to assimilate the formal principles of decorum and to add to the tradition through the uniqueness of his own poetic works. Pastoral poems are made of other pastoral poems. Beginning with Virgil's resourceful individualizing of Theocritus's parent form, we have a principle of continuity, shared meanings, and a poetic genre which, though it is highly conventionalized, permits and demands individual talent. Arcadia constitues a community of poets from Theocritus and Virgil, extending through the Renaissance and beyond, engaging in a dialectical process within the tradition with which they had identified themselves.

Although Theocritus is considered the first pastoral poet, the *Eclogues* of Virgil is the original source of Arcadia as the ideal landscape of the poet's imagination. Arcadia was in fact a region of Greece, but the Roman Virgil adopted this land of Pan as his fictive world and transformed it so that it became a continued metaphor for the poetic consciousness. Arcadia has a subjective symbolic landscape that combines nature's spontaneity with the sophisticated design of art. Virgil, like the pastoral poets who followed him, was able to explore his own mind through the fiction he created. If he could think of the shepherd as poet, then he could regard himself as a shepherd, and participate in his imagined pastoral landscape while creating it.

This fiction allowed him a retreat from the crises of practical affairs so that he could, through metaphor, symbol, and myth, create and contemplate a paradise of poetry. In the golden world of the pastoral, the life of the shepherd reveals the poet's contemplative and recreative ideals. The ideal of the good life is *otium*, a sense of well-being and self-sufficiency[1] that allows him to woo his pastoral Muse in the creation of art. As readers, we see the creation of music and poetry in a world of freedom. The leisurely shepherds, unconstrained by the disruptions of care and strife, play their songs, participate in singing matches, and carve verses on the bark of young trees. The avena and calamus, pastoral symbols of the poetic craft, are the pipe and pen. Twining a basket is a pastoral metaphor for the weaving of verses. Cups, with their decorative acanthus and figure of Orpheus, are symbols of the shepherd's poetic world.

The natural landscape of pastoral poetry is presented as objectively real but at the same time it functions subjectively. Nature in the golden world is restored nature created by art. While the objective pastoral setting is important in our understanding of pastoral imagery, the idealization and abstraction of nature are crucial in seeing how the poet strives to bring the human mind and nature into harmony.

In the Virgilian landscape, the nymphs and Muses, Pan and Orpheus embody the idyllic life of Arcadian poetry. Pan, the woodland spirit who incarnates the union of man and beast, communicates the music of nature that brings together poet and landscape. Orpheus, the prototype of pastoral singers, has the power to control nature through his enthralling song. Whereas Pan represents the elemental forces within nature, Orpheus symbolizes both inspiration and civilization. The pastoral poet imitates Pan's pipes and sees himself in a pastoral succession descending from Orpheus.

The poet bestows the human principle of order upon nature, and sees in it a reciprocity and benevolent sympathy with man. That the woods and groves echo the shepherd's song, and mountains and rocks weep for his loss is mere poetic feigning, a pathetic fallacy that has reality only in a golden world. Artificiality, then, is a predominant element in the form. Pastoral poets, as Peter V. Marinelli points out, have used art to pretend that nature is innocent, and have made art look like nature.[2]

The creator of the golden world was, of course, hardly a humble shepherd, but a sophisticated Roman living in an iron age of civil wars and social upheaval. Just as the Alexandrian court poet Theocritus had created an innocent bucolic fiction from the ironic perspective of urbane sophistication, so Virgil was aware of the discrepancies between simple, innocent Arcadia and complex, worldly Rome. As a poet who tried to discover the relationship between art and life, he saw the necessity of poetry for interpreting life.

While it may first appear that the Virgilian eclogue is an exercise in escape and nostalgia for the epicurean life of *otium*, it is primarily a vehicle by which the poet critically explores the relationship between the world of poetry and the empirical world. By creating an alternative world of the imagination, Virgil gained a persepctive from which he explored the values and attitudes of the real world. The pastoral fiction is used, then, as a touchstone by which one can test the raw material of reality. At the same time, however, the real world measures the effectiveness or adequacy of the fiction, and poetry generally, as a genuine criterion for evaluating human experience.

The *Eclogues*

Significantly, Virgil introduces his reader to the pastoral world through an eclogue that deals with the dispossession of that world. That is, the poet makes us aware from the very first that Arcadia, in spite of its poetry and peace, is a precarious state and in the process of dissolution. This first *Eclogue,* and the ninth, dramatize the theme of dispossession and show the fragility of pastoral *otium* when it is confronted by a world in which violence, corruption, and injustice exist. If pastoral poetry presupposes and expresses a retreat of the imagination from the experiential world outside its perimeters, then retreat risks indifference or sentimentality when it cannot resolve the dualities of art and life. In those eclogues concerned with love and death (2, 8, and 5), however, Virgil progressively includes the complications and disasters of man's life so that these elements resisting pastoral *otium* are incorporated and become the facts against which the meaning of poetry defines itself. The fourth, or golden age, *Eclogue* at first glance seems to violate the accepted norm, but because Virgil had made such a radical effort to adopt the visionary, historical theme into the pastoral framework, the result is a further enlargement of pastoral poetry. The seventh, third, and sixth *Eclogues* deal with the making of poetry itself, and how the activity of poetic creation, while exemplifying the freedom and play of Arcadia, also shows the circumscription of conventional pastoral song. The concluding eclogue brings together many of the themes of the preceding poems in a farewell to the pastoral. A theme that is interwoven throughout the *Eclogues* is the poet's criticism of the pastoral and his expressed need to abandon the confined world of Arcadia in order to follow the higher aspirations of the heroic poem, which both confronts the experiential world of history and inspires the nation to virtuous action. We have through the series of eclogues, then, a gradually developed and enriched revelation of the meaning of pastoral poetry.

When the resisting claims of actuality obtrude in the imaginative world of Arcadia, tensions arise because the problems of real life assert their arbitrariness and cannot be resolved by poetry.[3] The first *Eclogue* dramatizes these tensions as the outside world threatens and invades the poet's consciousness. Meliboeus meets Tityrus, the shepherd-poet, and tells him that the land on which his humble cottage stands has been confiscated by godless and barbaric soldiers. Meliboeus asks:

> impius haec tam culta novalia miles habebit
> barbarus has segetes.
>
> (70-71)

> (Is a godless soldier to hold these well-tilled fallows? a barbarian these crops?)[4]

He must leave his country and home, and go into exile. Now an outcast, Meliboeus views the aged Tityrus at ease lying under his spreading beech, teaching the woods to reecho his song about fair Amaryllis. Everything here in this pastoral world seems poignantly beautiful to the dispossessed Meliboeus because he perceives it through his sense of loss. Tityrus, on the other hand, may remain on his land and continue to be free from the coercions of the outside world. He is free to keep his pastoral *otium*, however, because he has been outside in the nonpastoral world and has been protected by "deus nobis," a young prince of Rome. His pastoral freedom, then, is indebted to the world outside, just as helpless Meliboeus's exile has been imposed from the outside. Meliboeus is aware of the turmoil outside the confines of the pastoral world,

> undique totis
> usque adeo turbatur agris
>
> (11-12)

> (such unrest is there on all sides of the land)

jeopardizing what is within it. While his world falls apart, even nature is no longer protective but shares the brutality of men. His suffering is aggravated when his goat drops and loses her twin kids on the naked flint.

Because Tityrus has not lost his *libertas,* he cannot empathize with Meliboeus's suffering. We know that when Meliboeus leaves the ideal, pastoral world for remote and barbaric lands, Tityrus, the *fortunate senex*, will continue to woo his woodland Muse on the slender reed. The question implicitly raised, however, is whether the protected Tityrus can exemplify the ideal poet if his private *otium* is based on a world that is unjust and unstable. Tityrus offers Meliboeus a night at his home before he starts a journey of despair. That final night in a world of private contentment suggests the precariousness and fragility of the pastoral myth because we see that it is in fact dependent on the outside world. The pervading atmosphere in this poem, as in many of Virgil's *Eclogues,* is melancholy because Meliboeus sees the beauty of his home but the longer shadows of the evening remind him, as the poem ends, that he must leave it.

The ninth *Eclogue* may be seen as a companion piece of the first because it completes the theme of dispossession, and develops the contrast between city and country, which is one of the distinctive elements in all pastoral poetry. This social contrast is based on the Art-Nature antithesis, but it is not so simple to align Art-City and Nature-Country as it first appears. In the country, the shepherds and their flocks have been made gentle by the arts of agriculture and poetry, and the community of shepherd-poets is characterized by humility and tender feeling. While the city is man-made, it symbolizes in these eclogues the world of hostile, ruthless forces that seek to destroy harmony and peace. Out of civilization emerge soldiers and officials who commandeer land and homes in the name of the authority residing in Rome.

Moeris is seen at the beginning of the ninth *Eclogue* leading his kids to a master who has confiscated his little farm. He and Lycidas feel impotent to survive before the encroaching power of the outside world. While the gifted fellow shepherd, Menalcas, could gain favor from that world through his extraordinary poetic skill, they acknowledge the fact that "amid the weapons of war" their own songs "avail as much as. . . . the doves of Chaonia when the eagle comes." Their situation is pathetic because their singing, which should be natural and spontaneous, is now strained. They yearn to sing as well as Menalcas because their fields and flocks literally depend on their skill. Lycidas recognizes that he cackles "as a goose among melodious swans," and Moeris admits that he has forgotten all his songs, and superstitiously believes his failure of voice to be the consequence of being seen by a wolf. Their naiveté, lack of talent, and hopelessness are presented in a humorous and pathetic way, but the pressure of a growing empire creates a bitterness in their world, and the desperation and dependence of the two shepherds exemplify the ineffectiveness of ordinary pastoral norms in coping with the contingencies of history and politics. The irony of their situation is that they, unlike Menalcas, do not have enough to maintain secure, self-sufficient lives.

Like the first and ninth eclogues, *Eclogue* 2 develops the city-country relationship, and like them, it shows the malign influence of the city, or outside world, on Arcadia. The shepherd Corydon has lost his beloved, the fair Alexis, to a wealthy suitor in the city. The unrequited passion of his love-complaint is reminiscent of Polyphemus's in the eleventh *Idyll* of Theocritus, for Corydon, too, is slightly comical and touching in his awkward eagerness. Because he feels scorned,

Corydon compulsively contrasts the simplicity and humility of his bucolic life with the advantages of the city. Yet his view of the pastoral gifts he would bestow upon Alexis reveals his own ambivalence about pastoral life; he recognizes on one hand that his world of "sordida rura / atque humilis habitare casas" (rude fields and lowly cots) cannot compete with sophisticated urban pleasures, but on the other hand he can see the emotional and aesthetic value of the "quinces, pale with tender down, and chestnuts" and "waxen plums" he gathers for his beloved. Moreover, it is the singing of poetry in Arcadia, rivaling the music of mythical Pan, that he perceives as most attractive. But finally, the once ardent Corydon comes to the unhappy realization that pastoral life is insufficient to attract Alexis, and that his passion was a "dementia" that had gripped him. He becomes preoccupied with the world that could destroy the fragility of pastoral peace and, more important, with the passage of time, which casts an ominous shadow over what he had wished to believe a timeless idyll of love and beauty. As in the first *Eclogue,* this poem concludes with the lengthening shadows of evening and with them a sense of imminent finality. The scorching heat and burning sun, which at the beginning of the poem suggested Corydon's passion, are no longer present, and in the end he feels only the futility of his desire and a final weariness.

It is clear from Corydon's experience that not all the threats to pastoral peace and harmony come from without; within Arcadia are forces inimical to *otium.* The elemental power of love, because of its irrational nature, resists the tranquillity necessary for a life of contemplation. The irrational passions of love disturb, and conflict with, the kind of harmony the shepherd needs if he is to pursue his sylvan Muse.[5] What we find in the eclogues that treat of love is the tendency to dramatize the conflict, and then to accommodate this emotion to the pastoral ideal.

Eclogue 8 is also a lament of unrequited love. Damon's lonely song of loss and pain protests the marriage of Mopsus, the singer's rival, and Nysa. The landscape of this eclogue, as in *Eclogue* 2, becomes a symbolic setting for the singer's state of consciousness. While Corydon's helplessness evokes the predatory wolf and the setting sun, Damon's more turbulent suffering turns the normal order of the pastoral world topsy-turvy:

> nunc et ovis ultro fugiat lupus, aurea durae
> mala ferant quercus, narcisso floreat alnus,
> pinguia corticibus audent electra myricae
> certent et cycnis ululae.
>
> (52-55)

> (Now let the wolf even flee before the sheep, let rugged oaks bear golden apples, let tamarisks distil rich amber from their bark, let owls, too, vie with swans.)

These *adynata*, unnatural reversals, reflect Damon's subjective sorrow, as does the "towering mountain crag" from which he threatens to "plunge into the waves."

Although the second and eighth *Eclogues* are poems about the tyranny of love that has the power to destroy the possibility of pastoral order, Virgil accommodates the emotions of frustrated, unrequited love to his sympathetic understanding and lyrical rendering of them. Through artistic detachment and the impersonal use of formal beauty, he objectifies feeling without diminishing its immediacy. Emotional power proceeds from his formal realization of highly personal elements. Before these poems subside to their carefully modulated conclusions, the poet has integrated the irrational passions of his characters into a controlled work of art. By momentarily relieving *otium* of its primacy, and allowing the passions of real life to be expressed with a lyricism and delicacy of feeling that do not ultimately violate the harmony of the pastoral, he enlarges and enriches his poetic world.

The mutability of the experiential world, through its assertions of arbitrary change, challenges the premise of timeless tranquillity in pastoral poetry. The vicissitudes of love exemplify this mutability, but perhaps it is the subject of death that best explores and tests the validity of the pastoral. By accommodating that force antithetical to the stable, permanent *locus amoenus*, Virgil creates a larger synthesis that includes oppositions, complications, and catastrophes.

Panofsky's seminal study[6] on the elegiac strain in representations of Arcadia shows how death intrudes upon the pastoral landscape: "Et in Arcadia Ego" (Even in Arcadia, I [Death] hold sway). In Virgil's fifth *Eclogue* the haunting image of Daphnis's tomb evokes this triumph of death even in Arcadia. The poem explores the relationship between the arbitrary fact of death in the universe and man's poetic consciousness. That this eclogue takes the form of a singing contest emphasizes the importance of poetry in trying to come to terms with death.

Virgil uses the two singers, Mopsus and Menalcas, to express contrasting responses to death, one lamentation and the other joy. In the first song, Mopsus bewails the "cruel" death of Daphnis, and he is preoccupied with the idea of loss and death in nature. While nature mourns the demise of Daphnis, it seems to him that the powers of beauty, creativity, and generation have gone with him, as "luckless darnell springs up and barren oat-straws. Instead of the soft violet, instead of the gleaming narcissus, the thistle springs up and the sharp-spiked thorn." The garden of Arcadia has become a weedy wasteland because the shepherd who embodied all the ideals of the pastoral world is dead. There is no hope for continuity in Mopsus's lugubrious dirge.

Menalcas tells the grieving Mopsus, however, that his song will "exalt . . . Daphnis to the stars." Subsuming the themes of Mopsus's elegy—which are nature, mortality, and death, Menalcas takes the role of poet-priest and elevates Daphnis to Olympus. After a brief revelation of heaven's threshold, a higher paradise that Arcadia foreshadows, Menalcas's song returns to the pastoral landscape. In his apotheosis of the shepherd-poet Daphnis, a humanized and deified nature celebrates joyfully:

> ergo alacris silvas et cetera rura voluptas
> Panaque pastoresque tenet Dryadasque puellas.
>
> (58-59)

> (Therefore frolic glee seizes the woods and all the countryside, and Pan, and the shepherds, and the Dryad maids.)

All nature enjoys a millennial peace as the predatory wolf gives up his cunning hunt for flocks and stags. The very woods, rocks, and groves ring out that Daphnis has become a god, and Menalcas himself joins the pastoral festivities. What had been a dirge becomes a triumph over mortality. Mopsus, who had been a disciple of Daphnis, is told that poetry does not die, and that Daphnis, the spirit of poetry, has been exalted to heaven through the newly created poetry of Menalcas. As Menalcas gives him the frail reed, Mopsus learns about the power of poetry, and in return he gives his friend and new teacher a shepherd's crook.

In the exaltation of Daphnis, Menalcas's song transforms death. His song complements the first song, and at the same time implicitly retracts the view of nature and death that Mopsus had expressed. The dirge and the apotheosis function as a pastoral debate, a dialectical process in which the reader follows the progressive development of thought from a meditation on nature's mortality, to joy in a restored nature and resurrected spirit.

The fourth or golden age *Eclogue*, which precedes the apotheosis of Daphnis, shares its religious concerns and ecstatic tone. It provides us with a vision of an ideal and universal Arcadia. This Arcadia is more like a celestial paradise than a place endangered by unrequited passion and death.

The dynamics of Virgil's attempt to reconcile the conflicting worlds of poetry and history, contemplation and action, pastoral and epic, enable him to reach beyond the limitations of the poetic idyll. More than any of the other eclogues, this one strikes an epic note. The praise of heroes and epic quests distinguish it markedly from the typical concerns of the pastoral mode. Pastoral Muse and political authority are not to be separated as they are in the first and ninth *Eclogues*. The realm of political action, which seemed alien and even hostile to pastoral *otium*, is to be reconciled with it.

Virgil's stance itself, his tone in "paulo maiora canumus" (let us sing a somewhat loftier strain), expresses his confidence that he will surpass Theocritus. His declaration dramatizes the shepherd-poet's idea of himself as inspired prophet and hero:

non me carminibus vincet nec Thracius Orpheus . . .
Pan etiam, Arcadia mecum si iudice certet,
Pan etiam Arcadia dicat se iudice victum.

(55, 58-59)

(Not Thracian Orpheus . . . will vanquish me in song . . . .
Even Pan, were he to contend with me and Arcady be judge,
even Pan, with Arcady for judge, would own himself defeated).

Virgil's level of diction suggests that he will not be bound by humility of manner since the grandeur of his subject, the pro- phecy of a divine child as king and the perfection of man and nature, demand his high, vatic expression. The language of prophecy must break out of his characteristic pastoral style as he broadens the range of the pastoral to embrace the oracular and heroic.

The baby boy of an actual, living person, the consul Pollio, will bring about universal peace. Accordingly, Virgil must ex- plore the nature of time, because in historical time there will be a return to the virtues of justice and peace so that the pre- sent iron age will be transformed and a golden age of im- mutable harmony be restored. In order to return to the original Golden Age of Virgo and Astraea, Virgil must simultaneously retrace history and move forward in time, to a second Argonautic expedition and another Trojan War. The return of the ideal *otium* of Arcadia to the whole world is brought about through heroic action.

The golden age is projected into the past and the future, but it is also very much like the idealized world of the pastoral. For all the movement backward and forward in time, and despite his recognition of the need for heroic action, Virgil did not leave Arcadia. What he envisions is not a political utopia, nor a great capital city, but a pastoral scene where

nec varios discet mentiri lana colores,
ipse sed in pratis aries iam suave rubenti
murice, iam croceo mutabit vellera luto:
sponte sua sandyx pascentis vestiet agnos.

(42-45)

(Wool shall learn no more to counterfeit varied hues, but of himself the ram in the meadows shall change his fleece, now to sweetly blushing purple, now to saffron yellow; of its own will shall scarlet clothe the grazing lambs.)

Unifying the pastoral world of simplicity and innocence and the historical world of experience and heroic action, the fourth *Eclogue* redefines the pastoral by presenting a third world, a sacred Arcadia, which has been achieved by pastoral *otium*, heroic action, and finally, spiritual contemplation.

Since Arcadia is a fictive place representing the golden world of poetry, Virgil, as pastoral poet, allows us to witness the creation of poetry.[7] In the seventh and third *Eclogues* we see the imagination in the process of play, and understand more clearly how poetry is a deliberate craft. By witnessing the activity of artistic creation, we see how a poem is an evolving entity. Both *Eclogues* take the form of singing matches, amoebaean pastorals in which two shepherd-poets compete in alternate song.

A combination of spontaneity and formality characterizes the amoebaean form specifically as it more generally does for pastoral poetry. The contending poet is free to imagine and spontaneously invent, but he is obliged to vary only slightly from the pattern set by his predecessor and then surpass him. The formality of the song patterns is more evident in *Eclogue* 7, for here Thrysis and Corydon are limited to symmetrically arranged quatrains.[8]

The two shepherds in the seventh *Eclogue* are described as being "ambo florentes aetatibus, Arcades ambo" (both in the bloom of life, Arcadians both), and these youthful Arcadians who are gifted in song participate in a playful, yet earnest, lyrical competition. The pastoral setting inspires the imagery of their alternating songs, and in them nature symbolically reflects the singer's emotions. "Now all nature smiles," sings Corydon, "but if fair Alexis should quit these hills you would see the very rivers dry." Thyrsis's lyrical response embellishes this imaginative shaping of pastoral nature:

Aret ager, vitio moriens sitit aëris herba . . .
Phyllidis adventu nostrae nemus omne virebit,
Iuppiter et laeto descendet plurimus imbri.

(57, 59-60)

(The field is parched; the grass athirst, dying in the tainted air . . . but at the coming of my Phyllis all the woodland will be green, and Jupiter, in his fullness, shall descend in gladsome showers.)

The amoebaean pattern of the singing match, which is itself set by Virgil's predecessor, Theocritus, enables the contending poets, while seeming to play against each other, in fact to play together. The songs of the match are in harmony, for the eclogue itself is a song made up of two songs in dialogue. Presiding over the singing match is Daphnis, who "had made his seat beneath a whispering ilex," and in bucolic repose he seems to incarnate the spirit of the shepherd-poet;[9] his presence in effect harmonizes the two songs and makes them one whole.

In the third *Eclogue* the meeting of Menalcas and Damoetas is marked by their rough and even surly tone to each other. The conversation of these herdsmen is full of teasing to arouse each other to a more combative mood. Menalcas taunts Damoetas about being a "hireling keeper" of Aegon's flock and milking the ewes twice an hour; Demoetas, in turn, accuses Menalcas of acting wantonly in a chapel. As the talk turns to their singing capabilities, they become boastful and more derisive. When Damoetas boasts that he beat Aegon in singing, Menalcas asks in scoffing surprise:

Cantando tu illum? aut umquam tibi fistula cera
iuncta fuit? non tu in triviis, indocte, solebas
stridenti miserum stipula disperdere carmen?

(25-27)

(You beat him singing? Why, did you ever own a wax-jointed pipe? Was it not you, Master Dunce, who at the cross-roads used to murder a sorry tune on a scrannel straw?)

When the two plain-speaking, competitive shepherds decide on a singing match, Palaemon agrees to be the judge. They seat themselves on the soft grass, and the pastoral setting itself, the green woods with every tree in bud, tempers their aggression just as the singing match seems to control and sublimate their instinct to brawl.[10] The formal rules of the poetic game demand the disinterestedness of art. Their lyrics are still competitive in that they try to surpass each other in their amorous praises of Galatea and Amyntas, but the pastoral love lyrics are removed from the discord of their previous bickering.

After the singing match is over, however, both shepherds observe a number of threats to the harmonious world about them: "a chill snake lurks in the grass," the bank seems to be crumbling, the stream is dangerous for the grazing goats, and the heat may make it hard to milk their animals. All these aspects of nature insinuate that the pastoral world is menaced by destructive forces. "Some evil eye," says Menalcas credulously, "bewitches my tender lambs." Then their judge, Palaemon, decides that neither contestant has won the singing match but that both deserve a heifer. There is, then, no decision, and while the two shepherds have played their songs together, the atmosphere suggests that nature is sinister and antagonistic.

These two singing match eclogues may be described as "recreative," to use one of E. K.'s classifications of Spenser's *The Shepheardes Calender*. That is, these are two poems in which the shepherds temporarily escape a world of care into a place where they may play in song. Although the spirit of *lusus* predominates in both, they intimate that the songs are escapes from real danger and loss.

In a number of the eclogues, however, Virgil, perhaps becoming restless with his period of youthful apprenticeship, expresses a discontent with the limitations of the pastoral, a poetic world circumscribed in its artifice. As if he has become more assured of his poetic capacity, he now wishes to progress to a greater world of experience. The pastoral allows him this impulse to explore higher aspirations. At the beginning of his golden age *Eclogue*, Virgil tells the Muses that he will lift his style from the more humble bucolic norm because his subject demands that he do so. In the eighth *Eclogue* he asks the consul, Pollio, almost impatiently:

> . . . en erit umquam
> ille dies, mihi cum liceat tua dicere facta?

en erit, ut liceat totum mihi ferre per orbem
sola Sophocleo tua carmina digna coturno?

(7-10)

(O will that day ever come when I shall be free to tell thy
deeds? O shall I ever be free to spread through all the world
those songs of thine, alone worthy of the buskin of Sophocles?)

These two epic gestures suggest that Virgil feels confined by
the mean estate of the shepherd and by subjects of the
pastoral. The sixth *Eclogue*, which specifically concerns itself
with poetry, opens with

Prima Syracosio dignata est ludere versu
nostra hec erubuit silvas habitare Thalia.
cum canerum reges et proelia . . .

(1-3)

(My Muses first deigned to sport in Sicilian strains, and blushed
not to dwell in the woods. When I was feign to sing of kings and
battles . . .)

The shepherd-poet then ambivalently resigns himself to "woo
the rustic Muse on slender reed," but the song he sings about
Silenus clearly exceeds the normal subject matter and manner
of the pastoral. The song of the shepherd is a description of
Silenus's song, and the subjects that Silenus sings of are cosmic,
mythological, and heroic. Virgil's disavowal of epic ambitions
at the beginning of the eclogue is ironically betrayed by the
song-within-the song. The power of Silenus's song, says the
shepherd, is greater than that of Apollo and Orpheus, the two
mythic singers of the pastoral world. Silenus sings of the Creation, of Saturn's reign, the theft and Prometheus, among other
great legendary events, and while they may constitute a poetic
program for Virgil himself, they are not pastoral; rather they
are an evocation of themes challenging a poet's highest aspirations. In this evocation of the poetic imagination, Virgil implicitly acknowledges the conditions and limitations of pastoral
poetry; it does not have the vast range of Silenus's song, which
echoes to the stars.

    In the concluding poem, Virgil brings together many of the

themes of the preceding eclogues. We have seen how in the recreative third *Eclogue*, Damoetas, after playing in a contest, observes a cold snake (frigidus angui) lurking in the grass. This ominous image suggests the incursion of the hostile world of real nature into the circumscribed world of pastoral art. Throughout the whole series of eclogues, one sees, in varying degrees, the imminent or actual invasion of the empirical world upon Arcadia, and the vulnerability of the pastoral myth.

It is perhaps the poet's own feelings regarding the pastoral that constitutes the greatest, and ultimate, resistance to its premises. This place of poetry is a reflection of the poet's attitudes and states of mind. The defining values expressed and enacted by the pastoral poet are simplicity, contentment, and contemplation. If he no longer can acquiesce in his role of youthful apprentice with its gestures of self-depreciation, and he rejects the ideals of the good life inherent in the pastoral, then he must abandon that kind of poetry. A desire for fame and glory, and the hope of inspiring one's nation to virtuous action are the premises on which not pastoral but epic poetry is built.

"Extremum hunc" (my last task is this), says the poet in the opening of the tenth *Eclogue*, to sing for Gallus, the shepherd-poet who has been deserted by his mistress. At first this subject seems similar to the complaints of unrequited love in the second and eighth *Eclogues*. But unlike Corydon, Damon, or Alphesiboeus, a flesh-and-blood person, Cornelius Gallus, has abandoned the Arcadia of poetry to enter the real world of politics and war. Heartbroken, he has given up Arcadia because pastoral well-being and contentment were no longer possible for him. Though the laurels and tamarisks wept for him as he pined in his unrequited love for Lycoris, he knew that he could not remain in a *locus amoenus* if he had no peace. When Gallus needed help, the pastoral Muses were not there, "for no heights of Parnasus or of Pindus, no Aonian Aganippe" made him "tarry." His sweetheart, Lycoris, had deserted Arcadia to follow another "amid snows and rugged camps." And Gallus, too, deserts his native Arcadia:

nunc insanus amor duri me Martis in armis
tela inter media atque adversos detinet hostis.

(44-45)

(But now a mad passion for the stern god of war keeps me
in arms, in the midst of weapons and opposing foes.)

He recognizes that Arcadia is the place of poetic creativity,
"soli cartare periti/Arcades" (32-33) (Arcadians only know
how to sing), and expresses both his love and judgment of the
pastoral world. His farewell to that world of innocence and
contemplation is full of regret: "ipsae rursus concedite silvae"
(63) (once more adieu, even ye woods.)

As in the first *Eclogue* when Meliboeus sees his pastoral
world for the last time, Gallus's farewell is a poignant expression of paradise lost. But Gallus chooses to abandon Arcadia
because he feels pulled by the world outside it, a world of injustice, strife, and suffering, but one that calls aspiring man to
heroic action.

Here, in the tenth *Eclogue*, we find a final symbolic confrontation of the opposing claims of innocence and experience,
country and city, nature and art, contemplation and action,
pastoral and epic. The dialectical tensions within the pastoral
have reached a critical point where the form becomes, to use
Stanley E. Fish's phrase, a vehicle of its own abandonment.[11]
In spite of the great potential of the pastoral for variation and
invention, the limits of imaginary Arcadia are too narrow for
Virgil, and the limits imposed upon Arcadia by the actual
world too confining.

At the end of the *Eclogues*, Virgil, speaking in his own voice,
declares that he, too, must leave the pastoral world. Address-
ing the Muses, he says

Haec sat erit, divae, vestrum cecinisse poetam,
dum sedet et gracili fiscellam texit hibisco,
Pierides.

(70-72)

(These strains, Muses divine, it will be enough for your poet to
have sung, while he sits idle and twines a basket of slender
hibiscus.)

But he must rise from his retirement and move on. He does not annul the imaginative truth of his pastoral eclogues, but he hints at new poetic forms that are more suitable to the maturity he has gained in Arcadia.

The melancholy elegiac atmosphere present in many of the eclogues pervades this final poem. This pagan *lacrimae rerum* comes from the intrusion of the real world, the unhappiness of lovers, or an awareness of man's mortality. But perhaps the melancholy of the pastoral world can be best explained, as Thomas J. Rosenmeyer says, by our apprehension that the world of imagination does not in fact exist.[12] The lengthening shadows that come at the conclusion of the first and second *Eclogues* evoke sadness and a sense of fragility. Evening comes at the end of the last *Eclogue* as the shepherd-poet watches through the falling shadows the coming of Hesperus, the evening star. This star brings the end of the Arcadian day, but it is a sign of hope, too, for some higher aspiration.

The *Georgics*

The ending of the *Eclogues* is implicit in the beginning of the *Georgics*. Exploring the place of the poetic imagination in the *Eclogues*, Virgil had engaged in a process of discovery whereby he came to terms with the limitations of the Arcadian ideal of *otium*. With what became self-discovery, his view of his own role as poet had changed, and the *Georgics*, a work of his middle career, constitutes his poetic realization of the kind of role he had to assume. Moreover, in response to the Augustan effort to regain the moral stability of Italy after a period of political and social cataclysm, Virgil agreed with the national policy, which urged a revitalization of the Italian agricultural economy.[13] Patriotic motives, then, compelled him to write a didactic poem that would be useful to his nation. A life of contemplation and play seemed frivolously idle when Maecenas, a man active in political affairs, persuaded him that his poetry could be useful to their nation.

The opening lines of *Georgics*, addressed to Maecenas, tell the reader what subjects his four books will develop:

Quid faciat laetas segetes, quo sidere terram
vertere, Maecenas, ulmisque adiungere vites
conveniat, quae cura boum, qui cultus habendo
sit pecori, apibus quanta experientia parcis,
hinc canere incipiam.

(1.1-5)

(What makes the crops joyous, beneath what star, Maecenas, it is
well to turn the soil, and wed vines to elms, what tending the kine
need, what care the herd in breeding, what skill the thrifty
bees — hence shall I begin my song.)

Following the model of Hesiod's *Works and Days*, Virgil writes
a poetic treatise on agricultural methods. He gives useful advice on plowing, crop rotation, manuring, growing olives and
grapes, animal husbandry, and bee-keeping. He sees all these
agricultural activities as important for the renewal of his nation and for creating the golden age in Augustan Italy.

Georgics describes a pastoral world that stands in opposition
to the defining values of Arcadia. The parting words of the sorrowing Gallus in the last *Eclogue* are "omnia vincit Amor"; in
Georgics, Virgil says "labor omnia vincit." These phrases suggest the underlying assumptions of the two pastoral poems.

Virgil's narrative of Orpheus and Eurydice, inset in the
poem and taking the form of an epyllion, is a story that expresses and exposes the weakness of Arcadian ideals, and
therefore of the ineffectiveness of pastoral poetry to resolve the
problems of life. Eurydice has been killed by the bite of a snake
in the deep grass as she was fleeing from the amorous
Aristaeus. The shepherd-poet Orpheus, symbol of Arcadian
idyll, descends into hell to win her back:

ipse cava solans aegrum testudine amorem
te, dulcis coniunx.

(4.464-65)

(But he, solacing love's anguish with his hollow shell, sang of
thee, sweet wife.)

When he regains her through the power of his lyre, we feel that
love and art have indeed triumphed over the finality of death.
But his victory is illusory, for having violated Proserpine's condition in looking back at his bride, Orpheus loses her a second

time. He must return alone in despair from his quest in hell. Poetry has failed him.[14]

The myth of Proserpine's death and return explains the eternal recurrence of the seasons. This myth has moral significance for Orpheus and all pastoral poets. He cannot disobey the laws of Proserpine. Nature will not change with the poet's moods as in Arcadia; it is not subject to the poet's wishes but has a deeper law to obey. The georgic poet recognizes, as the Arcadian poet does not, that mutability and the rhythmic cycles of nature are an inescapable part of human life.

In Virgil's brief account of the Golden Age (1. 125-28), he describes a life of *otium* in which man did not have to subdue the earth, for it freely and abundantly yielded its fruits. But Jove, desiring to strengthen him, imposed hardship and continual labor to teach him the use of his powers:

> pater ipse colendi
> haud facilem esse vian voluit, primusque per artem
> movit agros, curis acuens mortalia corda,
> nec torpere gravi passus sua regna veterno.
>
> (1.121-24)

(The great Father himself has willed the path of husbandry should not be smooth, and he first made art awake the fields, sharpening men's wits by care, nor letting his realm slumber in heavy lethargy.)

In the humble labor of plowing or manuring the soil, the farmer cooperates with the seasons and a divine plan.

Work on the land is a human endeavor that enables man to stay in touch with the rhythmic cycles and continuity of nature outside his mind. In the regular cycle of seasonal tasks that constitute the farmer's year, man works in accord with the dynamic harmonies of nature, and by participating with them he enters into partnership with the divine. This religious understanding of husbandry invests the most seemingly trivial kind of labor with dignity and sanctity. The descriptions of autumn's harvests, for example, are characterized by a sensuous imagery that expresses the bounty and divinity of nature. The *Georgics* evokes autumn in a celebration of the harvest, with a love of dynamic process and a serene joy in completeness:

spicea iam campis cum inhorruit et cum
frumenta in viridi stipula lactentia turgent

(2.314-15)

(the bearded harvest now bristles in the fields, and the corn
on its green stem swells with milk.)

nec requies, quin aut pomis exuberet annus
aut fetu pecorum aut Cerealis mergite culmi,
proventuque oneret sulcos atque horrea vincat.

(2.516-18)

(No respite is there, but the season teems either with fruits,
or with increase of the herds, or with sheaves of Ceres' corn,
loading the furrows with its yield and bursting the barns.)

The kinesthetic, tactile, and visual images particularize the
productive animation of the natural world working in harmony
with man and gods.

Bucolic repose is achieved by toil; it is not merely a literary
premise provided by a controlling artistic consciousness:

(speluncae vivique lacus et frigida Tempe
mugitusque boum mollesque sub arbore somni)
non absunt.

(2.469-71)

(Yea, the ease of broad domains, caverns and living lakes,
and cool vales, the lowing of the kine, and soft slumbers
beneath the trees — all are theirs.)

This *locus amoenus*, similar in many ways to that of Arcadia, is
different from it because it is not a creation of *homo artifex*,
but rather an objective, empirical nature working in partnership with *homo laborans*.

As a bridge to writing his epic, the *Georgics* afforded Virgil,
moreover, the opportunity to experiment with heroic themes
and epic conventions. He celebrates the political, social, and
religious ideals of his nation in history, and bases his glorifica-
tion of the Italian husbandman on a patriotic conception of
heroic virtue for his readers to imitate. In what Raymond
Williams calls Virgil's "epic of husbandry,"[15] the poet frequently elevates his tone and language above the humble man-

ner of customary pastoral, and his similes comparing farmers with soldiers endow the farmer with the dignity, knowledge, and virtue of an epic hero.

Although the advice he gives to the farmer may at times seem trivial, Virgil takes every opportunity to glorify the kind of knowledge the farmer has, the tools he uses, and the purposeful work he does.

> Quare agite o proprios generatim, discite cultus,
> agricolae.
>
> (2.35-36)

(Up! therefore, ye husbandmen, learn the culture proper to teach each after its kind.)

For Virgil, to be "able to win knowledge of the causes of things" (potuit rerum cognoscere causas [2. 490]) is one of the great benefits of working with nature on the land. While this knowledge has practical value for the farmer, it also elevates him to the level of philosopher, who comprehends the natural order of things.

Virgil refers to the farmer's implements as "weapons" (arma [1. 160]), and his epic simile suggests both the patriotic and heroic nature of agricultural work:

> ut saepe ingenti bello cum longa cohortis
> explicuit legio et campo stetit agmen aperto.
>
> (2.279-80)

(As oft, in mighty warfare, when the legion displays its companies in long array and the column halts on the open plain.)

These manly, gallant military maneuvers are compared to vineyard landscaping: omnia sint paribus numeris dimensa viarum. (284) (So let all your vineyard be meted out in even and uniform paths). He compares the farmers to courageous soldiers since they plan, struggle, and sacrifice for their nation's peace. He identifies Italian husbandmen as "Ausonia's swains," descended from the Trojan race (Troia gens missa [2. 385]), who exercise their military virtues, and like the Trojans help establish and settle Italy.

Virgil explores and uses those literary devices associated with the heroic poem, but because he is dealing ostensibly with humble concerns, the tone of his epic similes tends to be as playful as it is serious. Yet his views regarding the role of the Italian husbandman and citizen in rebuilding the nation compel him to idealize and make heroic their efforts.

Set in a framework of a treatise on bees is a miniature epic of warfare in which Virgil describes warrior bees in heroic terms. "Trumpet-blasts" call the bees to battle:

> et circa regem atque ipsa praetoria densae
> miscentur magnisque vocant clamoribus hostem.
>
> (4.75-76)

> (Round their king, and even by his royal tent, they swarm in throngs, and with loud cries challenge the foe.)

Mock-epic in tone, there is an element of aesthetic play in Virgil's battle of the bees, yet the poet is serious in his didactic exemplum of noble self-sacrifice for ruler and race:

> et saepe attolunt umeris corpora bello
> obiectant pulchramque petunt per volnere mortem.
>
> (217-18)

> (Often they lift him on their shoulders, for him expose their bodies to battle, and seek amid wounds a glorious death.)

The poet's playful interpretation of their chivalrous valor is based on a serious, national theme.

The *Georgics* is a work that transcends its expressed agricultural and patriotic intentions. The spiritual and aesthetic aspects of the poem are integrated with the more didactic elements, as in the prayer that concludes Book 1. In this prayer Virgil asks that, with the gods' aid, Augustus will save the world, which has been overrun by violence and evil:

> di patrii, Indigetes, et Romule Vestaque mater,
> quae Tuscum Tiberim et Romana Palatia servas,
> hunc saltem everso iuvenum succurrere saeclo
> ne prohibete!
>
> (1.498-501)

(Gods of my country, Heroes of the land, thou Romulus, and thou Vesta, our mother, that guardest Tuscan Tiber and the Palatine of Rome, at least stay not this young prince from aiding a world uptorn!)

In contrast to the unnatural and destructive character of soldiers in wars, the husbandmen, who also are "heroes of the land," represent the natural and creative:

> non ullus aratro
> dignus honos, squalent abductis arva colonis
> et curvae rigidum falces conflantur in ensem.
>
> (1.506-8)

(the plough meets not its honour due; our lands, robbed of the tillers, lie waste, and the crooked pruning-hooks are forged into stiff swords.)

But because "labor omnia vincit," the Italian countryside will be healed and restored by man's peaceful and productive work.

In his account of the bees, moreover, Virgil develops a theme of spiritual significance. He tells us at the beginning of the fourth book that he will discuss "aërii mellis caelestia dona" (1) (Heaven's gift, the honey from the skies), and his language here prepares us for his speculation on divine presence in the life of these bees:

> His quidam signis atque haec exempla secuti
> esse apibus partem divinae mentis et haustus
> aetherios dixere.
>
> (219-21)

(Led by such tokens and such instances, some have taught that the bees have received a share of the divine intelligence, or a draught of heavenly ether.)

The poet is particularly interested in the restoration of all living things after death:

> scilicet huc reddi deinde as resoluta referri
> omnia, nec morti esse locum, sed viva volare
> sideris in numerum atque alto succedere cealo.
>
> (4.225-27)

(Yes, unto Him all beings thereafter return, and, when unmade, are restored; no place is there for death, but, still quick, they fly unto the ranks of the stars, and mount to the heavens aloft.)

This theme of rebirth is an integral part of *Georgics* as a whole, as Virgil expresses his country's need for restoration after its moral death. It develops, moreover, his concern with the processes, rhythms, and continuity of nature, and divine manifestations in the natural order. His celebration of man's return to the land, then, encompasses politics, history, *amor patriae*, and religion.

The poet develops the theme of rebirth in the latter part of Book 4 of *Georgics* in the myth of the shepherd Aristaeus. When Aristaeus discovers that he is responsible for the deaths of Eurydice and Orpheus, he tries to propitiate Orpheus's spirit by sacrificing oxen. Virgil's narrative ends dramatically and symbolically:

> hic vero ac dictu mirabile monstrum
> aspiciunt, liquefacta boum per viscere toto
> stridere apes utero et ruptis effervere costis.
>
> (554-56)

(But here they espy a portent, sudden and wondrous to tell— throughout the paunch, amid the molten flesh of the oxen, bees buzzing and swarming forth from the ruptured sides.)

In the climax of the poem, this miraculous rebirth of the bees symbolizes the presence of the divine intelligence in nature.

The movement of the *Georgics* is primarily away from the subjective and contemplative, however, and advances purposefully toward an objective world of regenerating nature and nation. In the epilogue to the whole four books Virgil reviews his work:

> Haec super arvorum cultu pecorumque canebam
> et super arboribus.
>
> (559-60)

(thus I sang of the care of fields, of cattle, and of trees.)

When he was singing his pastoral song, "great Caesar thundered in war . . . and gave a victor's laws unto willing nations" (235-37). Both Caesar and Virgil were doing work for their nation, one active, political, and martial, the other contemplative and poetic. But the discrepancy between the heroic deeds of Augustus and his own meditative songs is too great. The poet looks in retrospect at his early career:

> illo Vergilium me tempore dulcis alebat
> Parthenope, studiis florentem ignobilis oti,
> carmina qui lusi pastorum audaxque iuventa,
> Tityre, te patulae cecini sub tegmine fagi.
>
> (563-66)

(In those days, I, Virgil, was nursed of sweet Parthenope, and I rejoiced in the arts of inglorious ease, and, in youth's boldness, sang, Tityrus, of thee under they spreading beech's covert.)

Returning to the *otium* of his first *Eclogue*, Virgil says, with some regret and more reproach, farewell to the idyllic life. While he does not tell us where he is going, he asserts explicitly what he had been implicitly saying about his relation to the pastoral; he has matured and outgrown it, and must progress to efforts more challenging and ambitious.

The *Aeneid*

Having emulated Theocritus and Hesiod, Virgil desired to equal Homer, and thereby complete and perfect his poetic career. In the experimental stage of composition, he prefaced his *Aeneid*:

> Illo ego, qui quondam gracili modulatus avena
> carmen, et egressus silvis, vicinu coegi
> ut quamvis avido parerent arva colono,
> gratum opus agricolis; at nunc horrentia Martis
> Arma virumque cano.
>
> (11.1a-1d, 1)

(I am he who once tuned my song on a slender reed, then,

leaving the woodland, constrained the neighboring fields to serve the husbandmen, however grasping—a work welcome to farmers: but now of Mars' bristling. Arms I sing and the man.)

These prefatory lines recapitulate Virgil's career as pastoral poet, and declare his new identity as heroic poet.

Virgil's moral purpose in writing his heroic poem is to teach Romans *pietas*, on which the perpetuation of their national glory is based. The hero of the *Aeneid*, while exemplifying some Homeric ideals, is also a new kind of epic hero. Virgil describes him as "insignem pietate virum" (a man of good so wondrous), and the moral and spiritual significance of *pietas* distinguishes him from Homer's Achilles, who bases his deeds on *areté*, a Greek concept defined by Werner Jaeger as "a combination of proud and courtly morality with warlike valour."[16] Although Virgil's hero has courage and prowess, his virtue is religious, involving a fulfillment of duty to the gods, and patriotic, requiring self-renunciatory duty to family and nation.[17] Embodying Roman *virtus* and *pietas*, Aeneas's epic heroism takes the place of the military virtues of Achilles. He is "Troius Aeneas, pietate insignis et armis" (6. 403) (Trojan Aeneas, famous for piety and arms).

Virgil's characterization of his adversary, Turnus, on the other hand, embodies the older Homeric qualities of the heroic. Indeed, the Cumaean Sybil tells Aeneas "Alius Latio iam partus Achilles" (6. 90) (Even now another Achilles is raised in Latium), thus explicitly identifying Turnus with the Homeric hero.[18] He is like Achilles in that he is motivated by a personal desire for glory, and pursues that glory impatiently, irresponsibly, and recklessly. His heroism, unlike that of Aeneas, is based on egotistical pride and primitive *areté*. Lacking the necessary *sapientia* and *pietas*, Turnus is doomed to lose in the struggle with Aeneas. His *hybris* brings him to defeat and death.

For Aeneas, ideals of practical public action conflict with contemplative piety. He must integrate *sapientia* and *fortitudo*. Called by fate to heroic action, he is sometimes hesitant and frequently melancholy about what he sees he must do. The Sack of Troy demonstrates Virgil's own feelings regarding the old heroic ideals of arms. The poet describes very precisely and in detail the reckless cruelty, madness, and pathos of war. Aeneas excels in the military virtues but he is also a morally sensitive, sorrowing man who feels forced into war, both in Troy and Italy.

In many ways, Aeneas has as much in common with the shepherd as with the warrior. His melancholy sensibility resembles that of Gallus in the tenth *Eclogue*. The "stern god of war" keeps Aeneas, like Gallus, "in arms, in the midst of weapons and opposing forces," but the savage conflict of war is not natural to Aeneas's contemplative, poetic temperament. As protector of his land, he suffers greatly when he beholds the indiscriminate devastation of pastoral peace. Aeneas describes himself on the rooftop looking at the destruction of Troy:

> excutior somno et summi fastigia tecti
> ascensu supero atque arrectis auribus adsto:
> in segetem veluti cum flamma furentibus Austris
> incidit, aut rapidus montano flumine torrens
> sternit agros, sternit sata laeta boumque labores
> praecipitesque trahit silvas; stupet inscius alto
> accipiens sonitum saxi de vertici pastor.
>
> (2.302-8)

(I shake myself from sleep and, climbing to the roof's topmost height, stand with straining ears; even as, when fire falls on a cornfield while the south winds are raging, or the rushing torrent from a mountain-stream lays low the fields, lays low the glad crops and labours of oxen and drags down forests headlong, spellbound the bewildered shepherd hears the roar from a rock's lofty peak.)

In having Aeneas compare himself to a "bewildered shepherd," the poet emphasizes his hero's innocence and tender feeling for his land as forces of destruction, relentless as the natural elements themselves, consume the georgic landscape.

He must witness the barbarous massacre of his fellow Trojans, must abandon burning Troy and lose his wife, Creusa, before he is compelled to pursue his way from his homeland to Italy. On the journey his father, Anchises, dies, and later in Carthage, he has no choice but to forsake Dido, who gave him

her love. With the Trojan remnant, "Pater" Aeneas fulfills his
destiny by founding the new city, but only after tragic sacrifice
and loss.

Destiny, coercion, and necessity are the forces that dominate
Aeneas's universe. A servant of fate, he can never free himself
from the entanglements of gods and history. The life of contemplation and pastoral *otium* is remote from the fate com-
pelling him to be a warrior and statesman. The *locus
amoenus* seems alien to the events of the *Aeneid*, voyages,
quests, warfare, and the building of the new city. Yet, in two
important episodes Aeneas does visit a pastoral world of retirement and contemplation. These Arcadias are pastoral
enclaves, enclosed within the mutable world of history and suffering.

Pastoral enclaves are traditional scenes in epic poetry, occur-
ring first in Homer's *Odyssey* when Odysseus visits the Gardens
of Alcinous. Following Virgil's epic, they make their appearance in Dante's *Commedia*, Ariosto's *Orlando Furioso*,
Tasso's *Gerusalemme Liberata*, Spenser's *The Faerie Queene*,
and, of course, Milton's *Paradise Lost*. Not mere digressions,
these pastoral enclaves have important thematic and narrative
functions in the heroic poem. Virgil uses the pastoral in his
Aeneid, for example, as an integral part of the epic's thematic
resolution.

The pastoral places that Aeneas visits have critical
significance for the poem as a whole. In both, Aeneas experiences a psychological crisis that helps give meaning to his
heroic quest. These enclaves, moreover, provide the pious
Aeneas with a greater contemplative understanding of both
divine purpose and his own religious, familial, and patriotic
duties. His pastoral experiences give him a new awareness and
strength preparatory to the heroic trials in which he must
engage. That impatient Turnus has no such contemplative experience suggests that his ambition for personal glory springs
from a mistaken sense of self-sufficiency, and that this pride
will lead to his defeat. True heroic action is based on com-
templation through which the hero can gain self-knowledge.

The first episode takes place in the Elysian Fields; the other
in the rural kingdom of Evander. The sixth book is the center

of the *Aeneid*, because it is the poem's literal mid-point and dramatizes a great psychological and spiritual crisis of the hero. Having completed his odyssey to Italy, he finds himself confronting both his past and his future. Before he learns what his future is destined to be, he must face his past and renounce what he once was.[19]

Guided by the prophetic advice of the Sibyl, Aeneas descends, gripping the golden bough, into the cave at Cumae. In Lugentes Campi (the "Mourning Fields") he meets the shade of Dido, who had killed herself for him. He tries passionately to convince her that he did not willingly desert her, that he was constrained by divine decree, but the "fiery, fierce-eyed queen" turns away in silence and flees from him. He then sees the mutilated, scarred specters of soldiers slain in the Trojan War. They remind him of the terrible violence, carnage, and sacrifice of war. The Sibyl, however, warns him: "nox ruit, Aenea; nos flendo ducimus horas" (539) ("Night is coming, Aeneas; we waste the hours in weeping") and Aeneas must leave behind him the "sad, sunless dwelling" of the Mourning Fields, and the memories of personal losses; and after wandering through the underworld nightmare of Tartarus with its tortured, sinful humanity, he ascends into the dawn light of the Elysian Fields.

The experience of his interior descent has been purifying, and now Aeneas is ready to be admitted to Elysium for a brief time to see his father, Anchises. Virgil describes Elysium as a *locus amoenus*,[20] but it is an Arcadia transformed into an unearthly paradise:

devenere locos laetos et amoena virecta
Fortunatorum Nemorum sedesque beatas.

(6.638-39)

(they came to a land of joy, the green pleasaunces and happy seats of the Blissful Groves.)

This place of pastoral beauty and happiness is unthreatened by the perils of mutability, and that it has its own sun and stars suggest it exists on a level that transcends the aesthetic Arcadia of poets. Bathed in "lumina . . . purpuro," roseate light, the meads of Elysium are a place for play, dance, and music:

> pars in gramineis exercent membra palaestris,
> contendunt ludo et fulva luctantur harena;
> pars pedibus plaudunt choreas et carmina dicunt.

> (642-44)

> (Some disport their limbs on the grassy wrestling-ground, vie in sports, and grapple on the yellow sand; some trip it in the dance and chant songs.)

While their recreative activities seem simple and innocent, those participating in them are exalted spirits who have gone through the purifying fires of experience, and have been refined by that purification to an enlightened innocence.

After his melancholy wandering on earth and through the dark night of lost souls, the Elysian Fields offer Aeneas relief and restoration. Among the happy souls who, unlike Aeneas, can remain in Elysium, he sees men who died for their country, pure priests, good bards, philosophers, inventors, and men who have served mankind. Museus, the "best of bards," describes for Aeneas their manner of existence:

>   lucis habitamus opacis
> riparumque toros et prata recentia rivis
> incolimus.

> (673-75)

> (We dwell in shady groves, and live on cushioned river-banks and meadows fresh with streams.)

Aeneas sees his father deeply contemplating the "imprisoned souls that were to pass to the light above." Unlike most of these souls, who drink of Lethe's waters and then return to new bodies, Anchises remains in the Elysian Fields forever. The profundity of Anchises' contemplation "deep in a green vale" (penitus convalle virenti [769]) gives the pastoral setting a greater spiritual significance. In "a sequestered grove and rustling forest thickets," Aeneas sees those spirits who, as Anchises explains, drinks at the stream of forgetfulness, awaiting their second bodies. The great number of these spirits are compared to bees:

> ac veluti in pratis ubi apes aestate serena
> floribus insidunt variis et candida circum
> lilia funduntur, strepit omnis murmure campus.
>
> (707-9)

(even as when, in the meadows, in cloudless summer-time, bees light on many-hued blossoms and stream round lustrous lilies and all the fields murmur with the humming.)

The tonal effect of this luminous image of bees recalls the poet's mystical interpretation of their regeneration in the *Georgics*. While the language is sensuously precise in its natural observation, the atmosphere evoked by Virgil suggests the mystical and visionary. Aeneas and Anchises are not in a temporal but in a sacred garden.

The Elysian Fields, for all its contemplative serenity and pastoral beauty, becomes for Aeneas the place where he learns his duty to a life of heroic deeds in history. The necessity of fate and history demand that Aeneas be founder and ancestor of Rome. Anchises speaks for destiny itself as he reveals to Aeneas a panorama of Roman myth and history. His son's role is to bear this destiny into the world. Through prophetic visions Aeneas learns of the future of Rome. After the prophecy of the Augustan peace, 'the fate of young Marcellus, Augustus's nephew and destined successor, casts a shadow on the future of the Empire.

> Atque his Aeneas (una namque ira videbat
> egregium forma iuvenum et fulgentibus armis
> sed frons laeta parum et deiecto lumina voltu).
>
> (860-62)

(And hereon Aeneas, for he saw coming with him a youth of wondrous beauty and brilliant in his arms— but his face was sad and his eyes downcast.)

Marcellus, who had aroused high national hopes, was dead when Virgil wrote these lines. The vision of history ends with this somber evocation of the young Marcellus. Anchises expresses his grief in a pastoral elegy:

> manibus date lilia plenis,
> purpureos spargum flores animamque nepotis
> his saltem accumulem donis et fungar inani
> munere.
>
> (883-86)

(Give me lilies with full hand; let me scatter purple flowers; let me heap o'er my offspring's shade at least these gifts and fulfill an unavailing service.)

The book ends in a melancholy and somewhat ambiguous mood. The elegiac tone of Anchises' final words, the overwhelming destiny that Aeneas must bear, and the enigmatic significance of the two gates of sleep all convey a sense of uncertainty and apprehension. Aeneas and the Sibyl depart from Anchises not through the gate of horn "given to true shades," but the gate of ivory. The ivory gate symbolizes false dreams, and therefore the truth of Aeneas's experience seems to be called into question. Virgil concludes the book without expressly clarifying the deceptive nature of dreams, but an inference may be drawn that the world of the Elysian Fields is real and true, whereas it is the mutable world of suffering, sin, and death that is illusory. Aeneas seems to be experiencing what Stephen Dedalus expressed in the phrase, "History . . . is a nightmare from which I am trying to wake." Dismissed through the ivory gate, Aeneas speeds his way into that tragic and insubstantial world of history.

The Arcadian kingdom of Evander is the earthly counterpart of the Elysian Fields. Here Aeneas experiences another psychological crisis as he advances toward the fulfillment of his destiny. Troubled by the threatening alliances of Italian warriors and the imminence of war, Aeneas wanders along the banks of the Tiber. In a complex, psychologically subtle figure, the poet reveals Aeneas's agitated mind:

> nunc dividit illuc
> in partisque rapit varias perque omnia versat:
> sicut aquae tremulum labris ubi lumen aenis

sole repercussum aut radiantis imagine lunae
omnia pervolitat late loca iamque sub auras
ergitur summique ferit laquearia tecti.

(8.20-25)

(as when in brazen bowls a flickering light from water, flinging
back by the sun or moon's glittering form, flits far and wide
o'er all things, and now mounts high and smites the fretted
ceiling of the roof aloft.)

These images of water and scintillating light suggest his state of
consciousness before sleep, and they foreshadow the emergence
of natural and divine forces at work in his dram. Falling
asleep, he sees the god of the river, Tiberinus, who speaks pro-
phetically and advises him to go to Pallanteum, the future site
of Rome, and seek aid from King Evander. The divinized river
Tiber guides him to the coast where exiled Arcadians under
Evander have chosen to live.

When he arrives in this rural kingdom, Evander and his
court are offering sacrifices to Hercules, commemorating his
heroic exploits. Although Evander rules a "scant domain," he
cordially welcomes Aeneas to a bucolic banquet:

dapes iubet et sublata reponi
pocula gramineoque viros locat ipse sedili
praecipuumque toro et villosi pelle leonis
accipit Aenean solioque invitat acerno.

(175-78)

(he orders the repast and cups, already removed, to be replaced,
and with his own hand ranges the guests on the grass seat, and
chief in honor he welcomes Aeneas to the cushion of a shaggy
lion's hide, and invites him to a maple throne.)

The Arcadians' courtesy and their attention to the solemn rites
of piety reveal the moral and spiritual strength of their lives.
The shepherd-king explains the meaning of their libations and
prayers to his Trojan guest by relating the sotry of Hercules' deliverance of his people from the "semihominis" (half-human)
Cacus, a monstrous incarnation of brutal violence, who had
assaulted their pastoral peace. Had it not been for the heroic
deeds of Hercules, their Arcadian enclave would have been

destroyed by an evil force. In a great battle with Cacus, the hero-god finally throttles him to death, and liberates the little kingdom.

Evander and his son, Pallas, soon became friends with Aeneas, and he receives military aid from the Etruscans, who have deposed their own tyrant and invited the Arcadian to become their new king. Aeneas receives, however, more than a military alliance from Evander. The transplanted Arcadian shows him Pallanteum, the grassy foundation on which Rome will be built, and this tour unifies its mythic past and present with its future, when the golden age will be restored after the battle of Actium. Following Evander through the sacred woodlands and groves, Aeneas's contemplative mood is like his father's in the Elysian Fields. The pastoral landscapes of both the Elysian Fields and Pallanteum are manifestations of divinity, and are invested with a religious significance that is an essential part of Aeneas's and Rome's place in history.

Evander assumes the role of Aeneas's moral teacher, who demonstrates and expresses the values of piety, humility, and courtesy. Aeneas must internalize the pastoral ideals of Arcadia before he returns to the iron world of history. These moral virtues are exemplified by Evander's humble dwelling, his hospitality, and the sacrifice and prayers offered to Hercules. He tells Aeneas

> aude, hospes, contemnere opens et te quoque dignum
> flinge deo, rebusque veni non asper egenis.
>
> (364-65)
>
> (Dare, my guest, to score riches; fashion thyself also to be worthy of deity, and come not disdainful of our poverty.)

and these words sum up Evander's pastoral wisdom. If Aeneas is to triumph over the Italians and be founder of Rome, he must combine the piety of Evander and the arms of Hercules.[21] But these ideals of pastoral contemplation and heroic action cannot always be reconciled.

As Aeneas seeks to regain Arcadian harmony and peace, he initiates warfare and bloodshed in Italy. The pastoral world that had offered him the possibility of happiness is subjected, because of his fateful mission, to war and death.[22] When Evander's beloved son, Pallas, goes to battle and is ruthlessly slain by Turnus, he becomes a sacrificial victim of arms. Grief for his loss is in effect a lament for the dissolution of Arcadia.

Although Virgil revisits Arcadia in his heroic poem, the pastoral world enclosed by the epic action is clearly not a return to pleasure, idleness, and the creation of pastoral song. Singing matches and love-complaints have no place in this redefined *locus amoenus*. These two episodes in Books 6 and 8 constitute enclaves within the heroic poem primarily because they suggest the inwardness of Aeneas's experience. They are visits to a paradise within. While they offer him a momentary escape from deeds, a serene bucolic interlude, they give him what is more important, illuminating insights that serve to integrate meanings from the troubling complexities of life.

Whereas rural Pallanteum is a moral Arcadia, the pastoral world of the Elysian Fields is visionary and celestial. Evander instructs Aeneas in those virtues necessary for the moral vigor of the Empire; Anchises speaks as his spiritual destiny. When he arrives in Elysium and Pallanteum he is in a state of psychological crisis; both give him the knowledge upon which he acts in significant turning points in his life. These pastoral experiences have the function of illumination, initiating Aeneas into the meaning of true heroism, so that as he leaves these places of retirement and contemplation, he is better able to act heroically in the real world.

One may retrace the dialectical progression in Virgil's pastoral poetry from the *Eclogues*, and the *Georgics*, to the *Aeneid*. Though the pastoral was considered to be at the low end of the generic scale from the epic, it consistently implies the heroic.[23] Indeed, Virgil dedicated a number of his pastoral eclogues to men of heroic action — Octavian, Pollio, Varro, and Gallus. In these poems, moreover, he expressed his growing discontent with pastoral themes and humble style, and in the fourth *Eclogue* he attempted to accommodate the heroic mode to his pastoral framework. From the first *Eclogue*, with its subversive implications regarding the unheroic pastoral, to the tenth, in which he more explicitly expressed the inadequacy of the pastoral, Virgil explored the tensions between pastoral and epic poetry. Heroic poetry both aroused his literary ambitions and called him to deal with the complex problems of the real world. The *Georgics*, while pastoral in setting, no longer conceived of life in terms of the contemplative and recreative. In this poem Virgil reached a half-way place between rural simplicity and the complex world of heroic action, between the Italian husbandman and Augustus Caesar. The next step in Virgil's progression to the heroic poem seems inevitable. But even in the *Aeneid*, Virgil needed his pastoral enclosures as stable reference points to help define and clarify the meaning of true heroic action.

Aeneas's visit to the Elysian Fields is a further step in the dialectical progression. Virgil and Aeneas have momentarily turned from heroic action to a state of visionary contemplation. This state has much in common with the pastoral ideal of *otium*, but it is a redefinition, refinement, and spiritualization of *otium* on a higher level of being. This desired state, unlike that of a esthetic pastoral poetry, must be won by spiritual achievement in the world. Anchises in Elysium represents an immortal life beyond mere heroic action and worldly fame and glory; it is essentially unworldly and contemplative. Aeneas may see this level of being for only a brief time, for he must return to the experiential world of turmoil and suffering, and fulfill his destiny through heroic deeds before he can regain the pastoral joy of enlightened innocence.

2

Spenser and the Pastoral

Virgil and the Renaissance Pastoral

PASTORAL poetry in the Renaissance had evolved in a way that developed certain elements incipient in Virgil's *Eclogues*, and resulted in new uses for the genre. The Renaissance humanists, notably Boccaccio, Petrarch, and Mantuan, made the pastoral eclogue a vehicle for didacticism, polemics, and allegory. Because they read Virgil's *Eclogues* in a way that threw his moral concerns and allegorical techniques into strong relief, their classical exemplar legitimized their own transformation of pastoral poetry.

Virgil's moral sensibility is manifest in his attempt to explore the relationship between poetry and the world. By defining moral problems with reference to his Arcadian fiction, he examined the discrepancy between the ideal and experiential, the imaginative and historical worlds. The pastoral afforded a perspective for exploring the real world, and that world in turn helped judge the virtues and limitations of the pastoral fiction. That Virgil had recognized that his Arcadian fiction was both vulnerable to experience and inadequate to deal with the world is abundantly clear in those eclogues which dramatize the ultimate insufficiency of withdrawal and retirement. Indeed, the anti-pastoral element in his *Eclogues* creates unresolvable tensions, and tends to subvert traditional pastoral premises and conventions.

The wrongs of the actual world can be rectified only by

heroic action, and that means the need to venture out beyond the circumscribed confines of an imagined Arcadia. While attempting to unite the epic with the pastoral, Virgil raised the form beyond its humble beginning, but he could not strain the form without destroying those ideals of contentment, self-sufficiency, and innocence which the pastoral requires. The poet could no longer return to the simple world of innocence that he himself had undermined and relinquished.

Virgil's pastoral poetry demonstrates his awareness of, and his preoccupation with the real world outside the *locus amoenus*. Whether in his sensitivity to its incursions into Arcadia or in his expressed need for heroic action to reform the iron age and make it golden, his continual readjustment of moral and generic tensions gives the *Eclogues* their singular richness and complexity of meaning.

A technique that Virgil uses in adapting the actual world to his pastoral fiction is allegory. The Arcadian world is itself a continued metaphor for the poet's state of mind, and the shepherd who tends his goats or plays his oaten reed is not a shepherd in the literal sense but represents among other things the pastoral poet. Some of the specific characters in this world of the imagination are allegorical, though at times Virgil's allusions to his contemporaries, as in the case of the consul Pollio or the poet Cornelius Gallus, are not at all allegorically veiled. Other characters, however, are given pastoral names, and some of them are allegorical in the sense that they suggest real living poets and political figures. At times it seems that Virgil himself assumes various pastoral personae, and it has been argued that he can be identified with a Tityrus or Menalcas. But the allegory is freely suggestive rather than based on a rigid one-to-one equation.

The Renaissance humanists, however, went far beyond Virgil's personal allusions or allegory to develop the moral and political themes of their pastoral poetry. The inherent possibilities of moral criticism and allegory in the *Eclogues* were made more explicit, and were extended and intensified in order to attack abuses in society. While Virgil obliquely criticizes the Roman policy of confiscation and other injustices, the chief exponents of the neo-Latin pastoral made denunciatory attacks on vice, folly, and incompetence central to their poems. Whereas Virgil's disclosure of injustice is somewhat passive and lyrical, focusing on the victims, the Renaissance pastoralists are typically aggressive and satirical in their exposure of the perpetrators. The Renaissance development of the form used the pastoral fiction primarily in a self-protectively allegorical way in order to expose the corrupt world of city, court, and church. The simple life of ease and contemplation diminished in significance as the Renaissance shepherd-poets assaulted the real, experiential world through satire and polemics. Their use of conventions, then, served mainly as an implicit norm, while in others these ideals become incidental to the poem and are reduced in their thematic significance until only pastoral conventions remain.

In this transformation of the pastoral in the Renaissance, the equation of priest and shepherd constitutes a governing metaphor. This pastoral equation was derived from biblical sources, beginning with the shepherd Abel, and continuing with the shepherd David and the imagery of the twenty-third Psalm, the Song of Solomon, the prophetic denunciations of unfaithful shepherds in Jeremiah and Ezekiel, Christ the Good Shepherd, the Lamb of Revelation, and in all the persistent metaphors of pastor and flock in the Church. Petrarch, Spenser, and Milton were able to exploit this pervasive pastoral language in writing their pastoral allegory and religious satire.

Virgil's golden age *Eclogue*, of course, provided the classical link with the biblical tradition. Christian interpreters of this *Eclogue* perceived echoes of the Hebrew prophets and prefigurations of Christian revelation. The Virgilian theme of the divine child-savior and the coming of the new golden age was inevitably taken over by Christian pastoral poets, who saw particular significance in the simple shepherds who first heard of the divine birth and who represented the exaltation of Christian humility. This simplicity and humility are characteristics of the ideal priest as he dedicates his life's work to the care of his flock.

The great potential of the pastoral for variation and invention allowed Petrarch and Boccaccio the freedom to transform the poem of Arcadian *otium* into a polemical instrument of satire and invective on the corruption of Rome. Their Latin eclogues are vehicles for didacticism and personal allegory. Battista Mantovano, known as Mantuan, further developed the didactic and allegorical pastoral in the sixteenth century, continuing to use it for satire on abuses in the Church. Mantuan's purpose and tone, like Petrarch's, are clearly different from Virgil's. Because Mantuan preserves the figure of the shepherd as dramatic persona, his poems have superficial similarity with Virgil's *Eclogues*. Assuming the role of simple shepherd, he exposes the worldliness, ambition, and vanity of the court. Rather than retreating from the world into Arcadia, he leaves Arcadia far behind him in order to engage in combat with the social and political world of his time.

In their definition of the pastoral, the Elizabethan critics Webbe and Puttenham were influenced by the Continental humanists and Virgil. They insisted that in the hierarchy of literary kinds, pastoral was the most humble form of poetry, epic the highest. At the same time, however, they showed how the pastoral does in fact border upon greater matters in the nonpastoral world of ecclesiastical and political history. Though the problem of stylistic decorum in the allegorical pastoral had troubled these theorists because they saw an incongruity between high matters and the rude and homely manner of uncouth swains, they attempted to explain it away by insisting upon an allegorical "cloake of simplicitie." Puttenham's *The Arte of English Poesie* exemplifies the Renaissance understanding of the pastoral poem:

> the Poet deuised the *Eglogue*. . . not of purpose to counterfait or represent the rusticall manner of loues and communication, by vnder the vaile of homely persons and in rude speeches to insinuate and glaunce at greater matters, and such as perchance had not bene safe to haue been disclosed in any other sort, which may be perceiued by the Eglogues of *Virgill*, in which are treated by figures matters of greater importance than the loues of *Titirus* and *Corydon*. These Eglogues came after to containe and enforme morall discipline, for the amendment of mans behauior, as be those of *Mantuan* and other Poets.[1]

The moral idealism of the Renaissance pastoral poet and his use of the genre to confront the experiential world, with its evil and corruption, constitute a movement from Arcadian innocence and contemplative withdrawal toward an active and critical participation in society, exposing its wrongs for the public good. These ideals are similar to the moral seriousness of the poet who wishes to write heroic poetry that would inspire a nation to virtuous action. Yet, by maintaining some pastoral themes and many conventions, the poet preserves the protection of humility, self-deprecation, and allegory.

Ambivalent motives compelled Spenser to choose the pastoral form when he wrote *The Shepheardes Calender*. On the one hand, he emphasizes the traditionally humble rank of pastoral by concealing his identity under the pseudonym of "Immerito"; on the other, he is introduced as "our new poete,"[2] and he includes E. K.'s complicated machinery of erudite gloss and commentary as if to encourage the reader to think that this poem is a major contribution to world literature.[3] Furthermore, he expresses in the poem his discontent with the narrowness of the pastoral's range and his ambition to write a work with a higher mission. By urging comparison with both Virgil and Chaucer, Spenser shows us that he continues the artistic purpose of his great predecessors, and by placing himself at once in a great tradition, invites us to see his poetic career as following Virgil's, progressing from apprenticeship to maturity, humility to ambition, contemplation to action, and from pastoral to heroic.

The Shepheardes Calender

The Shepheardes Calender is a complex poem that explores and clarifies the nature of pastoral poetry, the role of the poet and his relation to the experiential world of nature, love and death, society, and religion. The pastoral tradition Spenser inherited, classical and Renaissance, enabled him to create a poem of complex unity that defines and comprises the diversity, contradictions, and harmonies of pastoral experience.[4] He had canvassed the whole range of pastoral poetry, from Theocritus and Virgil to Mantuan and Marot, and he used themes and conventions that the genre provided. In its Renaissance development, the pastoral poet could venture out of Arcadia to explore all of human experience, in court and city, through the use of conventional pastoral perspectives. Unlike many of those harshly didactic and allegorical poems which tended to impoverish the imaginative beauty of Virgil's original Arcadia, Spenser's *Shepheardes Calender* enriched the pastoral tradition by uniting aesthetic pastoral song and polemical satire, contemplation and action.

E. K.'s classification of the eclogues into "plaintive," "recreative," and "moral" helps place *The Shepheardes Calender* in a clarifying perspective. While the idea of three "formes or rankes" simplifies the complex unity of the whole poem, it enables the reader to trace its overall pattern with greater ease and understanding.

The recreative eclogues, "March," "Aprill," and "August," are about the making of poetry. They are the most Arcadian in the sense that they take place in the timeless, fictive golden world where humble shepherd-poets have freedom and *otium* to create poetry. These idyllic eclogues share the purpose and mood of Virgil's third and seventh *Eclogues* in their playful singing matches, their combination of freedom and form. In these eclogues young Spenser, like Virgil before him, tests his poetic craft through imitating and individualizing the pastoral lyric tradition.

The moral eclogues, "Februarie," "Maye," "Julye," "September," and "October," examine the relationship between the poet and the world outside the circumscribed artifice of Arcadia. The shepherd-poet becomes a moral pastor who is concerned with the problems of the fallen, experiential world. In these eclogues, the didactic, allegorical, and satirical strains are developed as a way of critically exploring the anti-pastoral world while still maintaining pastoral conventions. These eclogues, closest in outlook and technique to those of the Renaissance humanists, Mantuan in particular, use the pastoral to reduce the complexity of the iron age by the conventions of form and by allegorizing the political and religious condition of England.[5] The "October" eclogue explores in specific terms the responsibility of the shepherd as poet-pastor. While the recreative eclogues demonstrate the aesthetic pleasure to be derived from poetry, the moral eclogues insist upon the obligaton of poetry to serve the public good.

The plaintive eclogues, "Januarye," "June," "November," and "December," deal with the disasters of love, death, and grief. The shepherd is seen as lover and poet, but primarily as a human being who is part of the natural order, and therefore involved by his mortality in the cycle of mutability and death. As lover the shepherd experiences the pangs of unrequited love for unfaithful Rosalind; as humble poet he suffers unfulfilled ambition; as man he is victim of fallen nature and mutability. That the *Calender* begins and concludes with the plaintive eclogues sets the pervading melancholy tone for the whole poem. The theme of rebirth, however, emerges from Spenser's consideration of mutability, and it constitutes an integral part of the poem's pattern; it is an implicit intention of the calendar form itself.

E. K. explains why Spenser begins his calendar year with the month of January rather than March, when the official year began, by focusing on the religious theme of rebirth:

> for the incarnation of our mighty Saviour and eternall Redeemer, the Lord Christ, who, as then renewing the state of the decayed world, and returning the compasse of expired yeres to theyr former date and first commencement, left to us his heires a memoriall of his birth in the ende of the last yeere and beginning the next.

Here E. K. underscores the importance of the Nativity in the *Calender*. It suggests the historical as well as mythic confrontation between the pagan and Christian traditions. Pagan in origin, the classical pastoral is characterized by *lacrimae rerum*, a melancholy perception of man's fragile existence in the fallen world of nature. The Christian pastoral, however, with its faith in an order of grace and eternity, understands that man is able to transcend the world. Virgil's fourth *Eclogue*, in celebrating the regeneration of man and nature, provides the Christian pastoral poet with the necessary link between the Nativity and the return of the golden age. Without hope and faith, Colin, like those "heathen philosophers" who could not conceive of the Incarnation, is vulnerable to the tormenting pressures of existence and he falls into faithless despair. Had he turned from the pagan Pan to Christ, the greater Pan and shepherd-King, he would have awakened from his death-in-life.

Spenser gave Colin so much psychological reality as the thwarted lover and disillusioned poet in the *Calender* that many readers accept E. K.'s identification of Colin with Spenser in the "Dedicatory Epistle." Colin's abandonment of the pastoral world in some sense prefigures Spenser's, but Spenser, unlike his shepherd protagonist, leaves Arcadia in order to progress to a higher mission, writing heroic poetry. Colin, on the other hand, is paralyzed by his introversion and despair, and is incapable of any creative productivity. Most important, whereas Colin's despair has a pagan sadness, Spenser's faith is founded on the Christian order transcending time.

Clearly, Spenser could go outside himself and into the minds of various personae. Just as Virgil should not be identified merely with Tityrus or Menalcas, so Spenser does not limit himself to any one of his personae. Spenser, moreover, does not use the names of his characters with any uniformity. He is as much Piers or Diggon Davie as he is Colin Clout; he is both the young Cuddie and aged Thenot in the "Februarie" eclogue. Spenser uses all these roles to explore various pastoral perspectives, to play with attitudes and reveal states mind. Other characters, even oafish Thomalin and cynically frivolous Palinode, are facets of the controlling consciousness of the poem because Spenser is sensitive to the diversity and contradictions of pastoral experiences. From eclogue to eclogue, these attitudes and perspectives receive varying degrees of emphasis. Spenser assumes the imaginative identity of "Immerito," not any one shepherd, and as Immerito he ranges the entire poem. The "I" of the prologue and epilogue is Spenser as Immerito, the controlling voice of the *Calender*.

It is the artistic consciousness and shaping imagination of Immerito that unifies the whole work. Introduced as the New Poet, Immerito demonstrates his humility as an apprentice to the tradition and his professional craftsmanship in the sophisticated use of a variety of modes and verse forms. Comprehensive in scope, *The Shepheardes Calender* is a mosaic of diverse pastoral materials. In one collection of twelve eclogues Spenser brings together nearly every aspect of Renaissance pastoral, love complaint, debate, singing match, panegyric, elegy, allegory, and religious satire. His stylistic virtuosity is manifest, moreover, in his innovative use of many prosodic forms, from old-fashioned alliterative verse, fourteeners, and sestina, to the experimental stanzaic forms in "Aprill" and "November." While the Renaissance humanists, following Virgil's example, adopted the hexameter as the proper meter for the pastoral eclogue, Spenser's experimentation and versatility identify him as the "new poete" who in the *Calender* gives promise of a new age in English poetry.

Indeed, it was the Englishness of his poem in particular that won approval from his contemporaries. Borrowing for all pastoral sources, Theocritus, Bion, Virgil, Mantuan, and Marot, Spenser individualized and naturalized the pastoral genre by his original use of native elements of the language. One achievment, according to E. K., was Spenser's restoration of "good and natural English words as have bene long out of use and almost cleare disinherited." Mircea Eliade has pointed out in his studies of mythic archetypes that all poetry is "effort to recreate the language" as it journeys back to the "perfection of the beginning of things," a mythic golden age.[6] For Spenser, the *illud tempus* is Chaucer's time, and the archaic language he tries to re-create is the language of the original paradisal age of English poetry.

Chaucer and his language, called by Spenser in *The Faereie Queene* the "well of English undefyled" (4. 2. 32), provide the national and poetic authority for his poem, placing the new poet as successor to the great old master in a poetic line. Calling Chaucer his master, Spenser deliberately overlooks the great span of time separating himself from that "loadstarre of our language," considered to be the first and only great English poet. While he imitates pastoral themes and conventions of Theocritus, Bion, and Virgil, and adapts material from Mantuan and Marot, it is his recurrent strategy to express indebtedness only to Chaucer. Throughout the *Calender*, from the prologue "To His Book" to the concluding "Envoy," he echoes, borrows from, and alludes to the English poet. In the two framing poems, the prologue and epilogue, Spenser imitates and transforms Chaucer's farewell to *Troilus*. Spenser's introductory poem suggests that the new poet begins where the old poet left off, and in the "Envoy" he ends where he began, completing the whole cycle of the year and poem.[7]

In both the "Februarie" and "June" eclogues the dedicated apprentice pays homage to his master, Chaucer. Before the old shepherd, Thenot, in "Februarie," relates to young Cuddie the illustrative moral fable of the Oak and the Briar, he tells him that he had heard it in his youth from Tityrus, who kept sheep on the hills of Kent. Even Cuddie knows the reputation of Tityrus and has heard some of his tales: "They bene so well thewed, and so wise,/ What ever that good old man bespake" (96-97). Thenot describes Tityrus's tales: "Many meete tales of youth did he make,/ And some of love, and some of chevalrie" (98-99), and he remarks that he sees particular applicability of his fable of the Oak and the Briar to the debate on age and youth in which the two shepherds are engaged: "But none fitter than this to applie,/ Now listen a while, and hearken the end" (100-101). This fable, exploring the relationship between old and new, originated with a "good old man" who could tell "tales of youth": that is, Tityrus-Chaucer, represented by the Oak, bestows upon the younger shepherd-poet, Spenser, who is a wise briar, an ample shelter of wisdom and poetic tradition. The new poet, for all his innovative talents, expresses his dependence on, and reverence for, the great Oak of English poetry.

The very fact that Spenser acknowledges his indebtedness here reconciles the difference between old and new, resolving in advance the fable's conflict between youth and age. Moreover, in E. K.'s gloss, which equates Tityrus and Chaucer, the editor sustains Spenser's esteem for the old poet with his own eulogy:

> I suppose he meanes Chaucer, whose prayse for pleasaunt tales cannot dye, so long as the memorie of hys name shal live, and the name of poetrie endure.

Because it was believed in Spenser's time that Chaucer had written the ecclesiastical satire *The Ploughman's Tale*, and because the genuine *Canterbury Tales* develops moral and satirical themes, Spenser praises his great predecessor in the first of his moral eclogues.

Spenser praises the plaintive strains of Chaucer's poetry as well as the moral. Colin laments Chaucer's death in "June," a plaintive eclogue about love and the writing of poetry:

> The god of shepheardes, Tityrus, is dead,
> Who taught me, homely as I can, to make.
> He, whilst he lived, was the sovereigne head
> Of shepheardes all that bene with love ytake:
> Well couth he wayle his woes. . . .
>
> (81-85)

Colin's self-regarding withdrawal is contrasted with the healthy and productive vitality of Tityrus, whose tales of love and chivalry transfigure experience and transcend private suffering. As artist and lover, Tityrus-Chaucer has reconciled poetry and love; Colin has not.

In W. J. Bate's terminology,[8] Chaucer is Spenser's parental, and Virgil, his classical-ancestral, past. Whereas "Tityrus" is the name given Chaucer, Virgil in the "October" eclogue is called "the Romish Tityrus," a derivative title suggesting his subordinate position. In the "Envoy," however, Spenser reconciles and unites the Roman Virgil and English Chaucer as he tells his *Calender*: "Dare not to match the pype with Tityrus hys style." Here both poets are subsumed under one pastoral name, and in the concluding lines,

> Nor with the Pilgrim that the Ploughman playd awhile:
> But followe them farre off, and their high steppes adore:
> The better please, the worse despise; I aske no more,

he continues his role of humble, self-deprecating Immerito, as he identifies Chaucer's Pilgrim Ploughman with Langland's *Piers Plowman*. These are two English vernacular poems which, like the moral eclogues, make full use of pastoral allegory to satirize the corruption of a worldly priesthood. Of course Spenser, while explicitly eschewing comparison with Virgil, Chaucer, or Langland, implicitly encourages his reader to identify him as their literary heir and as a new member in the community of great pastoralists. Eager to acknowledge his role of disciple and his indebtedness to the literary past, Spenser does not feel intimidated or inhibited by his masters. While he is self-conscious about his use of predecessors, he feels assured of his ability to merge English poetry with the European tradition, and of the uniqueness of his own contribution to pastoral poetry.

Of the three recreative eclogues, two are attributed to the "nightingale of the shepherds," Colin himself. The hymn-strophes of "Aprill" and the highly formal sestina of "August" both demonstrate Colin's sophisticated poetic skills. The "Aprill" eclogue epitomizes the paradise of poetry that the pastoral world, free from compulsion and the necessities of life, can be. Recreative poetry is the poetry of *otium*, revealing the shepherd-poet's love of song and life of enjoyable ease. We are told by Hobbinol, however, that Colin sang this song before he was rejected by Rosalind and broke his shepherd's pipe. Even here, in an eclogue that provides us with an Elizabethan version of the golden age, we have a reminder of Colin's melancholy. While his melancholy does not permeate the hymn of praise itself, the frame of the eclogue refers to Colin's present psychological state, for he is oppressed by worries and cares. The golden age ode of "Aprill" is seen from the perspective of the past, of a poet's paradise lost. After Hobbinol sings Colin's elevated hymn of a timeless order, we are abruptly let down to a homely, dejected, and somewhat prosaic world.

Spenser's assimilation of Virgilian elements is apparent in this poem. The characterization of the rejected shepherd-lover, with its reminders of Corydon and Gallus, the two Virgilian emblems concluding the poem, and of course the ode itself, which thematically and generically is indebted to Virgil's fourth *Eclogue*, all serve to classicize the poem. Like Virgil's golden age *Eclogue*, "Aprill" integrates the experiential world of history and politics by pastoralizing it, and elevating it to a mythic level. Rather than divorcing the *locus amoenus* from the real world, the poet harmonizes them by insisting upon the interrelationship of the social and artistic order.[9]

Despite his assimilation of classical themes and conventions, Spenser shows his independence from Virgil by emphasizing particularly national, English aspects of his golden age. While Elisa is presented as the shepherds' goddess, Spenser never lets us forget she is also Queen of England. The "laye of faire Elisa" is therefore a patriotic hymn as well as pastoral love song. Comparing the complexion of Elisa's "angelick face" to red and white roses, the poet both draws from the conventions of love poetry and emblematically alludes to the Houses of Lancaster and York. The introduction of the "Ladyes of the Lake" in his pastoral procession of mythic deities evokes the allegorical pageantry of Queen Elizabeth's royal entertainments at Kenilworth. While Elisa is transformed into Astraea, she is still the Virgin Queen of England. The Pan-Syrinx myth, classical in origin, also carries national allegorical meanings:

> Pan may be proud, that ever he begot
>   Such a bellibone,
> And Syrinx rejoyse, that ever was her lot
>   To bear such an one.
>
> (91-94)

In this mythological genealogy, which identifies her as offspring of Pan and Syrinx, Elisa is an appropriate subject for pastoral song. Yet we are told by E. K. that "Pan is here meant [to stand for] the most famous and victorious king, her highnesse father, late of worthy memorye, King Henry the Eight." Moreover, the nymphs and graces dance in an English countryside profuse with native flowers. This pastoral panegyric, for all its sophisticated courtliness, has the simplicity of popular and native country song. Spenser cultivates English homeliness through the shepherd singer's rustic diction:

> Soone as my younglings cryen for the dam,
> To her will I offer a milkwhite lamb:
>   Shee is my goddess plaine,
>   And I her shepherds swayne,
> Albee forswonck and forswatt I am.
>
> (95-99)

Through "Aprill" the poet moves from Virgil's Arcadia to the England of Chaucer and Langland, and then to the age of

Elizabeth, the royal entertainments, and a new age of poetry. The whole tone of "Aprill" is one of play, at once sophisticated and spontaneous, uniting what Johan Huizinga calls the "two play-idealizations *par excellence*" of the Renaissance, the "two 'Golden Ages of Play,'" which are "the pastoral life and the chivalrous life."[10]

Without transition, the poet turns from the playfully rustic diction of that stanza to a heroic mode: "I see Calliope speede her to the place,/ Where my goddess shines" (100-101). The Muse of epic poetry responds to Elisa's presence because she represents the heroic as well as the pastoral ideal. As divinely anointed ruler of the body politic, she embodies justice and order. To the iron world, with its injustices and conflicts, she brings heroic deeds worthy of an epic voice, and she restores a golden age of peace and harmony.

In this golden age nature, too, is restored. Through deliberate artifice the poet heightens and idealizes nature:

> "Bring hether the pincke and purple cullambine,
>   With gellifloures;
> Bring coronations, and sops in wine,
>   Worne of paramoures;
> Strowe me the ground with daffadowndillies,
> And cowslips, and kingcups, and loved lillies."

> (136-40)

These flowers are not part of fallen nature and therefore not seasonal; they are decorative flowers that exist timelessly in a golden world of art. The progression of the seasons in the calendar's year has nothing to do with a bouquet gathered in timeless Arcadia.

Sidney's famous definition of poetry in "An Apologie for Poetrie" has important implications for Spenser's golden age eclogue and pastoral poetry in particular. Sidney argues that poetry provides mankind with an ideal world:

> Nature neuer set forth the earth in so rich tapistry as diuers Poets haue done, neither with plesant riuers, fruitful trees, sweet smelling flowers, nor whatsoeuer els may make the too much loued earth more louely. Her world is a brasen, the Poets only deliuer a golden.[11]

The poet's purpose, according to Sidney, is the creation of a golden world of art not by imitating nature, but by heightening and idealizing it in a verbal construct of his vision. A golden world that is timeless, ordered, and artificial can be created outside and above the ordinary time of the fallen, brazen world.

According to Sidney, fallen man has lost a golden Eden and his will has been "infected." Man's essential "erected wit," however, is able to sanction and confirm a golden world on earth. This world provides a pattern of and for man's erected wit. Spenser's description of Elisa ascending with the Graces to heaven represents the transforming power of divine art in reordering the life of nature and man. She is the fourth Grace, artistic inspiration. She may aid the poet in his attempt to harmonize art and nature, poetry and society, pastoral and heroic. The "Aprill" eclogue exemplifies Sidney's doctrine that the moral purpose of visionary poetry is to redeem man and restore him to his golden world.

The "August" eclogue shares with "Aprill" a delight in the making of poetry for its own sake. Here, too, we fine the *otium* that frees the shepherd-poet to pursue his pastoral Muse. In both of these recreative eclogues Spenser calls attention to his artifice, to pastoral conventions and especially to the complex verse forms of hymn and sestina, which suggest the time and careful attention Colin had at one time given to his poetry. In the "August" eclogue also, the song is not sung by Colin himself but by another shepherd. The song Cuddie sings, however, is a lament of love and reveals in its tragic tone the decline of Colin's spirits since April.

Divided into two parts, the "August" eclogue is comprised of contrasting songs, the improvisatory, amoebaean singing match between Perigot and Willye, and the formal sestina of Colin's. The tone of the singing match is playfully light hearted, but Willye's pledge cup, "a mazer ywrought of the maple warre," hints at a natural world that is aggressively hostile and inimical to pastoral *otium*. Two scenes are preprsented on the panels of the mazer: "beres and tygres, that maken fiers warre" and a shepherd running to save an innocent lamb from a wolf's jaws. Spenser's description of the cup stresses its crude style, for it is unlike the elegant cups in Theocritus and Virgil. The ruthless beasts of prey pictured on the shepherd's mazer intimate, as did the chill snake lurking, after the singing match in Virgil's third *Eclogue*, a sense of menace and imminent disaster.

After the pastoral conventions of the challenge, the pledges, and the election of Cuddie as judge, the two contestants engage in a traditional singing match in the amoebaean pattern of Theocritus and Virgil. A sense of formal play pervades their poetry-making, as Perigot initiates a subject for his song and Willye invents a variation, improvising something new to surpass him. In a gay rhythm the brief, rapid, and alternating lines of the two contestants create a sense of spontaneity and harmony. Their roundelay in praise of love is playful in tone, treating lovesickness in a comic or mock-tragic way.[12] The pastoral world of the two shepherds is innocent, a timeless world of *lusus*, with formal rules but no perils.

After their "roundels fresh," Colin's "doolefull verse of Rosalind," sung by Hobbinol, makes a dramatic tonal contrast. This "heavy laye" is also about love, but it is neither merry nor impromptu. Written in elaborate sestina form, the poem is superior in artistry to the simple roundelay, and it expresses passion, not play. Perigot and Willye are hushed by Colin's song, and the sunlit Arcadian world is darkened by the lugubrious tones of Colin's despair. At the conclusion of the song, Colin identifies himself with the nightingale,

> That blessed byrd, that spends her time of sleepe
> In songs and plaintive pleas, the more taugment
> The memory of hys misdeed, that bred her woe,
>
> (183-86)

and through this allusion to the legend of Philomela and Tereus, the poet presents himself as a violated, tormented singer of loss and darkness. He is a nightingale, perhaps, singing in the wild and savage world engraved on Willye's mazer.

Just as there is in "August" a contrast of tone between a popular roundelay and an elegant Italianate sestina, so the "March" eclogue contrasts opposing modes, the homely realism of Chaucer and the artificial Cupid-idyll of Bion. Only in the "holiday" world of recreative poetry can Spenser have such a free field for the imaginative play of incongruities. Like Theocritus, he evokes and exploits his characters' rustic language and behavior for comic purposes, and the comedy is intensified when Thomalin, a simple country bumpkin, is placed in a situation beyond his naive, literalistic understanding. Initiated by Cupid into the mysterious rites of love, he cannot, for all his blustering pretentions, understand the meaning of his experience.

The contrast between loutish Thomalin and the exotic little god with golden quiver and silver bow is comically incongruous, as is Thomalin's ineffectual attempt to pursue his quarry and shoot an immortal spirit. Because he does not understand the nature of his adversary, Thomalin relies completely on physical means to capture the "winged lad." But when Thomalin recalls the adventure, he earnestly assumes the role of epic narrator and hero. Being a braggart, he exaggerates his hunter's deeds so that his tale as a result is boasting, even mock-heroic in tone:

> But were it faerie, feend, or snake,
> My courage earnd it to awake,
> And manfully thereatt shotte.
>
> (76-78)

In contrast to the eclogues in which the poet seriously introduces the high matter and style of the epic, "March" plays with the incongruity of false heroics in the pastoral setting of real rustics. Thomalin, unlike the singers in "Aprill" and "August," fails as a shepherd-poet. Because he is incapable of either heroic action or heroic narration, his tale exposes the inability of the artless bumpkin to enter the heroic world.

If the recreative eclogues offer an idealization of pastoral *otium*, they can provide only a temporary relief. The moral eclogues increasingly demonstrate the existence of evil in the fallen world, and the inadequacy of pastoral poetry to deal with that evil. As the reader turns from the recreative to the moral eclogues, he leaves a timeless holiday and enters a time-haunted world that reflects more clearly the problems of real life.

"Februarie" is not so harshly satirical or denunciatory as the later moral eclogues, but like them it centers on a debate, and it also makes use of allegory, though that allegory is, as E. K. remarks, "rather morall and generall then bent to any secrete or particular purpose."

The thematic conflict between tradition and innovation in Thenot's tale of the Oak and the Briar has direct relevance to the shepherd both as poet and as pastor. All new poets, particularly pastoral poets like Spenser himself in *The Shepheardes Calender*, must recognize and use the rich resources of the pastoral tradition and at the same time contribute to that tradition by writing poems that are expressions of individual talent. But the tale of the Oak and the Briar also illustrates the dangers of excessive love for age and tradition, which can be perverted into blind superstition. It is foolish to venerate a decayed tradition that has lost its vitality:

> For it had bene an auncient tree,
> Sacred with many a mysteree,
> And often crost with priestes crewe,
> And often halowed with holy water dew.
> But sike fancies weren foolerie,
> And broughten this Oake to this miserye.
> For nought mought they quitten him from decay.
>
> (207-13)

This satirical image of heathen tree-worshipers has, of course, an allegorical function that is more specific than general. In its implications regarding a degenerate priesthood, it anticipates "Maye," "Julye," and "September," moral eclogues that develop and intensify Spenser's satirical attack upon bad shepherds and the corruption of the purity of the Christian priesthood.

Spenser introduces the theme of a worldly priesthood in the "Maye" eclogue. While the bad shepherd wants to enjoy a pastoral life free from care and responsibility, the good shepherd reminds us that the pastoral world of innocence is compassed round by the fallen world, and the corrupting influence of that world has already affected shepherd-pastors who have betrayed their vows and exposed their flocks to the invasion of deceitful, devouring wolves. With "some Satyrical bitterness," as E. K. terms it, Spenser writes an allegory of the religious condition of England. Milton read the "Maye" eclogue as a religious satire, and he remarked in his *Animadversions:*

> that false Shepheard *Palinode* in the Eclogue of May, under whom the Poet lively personates our Prelates, whose whole life is a recantation of the pastorall vow, and whose profession to forsake the World, as they use the matter, boggs them deeper into the world: Those our admired *Spencer* inveighs against, not without some presage of these reforming times.[13]

Piers and Palinode, two shepherd-pastors, debate about the role of priest in the world. Spenser characterizes Palinode as an irresponsible and hedonistic pastor, and Piers as a dutiful and austere one. A conscientious pastor dedicated to the welfare of his flock, Piers is probably named after Piers Plowman, whose name since the English reformation was synonymous with the good spiritual shepherd. E. K. interprets the characterization of the two shepherd-pastors in specific allegorical terms. They represent, according to him, "two formes of pastoures or ministers. . . the Protestant and Catholique." His gloss, moreover, elaborates upon what he sees as a satirical attack on Catholicism, specifically "the Pope, and his Anti-christian prelates, which usurpe a tyrannical dominion in the Churche," and "the false and faithlesse Papistes." While the ecclesiastical allusions in the eclogue do suggest Palinode's love for paganism in the medieval church, he is presented in a more general way as a false pastor who has been seduced by the sensual pleasures of this world and has betrayed his spiritual calling.

May Day elicits from Palinode an instinctive desire to participate with "yougthes folk" in their pagan revelries. Instead of tending his flock, he wants to sing and dance to the lusty music of horn and tabor, and worship the wanton Lady Flora, a parody of the Virgin Queen. Palinode would prefer to be a pagan and throw off the responsibilities of the priesthood by playing in the May games of Merrie England. Not willing to admit that mankind no longer lives in a pagan golden age, he praises the ideals of pastoral *otium*, pleasure, "ease and leasure," but defined against Piers's sense of pastoral duty,

Palinode's love of licentious pleasure is a corruption of the concept of *otium*. To Piers's gloomy admonitions he responds lightheartedly:

> Sorrowe ne need be hastened on:
> For he will come, without calling, anone.
> While times enduren of tranquilitie,
> Usen we freely our felicitie.
>
> (152-55)

Palinode seems frivolous in his gaiety, "a worldes child," and dangerously irresponsible as a pastor. Piers sees that the shepherd who does not feed his sheep and lets them run at large alone has forsaken his duty, and misgoverned "all the welth and the trust/ That his father left by inheritaunce." Lulled by false feelings of security, the selfish pastor will abandon his vulnerable flock to wolves in sheep's clothing:

> . . . under colour of shepeheards, somewhile
> There crept in wolves, ful of fraud and guile,
> That often devoured their owne sheepe,
> And often the shepheards that did hem keepe.
>
> (126-29)

Piers's warning, of course, echoes Matthew 7:15, "False prophets, which come to you in sheep's clothing, but inwardly are ravening wolves." Unlike Palinode, Piers sees that the real world is fallen, and malicious wolves roam the English countryside. Because the shepherd must constantly be vigilant against imminent attack, he cannot deceive himself into spiritual complacency.

In both the "Julye" and "September" eclogues, Spenser borrows themes from Mantuan, the pastoral satirist of the Catholic clergy. The "Julye" eclogue, derived from Mantuan's eighth eclogue, dramatizes a debate between ambition and lowliness. Humility, the low estate, is, of course, a major pastoral premise, for all shepherd-poets acknowledge the humbleness of their lowly subjects and homely manner. But here, in moral eclogues that deal with the shepherd as priest, the concept of lowliness is an ideal of the Christian faith and Christian clergy.

Morrell tries to justify man's aspiring mind by using the imagery of the sacred hill and mountain, alluding to St. Michael's mount, Parnassus, and Mount Olivet, and arguing that "hills bene nigher heaven." In contrast, Thomalin praises the humility of true shepherds, and warns Morrell of the dangers of ambition: "Great clymbers fall unsoft." He uses the symbolic image of the valley and "lowly playne" in his advocacy of pastoral meekness and simplicity, and interprets Morrell's "aspiration" as being spiritual pride: "And he that strives to touch the starres/ Oft stumbles at a straw" (99-100). He soon recognizes, however, that good men have lived on hills, shepherds such as Abel, Jacob's sons, and Moses, who kept "the flockes of Mighty Pan." But now, he argues, shepherd-priests are not like those biblical shepherds in the golden age. They exploit others for their own profit and, becoming wealthy, pamper themselves in pleasure. Selfishly fattening themselves, they misuse their flock: "Theyr sheepe han crustes, and they the bread."

In "September," the most satirically bitter of the moral eclogues, Spenser borrows his dramatic situation from Virgil's first *Eclogue*. The wandering shepherd, Diggon Davie, has just returned home from a trip abroad, disillusioned and poor. He reports the moral corruption and spiritual pride he has seen abroad to Hobbinol, who has remained peacefully at home. He has witnessed the unscrupulousness of pastors and parasitical courtiers who have made themselves wealthy with church property.

Attempting to moralize on the dangers of restless ambition, Hobbinol praises the ideal of *otium*:

> Content who lives with tryed state
>   Neede feare no chaunge of frowning fate:
>   But who will seeke for unknowne gayne,
>   Oft lives by losse, and leaves with payne.
>
> (70-73)

Diggon admits to Hobbinol that he had been guilty "with vayne desyre and hope to be enricht." Hobbinol recognizes the dangers of pride and ambition, but his speech about contentment in the face of Diggon's bitter experience seems to avoid

important moral issues. Like Tityrus in Arcadia, Hobbinol is
not willing to address himself to the existence of evil in the
world. *Otium* is under the threat of imminent attack since
there are ravening wolves in sheep's clothing roaming the
world. His contentment, therefore, is precarious. Hobbinol's
pastoral paradise, cloistered from the world, is made all the
more vulnerable because of his inability to recognize evil.[14]
This inability reveals the narrowness of his view, which
precludes moral responsibility.

Diggon Davie does not limit his recognition of evil to corruption abroad; he attacks established institutions at home for
their moral degeneration. When Diggon becomes rather
specific in his accusations against bad English shepherds and
the "bigge bulles of Basan," Hobbinol becomes fearful:

> Nowe, Diggon, I see thou speakest plain;
> Better it were a little to feyne,
> And cleanly cover that cannot be cured:
> Such il as is forced mought nedes be endured.
>
> (136-39)

A desire for an idyllic peace leads to his political temporizing
and toleration of the world's evils. For all Diggon's warnings,
Hobbinol wishes or pretends to believe that there are no
ravenous wolves in England:

> Fye on thee Diggon, and all thy foul leasing,
> Well is knowne that sith the Saxon King,
> Never was Woolfe seene many nor some,
> Nor in all Kent, nor in Christendom.
>
> (150-53)

Diggon's cautionary tale of Roffy proves the presence of
wolves among their English sheep, and shows how even the
wise, Argus-eyed Roffy and his watchdog Lowder are deceived
by a wolf's malicious intent. Hobbinol, not willing to recognize
the presence of wolves, is more defenseless and vulnerable to
attack. His response to Diggon's woeful tale, like that of
Tityrus upon hearing the lament of dispossessed Meliboeus, is
to offer him a temporary shelter:

But were Hobbinol as God mought please,
Diggon should soone find favour and ease.
But if to my cotage thou wilt resort,
So as I can I wil thee comfort.

(252-55)

Although Hobbinol's hospitality reveals human decency, his optimism is shallow, and he cannot give an adequate answer to Diggon's moral outrage.

The "September" eclogue dramatizes the moral impossibility of contentment and withdrawal when evil infiltrates the shepherd's consciousness in Arcadia. Exploring the declining moral conditions in England, the moral eclogues exemplify the poet's need to reject the pastoral life in order to confront the iron world, and to expose those wrongs which infect it. That these wrongs require remedy and retribution becomes more clear as the moral eclogues insist upon the public and social mission of the poet. The poet's problem, then, is how he can participate in a corrupt world without being infected by its evil, and how he can assume a role in serving the public good.[15] The shepherd as pastor and poet has only a limited function since he continually withdraws from the iron world into the contentment and security of his *locus amoenus*. Instead, he must be prepared to reject *otium* and ambitiously dedicate himself to the poetry of heroic achievement, to call his nation to virtuous action by memorializing the hero and his epic deeds.

"October," the concluding moral eclogue, addresses itself to the problem of the responsibility of the poet. Like the preceding moral eclogues, it dramatizes a debate and expresses a complaint against the iron world, but unlike them, it provides a poetic that resolves the dialectical tensions between contemplation and action, art and life.

In the first section of the debate, Cuddie complains that his poetry goes unrewarded, "And my poore Muse hath spent her spared store, / Yet little good hath got, and much less gayne" (9-10). He regards his singing only the worthless summer play of the grasshopper. Piers tries to encourage him: "Cuddie, the prayse is better then the price, / The glory eke much greater then the gayne" (18-19). Piers's concept of the poet's role is clearly more idealistic than Cuddie's, for he perceives that poetry has a didactic function: "O what an honor is it, to restraine/ The lust of lawlesse youth with good advice" (21-22). He reminds Cuddie, who fears that nature and time will master him, that his great predecessor Orpheus tamed "the hellish hound" and brought Eurydice back "from Plutoes balefull bowre" by the power of his music. The ideal poet, according to Piers, can conquer time and even death through lasting fame.

Piers exhorts the disenchanted Cuddie to abandon the pastoral for a serious confrontation with the heroic world:

> Abandon then the base and viler clowne,
> Lyft up thy selfe out of lowly dust
> And sing of bloody Mars, and giusts,
> Turne thee to those, that weld the awful crowne.
>
> (37-40)

Here, in this passage, the guiding principle is the poetry of the active life, and the way is directed to the epic. Of course, Spenser had the Virgilian model in mind. The aspiring poet must progress beyond his apprenticeship to the pastoral and, like Virgil, adopt the heroic poet's public and social mission as spokesman for his nation, crowning his career by writing an epic that will inspire men to virtuous action. By serving "fayre Elisa," the heroic poet can fulfill the role of pastor in morally influencing the nation.

Piers, while elevating the rewards of poetry — "our Cuddie's name to heaven sownde" — turns to its theme and inspiration. He believes that the mature poet reaches beyond the role of humble shepherd, and Cuddie recognizes that this ascent imitates "the perfecte paterne of a poete." Cuddie responds by drawing a parallel with Virgil's progress from pastoral to epic poetry:

> Indeede the Romish Tityrus, I heare,
> Through his Mecoenas left his oaten reede,
> Whereon he earst had taught his flocks to feede,
> And laboured lands to yield the timely care,
> And eft did sing of Warres and deadly drede,
> So as the heavens did quake his verse to here.
>
> (55-60)

Glossing this stanza, E. K. notes that "the three severall workes of Virgile" are intended, "For in teaching his flocks to feede, is meant his Aeglogues. In labouring of lands, is hys Bucoliques. In singing of wars and deadly dread, is his divine Aeneis figured." By implication, Spenser expresses his own readiness to progress from pastoral poetry to epic poetry that has the didactic function of celebrating deeds of greatness and thereby improving the commonwealth.

Cuddie complains, however, that in this iron age there are no grateful patrons like Virgil's Maecenas, and no worthy subject like Augustus:

> But ah! Mecoenas is yclad in claye,
> And great Augustus long ygoe is dead,
> And all the worthies liggen in leade,
> That matter for poets on to play.
>
> (61-64)

Bewailing the loss of an age of heroism and heroic poetry, Cuddie grumbles that in this degenerate time he must sing "rymes of rybaudrye" or abdicate to Tom Piper.

As Piers redefines the nature of poetic inspiration, Spenser's language, like Virgil's in his fourth *Eclogue*, is elevated beyond the normal level of diction in pastoral poetry and becomes heroic. E. K. is aware of the problem of stylistic decorum in this eclogue, and he remarks in his gloss that Spenser's style is properly "more lofty than the rest, and applied to the heighte of poeticall witte." Piers's understanding of poetic inspiration is platonic and prophetic. While his theory reveals the close relationship between poet and priest, he sees that ideal love is the source of inspiration for poetry:

> . . . for love does teach him climbe so hie,
> And lyftes him up out of the loathsome myre,
> Such immortal mirrhor as he doth admire
> Would rayse ones mynd above the starrie skie,
> And cause a caytive corage to aspire.
>
> (91-95)

Whereas love in the plaintive mode of the pastoral humbles the shepherd-poet, Piers's concept of love inspires and elevates the heroic poet. In this "perfecte paterne of a poete," Piers unites love with moral responsibility and heroic courage. This union anticipates Spenser's statement of purpose in the opening stanza of *The Faerie Queene*: "Fierce warres and faithfull loves shall moralize my song."

Cuddie's humorous misconception of inspiraton, however, is limited by his own inexperience, and he can only imaginatively approximate the kind of elevation Piers speaks of by recalling how it is to feel exhilarated by "Bacchus fruit": "And when with wine the braine begins to sweate,/ The nombers flowe as fast as spring doth ryse" (107-8). Quite abruptly we are brought back down from Pier's high conception of poet as *vates*, to the lowly pastoral world with Cuddie's pleasant but unheroic concerns:

> But ah! my corage cooles ere it be warme;
> Forthy content us in thys humble shade,
> Where no such troublous tydes han us assayde.
> Here we our slender pipes may safely charme.

(115-18)

If the pastoral world had momentarily dissolved, it returns with Cuddie's shrug. He notion of content and safety defines the old ideal of withdrawal and idle ease. Their "slender pipes" can play a lovely tune, but cannot make that cosmic music of which Piers sings. The two shepherds will play their recreative pipes in the "humble shade," rather than soar "above the starry skie."

The Colin exemplum in "October" links it with the plaintive eclogues, as does the broader theme of the relationship between love and poetry.[16] Colin, unlike Piers's ideal of the love-inspired poet, has been disillusioned in love, and as a result has broken his shepherd's pipe. Cuddie says of Colin, "He, were he not with love so ill bedight,/ Would mount as high and sing as soote as swan" (89-90). Piers believes that the "immortal mirrhor" of lofty love will lift Colin "up out of the loathsome myre." The "Januarye" eclogue, however, reveals that Colin's unrequited love forces him deep into the mire of melancholy and despair. Instead of beholding the immortal mirror, he compulsively gazes at nature's mirror which reflects his own inner state: "Thou barrein ground, whome winters wrath hath wasted,/ Art made a myrrhour to behold my plight" (19-20). Although Colin sees the analogy between nature and his state of consciousness, he cannot learn the lesson that the progress of the seasons can teach him. Too eager to make the landscape a subjective symbol, he forgets that it has an objective reality. His present state of wintry barrenness is reflected in the naked trees, frost, and icicles of January, but he is young and it will not always be winter:

> Such stormy stoures breake my balefull smart,
> As if my yeare were wast and waxen old.
> And yet, alas! but now my spring begonne,
> And yet, alas! yt is already done.
>
> (27-30)

Colin does not perceive that if he lives according to nature, he will free himself from his premature winter. That he is experiencing a dark psychological state on a "sunneshine day" and a winter in the spring of his life in unnatural.[17] Both the day and his youth should suggest the possibility of renewal, but Colin does not have enough self-knowledge and foresight to hope. Winter for him need not be perpetual; the shepherd's calendar tells him that. But he returns from Pan, the shepherd's god, and rejects the sympathetic Hobbinol, who, like Virgil's Corydon, offers "clownish gifts" of "his kiddes, his cracknelles, and his early fruit." The shepherd-poet withdraws from the pastoral world into a state of neurotic despondency.

Obsessed as he is with faithless Rosalind, who hates shepherds and scorns his "rural musick," Colin neglects his own flock and then breaks his shepherd's "oaten pype." This "pensife boy," trapped by the irrationality of his emotions, falls into a spiritual death of his own making. Only if he liberates himself from his bondage to pastoral life and, like Virgil's Gallus, embarks on a life of ambitious striving and heroic action, can he escape his psychological confinement; and only if he turns from his unredeemed existence in Arcadia to address himself to a greater Pan can he transcend the narrow, mutable world of nature.[18]

The "June" and "November" eclogues dramatize these possibilties of freedom for Colin as poet, lover, and man.

Spenser traces the life cycle of his shepherd as poet and lover, and we see, as Colin does not, the way out of despair — through the active life of heroic poetry in "June," and in "November" through a faith in rebirth outside the natural order.

The "June" eclogue continues to explore Colin's melancholy introduced in "Januarye." The situation in "June" is a variant of Virgil's first *Eclogue*, in which Tityrus and Meliboeus discuss the retired life and the active life. The relation between Hobbinol and Colin resembles that between Tityrus and Meliboeus, and Hobbinol's life of *otium* corresponds to Tityrus's contemplative way of life.

Colin sees that pastoral life is impossible for him; it is like the paradisal Eden that Adam lost: "O happy Hobbinol I blesse thy state,/ That Paradise hast found, whych Adam lost" (9-10). If Arcadia constitutes spiritual contentment, then Colin, like Adam, is banished from it, as he is pursued "from coste to coste" by "angry gods," and he cannot recover his lost Eden. Although he regretfully recalls the delights of his youth in "a garden of pleasure," the older Colin recognizes that with his loss of Rosalind, pastoral life has no meaning for him.

Hobbinol praises Colin's poetry, remembering how he was able to teach the birds to sing, and when the Muses heard him, "They drewe abacke, as half with shame confound,/ Shepheard to see, them in theyr art outgoe" (63-64). While Hobbinol's advice to leave Arcadia for the court may reflect Colin's poetic ambitions, Colin paradoxically denies the ambitious implications of his praise:[19]

> Of Muses, Hobbinol, I conne no skill:
> For they bene daughters of the hyest Jove,
> And holden scorne of homely shepheards quill.
>
> (65-67)

He argues that he is a humble, simple shepherd who has no ambitions. When he tells Hobbinol, "I play to please my selfe, all be it ill," what sounds like pastoral self-sufficiency is in fact a perversion of it, for in his despondent state his playing merely to please himself is symptomatic of his introversion.[20] Colin does not want the poet's responsibility to his public, to share the Arcadian vision as a socially relevant ideal. He would prefer a life not of sweet content but of sweet discontent.

Yet, by proudly identifying himself as the disciple of great Tityrus, he admits being an heir to a poetic tradition that is socially responsible and to a creative spirit who can "lightly slake" the flames of love, and tell "mery tales, to keepe us awake,/ The while our sheepe about us safely fedde" (87-88). Colin does have poetic ambitions, but he is not fully willing to acknowledge them. He is too preoccupied with is own emotions — his hatred of Rosalind — to be either a pastoral or heroic poet.

The elegy on Dido in the "November" eclogue, like the lay of Elisa in "Aprill" or the sestina in "August," is Colin's own song. Colin himself sings the elegy in the present. The elegy is significant in revealing his character as man and poet, for it demonstrates the role he has forsaken, the ambivalence with which he regards the pastoral world, and his preoccupation with death.[21]

Thenot urges Colin, whom he calls "the nightingale," to sing once more, for his "Muse to long slombereth in sorrow." Colin says that now that "sadde winter" is upon him he cannot sing "light virelayes, and looser songs of love." Thenot initiates the singing by expressing grief over the death of Dido, and the elegiac tone of this song appeals to Colin's melancholy and tempts him to start. As humble shepherd, Colin modestly apologizes for his "rugged and unkempt rymes" before he sings his song, with its intricate stanzas and measured refrains.

In this song about Dido, Spenser follows Marot and adopts the thematic structure of the pastoral elegy that has Virgil's fifth *Eclogue* as its source. The elegy is two-fold: the first part, like Mopsus's funeral dirge, expresses sorrow for the loss of Dido, and the second, like Menalcas's exaltation of Daphnis, voices the consolation of contemplating her happiness in celestial paradise.

The first part of the pastoral elegy reflects Colin's sorrow, not just for "the death of some mayden of great bloud," but for himself as a victim of nature's mutability. In Dido's death he sees the symbol for his own loss of love and poetry, and his

alienation from the pastoral world. Spenser's ritualized lament
uses features of conventional elegy: invoking the Muse, asking
others to wail, describing the effects of Dido's death on nature,
the procession of the nymphs, and the dramatic turn from grief
and questioning doubt to joyful assurance.[22]

When Colin cries, "Why do we longer live, (ah, why live we
so long?)" his grief is deeply personal, and "Now is time to die"
reveals his own impatience with a life that has lost meaning. As
in Mopsus's dirge, Colin describes nature mourning the death
of a human being:

> The feeble flocks in field refuse their former foode,
> And hang theyr heads, as they would learne to weepe:
> The beares in forest wayle as they were woode,
> Except the wolves, that chase the wandring sheepe.
>
> (132-35)

The predatory wolf in the moral eclogues returns to assault the
vulnerability of innocence in Arcadia. As nature becomes
humanized in its mourning, so Colin asssumes once more the
voice of the nightingale, "Philomele her song with teares doth
steepe."

Colin's lament for the death of Dido is also a lament for the
decay of poetry: "The Muses, that were wont greene bayes to
weare,/ Now bringen bitter eldre braunches seare" (146-47). It
seems to him that now the powers of creativity and generation
have withered, and this elegy is the last song that he or any
shepherd-poet can sing. Colin's elegy is as much for his loss of-
creativity and of Arcadia, the place of poetry, as it is for Dido's
death.

Within the natural order Colin can find no consolation for
his grief:

> Now have I learn'd, (a lesson derely bought)
> That nys on earth assurance to be sought:
> For what might be in earthly mould,
> That did her buried body hould.
>
> (156-59)

Man is part of nature, and belongs to the natural cycle of
mutability and death. Yet nature manifests signs of rebirth as

well, and man may share in that.[23] This rebirth for man, however, must be outside the natural order. In the turning point of the elegy, Colin comes to the realization that we should not continue to grieve because "Dido nis dead, but into heaven hent." Like Virgil's Menalcas, Colin acts the role of poet-priest as he elevates Dido to heaven:

> She raignes a goddesse now emong the saintes,
> That whilome was the saynt of shepheards light:
> And is enstalled nowe in heavens hight.
> I see thee, blessed soule, I see,
> Walk in Elison fieldes so free.
>
> (175-79)

E. K. explains that the *"Elysian Fieldes* be devised of poetes to be a place of pleasure like Paradise, where the happye soules doe rest in peace and eternal happynesse." The poet, however, makes it a Christian Paradise. His language here becomes Christianized ("saynt," "soule") as Colin envisions the soul's release from the cycle of mutability through resurrection. These Elysian Fields, like Virgil's description of them in Book 6 of the *Aeneid*, is a *locus amoenus*, otherworldly and supernatural but still a pastoral landscape. A place of immutable *otium*, no dangers may befall the shepherd there:

> No daunger there the shepheard can astert:
> Fayre fieldes and pleasaunt layes there bene,
> The fieldes ay fresh, the grasse ay greene.
>
> (187-89)

Dido lives in this Arcadian landscape

> . . . with the blessed gods in blisse,
> There drincks she nectar with ambrosia mixt,
> And joyes enjoyes that mortall men doe misse.
>
> (193-95)

With Dido's resurrection nature and time have been defeated, and celestial paradise is described as a place where the exalted spirits live in eternal contemplative *otium*. Colin's emblem is "Ma mort ny mord," since Christ is "one that dyed for all."

While both the "October" and "November" eclogues reflect

the declining cycle, they demonstrate the powers of the human imagination to escape from, and transcend, mutability and death.[24] Man may be lifted up "out of the loathsome myre" and raised "above the starry skie" by his love, his art, and his faith.

In the final eclogue, "December," Spenser returns to Colin alone, and writes another monologue in the same stanzaic form as "Januarye," completing the cycle of the year. The year is nearly over and Colin is now old. Awaiting death, he sums up his experiences by comparing stages of his life to the four seasons of the year. In his "green cabinet," the enclosure of his "rurall song," Colin distills his life. The song begins with a memory of carefree *otium*, but it is sung by a "carefull" shepherd. In the spring of youth he had innocent freedom and joy, and was inspired by the Muse "to song and musicks mirth." He had learned his craft then, "by arte more cunning." The "wiser Muses" had followed his pipe, for he even excelled Pan in his pastoral song. In the "sommer season" he fell in love with Rosalind, and felt love's pain, losing his early freedom from care. As summer passed, and with it his "yougthly prime," he tried to apply himself "to thinges of ryper reason." His emotional bondage to faithless Rosalind was too great, however, and he perceived that his summer was "worne and wasted," and that the harvest of his maturity "was nought but brakes and brambles to be mown." He had been highly promising in youth, but now in his autumnal garden the fruit is fallen to the ground and the fragrant flowers are withered; he has reaped in his wasteland only "a weedye crop of care." Colin then telescopes his life story:

> So now my yeare drawes to his latter terme,
> My spring is spent, my sommer burnt up quite,
> My harvest hasts to stirre up Winter sterne,
> And bids him clayme with rigorous rage his ryght.
>
> (127-30)

Wrinkled with deep furrows and hoary as frost, Colin stands alone in the bleak landscape, destroyed by the winter that reigns in his heart. The sun no longer shines as it did in January when he had the opportunity for renewal. In the dying day and year, he is bitterly resigned to his death: "Winter is come, that blowes the balefull breath,/ And after winter commeth timely death" (149-50). Colin's melancholy nostalgia for the pastoral world echoes both the exiled Meliboeus and departing Gallus in Virgil's *Eclogues* as he says adieu to his delights, to his love, to his flock and woods, and to his faithful friend, "good Hobbinol." They all constitute the Arcadian world of the poetic imagination which, paradoxically, has been given permanent form by Colin, the calendar, and Spenser's pastoral art.[25]

Colin's missing emblem and Spenser's "Envoy" make explicitly clear how art both contradicts and transcends mutability. E. K. explains that the meaning of Colin's emblem is "that all thinges perish and come to theyr last end, but workes of learned wits and monuments of poetry abide for ever." In his "Envoy," Spenser describes what he has done:

> Loe! I have made a Calender for every yeare,
> That steele in strength, and time in durance, shall outweare,
> And if I marked well the starres revolution,
> It shall continue till the world's dissolution.

Spenser used the metaphor of the calendar as a regulative fiction imposing structure and meaning on man's temporal life so that it has an orderly succession.[26] The calendar metaphor provided him with a way of exploring the meaning of human experience in nature and time. But when the metaphor loses its effectiveness, the poet breaks out of his frame of reference by demonstrating the timelessness of art and the eternity of heaven.

Colin suffered despair through the metaphorical year of his life from a disillusionment in love so painful that he gave up any creative participation in the world. Though he had been given time and experience, he never achieved real self-knowledge and he surrenders gloomily to the seasonal cycle, awaiting death alone in the bleak landscape of December. The calendar framework of the poem, however, tells the reader something else; it tells him about nature, art, and religious belief. What the calendar does is to integrate the contingencies of the actual world in a satisfying, coherent design by an act of the imagination.

While the world of nature is fallen, and winter and age are destructive, there is in the cycle of seasons an orderly balance between autumn and winter and the birth and growth or spring and summer.[27] If there is an analogy between man's life and the order of the calendar year, then man must procreate and survive even if he must ultimately die. Second, the poetic calender itself is a formal work of art that transcends time, mutability, and death by its permanence. A symbol of time's progression, it is also an analogue of eternity. Finally, the theme of death and rebirth, implicit in the framework of the Nativity and manifest in the pastoral elegy of "November," insists upon Christian faith in man's resurrection. From *sub specie eternitatis* man's spiritual life is perceived as unlimited by time and mutability, for the living soul can be liberated from the confines of the unregenerate world.[28]

3

The Faerie Queene

W HEN E. K. introduced the "new poete" in his "Dedicatory Epistle" to *The Shepheardes Calender*, he asserted that a young poet should begin his literary career by writing pastoral poems, for "this kind of wryting, being both so base for the matter, and homely for the manner" is most appropriate for beginning poets when they first "trye theyr habilities." It follows, moreover, "the example of the best and most auncient poetes, which devised this kind of wryting." E. K. makes a list of poets who wrote pastorals before they progressed to more serious poetry:

> So flew Theocritus, as you may perceive he was all ready full fledged. So flew Virgile, as not yet well feeling his winges. So flew Mantuane, as being not full somd. So Petrarque. So Boccace. So Marot, Sanazarus, and also divers other excellent both Italian and French poetes.

The earlier pastoral poems in the careers of Renaissance heroic poets were, to a great degree, preliminary exercises in the craft of poetry preparatory to attempting the most exalted kind of poem. Petrarch's *Africa*, Boiardo's *Orlando Innamorato,* Ariosto's *Orlando Furioso*, and Sannazaro's *De Partu Virginis* had all been written after an apprenticeship to pastoral poetry.[1] Spenser also progressed to the heroic poem following the Virgilian pattern. He began writing *The Faerie Queene* a year after *The Shepheardes Calender* appeared.

Renaissance poets demonstrated what the critics had theorized, that the epic was the most highly respected form in the generic hierarchy. The epic had the greatest prestige because it was a poem encyclopedic in its world view, demanding of the poet a grasp and mastery of all human knowledge. Only in a poem of great size and scope could the poet integrate and synthesize a coherent view of man, history, and the universe. The heroic poet, moreover, must know the epic tradition, and by studying the ancients he could emulate and surpass them. In addition, he had to have a conception of heroic virtue and action in order to create and glorify the ideal so that his epic would have educative value. Just as the epics of Homer and Virgil were believed to be morally instructive, so the intention of the Renaissance heroic poem was to instruct and edify the reader through examples of virtuous actions that he would want to emulate.

Spenser's Virgilian intentions are clearly expressed in the opening lines of *The Faerie Queene*. He echoes the prefatory lines of the *Aeneid* printed in Renaissance editions:

> Lo! I the man, whose Muse whylome did maske,
> As time her taught, in lowly shephards weeds.
> Am now enforst, a farre unfitter taske,
> For trumpets sterne to chaunge mine oaten reeds.

Spenser's point of view here is both retrospective and prospective, for he establishes for his reader and himself the fact that *The Faerie Queene* is a work marking the end of a pastoral stage and the beginning of a new one as heroic poet.

Harvey's commendatory verse written "To the Learned Shepheard," while preserving the pastoral names of the *Calender*, Colin and Hobbinol, congratulates Spenser on his abandonment of "the layes that longs to lowly swaynes" in order to follow his "sacred fury. . .that lifts thy notes from shepheardes unto Kinges." The "Fairy Queene" herself, Harvey says, has infused

> Such high conceites into thy humble wittes,
> As raised hath poore pastors oaten reede,
> From rustick tunes, to chaunt heroique deedes.

In his "Letter" to Raleigh, the poet describes the "generall intention" of the poem:

> The generall end therefore of all the booke is to fashion a gentleman or noble person in vertuous and gentle discipline.

This passage defines the guiding principle of the poem as the poet explains both its theme and purpose. He makes his general intention more specific in the "argument" of the poem, in which he indicates that the type of gentleness and nobility is "that true glorious type" of Queen Elizabeth. He explains in the letter, moreover, that as he "fashions" or represents his virtuous noble person, Arthur, "the image of a brave knight" perfected in moral virtues, his poem will "fashion" of affectively mold a gentleman or noble person who is also the reader, in "vertuous and gentle discipline."[2]

For Spenser, as for Sidney and other Renaissance poets and theorists, the heroic poem had significant moral and educative value. For this reason, as well as for its comprehensiveness and universality, the epic was considered to be the crown of an aspiring poet's accomplishment. Sidney's praise of heroic poetry is typical of the age, and his defense of it shares Spenser's conception of his purpose:

> But if any thing be already sayd in the defence of sweete Poetry, all concurreth to the maintaining the Heroicall, which is not onely a kinde, but the best and most accomplished kinde of Poetry. For as the image of each action styrreth and instructeth the mind, so the loftie image of such Worthies most inflameth the mind with desire to be worthy, and informes with counsel how to be worthy.[3]

With such an exalted view of the epic, it is a small wonder that Renaissance poets thought of their pastoral poems as products of an apprenticeship to art and as a necessary preparation for the mature poet's heroic struggle to climb the height of literary achievement.

The *Aeneid* has been understood by Renaissance commentators as morally edifying and instructive, for the epic deeds of Aeneas glorified ancient virtues, and Virgil's hero was thought to provide a worthy example for the reader to emulate. Furthermore, they viewed the *Aeneid* as a national epic patriotic in purpose and theme. *The Faerie Queene*, like Virgil's epic, was to provide a story "doctrinal to a nation." As Augustus is prefigured in Aeneas, so Queen Elizabeth is foreshadowed in Gloriana; as Aeneas and his companions serve as models for the patriotic Roman, Prince Arthur and the titular knights of each book provide "ensamples" of virtuous conduct for the patriotic Englishman. The moral, educative, and patriotic values of the poem derive from the poet's concept of the hero, and Spenser attempted to create heroes that would inspire his reader, the gentleman or noble person, to virtuous actions.

In his Virgilian treatment of Arthur, chief of the Nine Worthies, Spenser made the heroic quest central to his epic. Since the quest is appropriate for both the chivalric romance and the soul's journey toward sainthood, he made his hero's knightly quest operate on many levels, literal and allegorical, active and contemplative. Virgilian commentators had interpreted the *Aeneid* as an allegorical epic that showed, through the deeds of the hero, both active and contemplative ideals. Landino and other Renaissance Neoplatonic commentators read Virgil's poem as a Christian allegory of the soul's progress in which Rome was a type of the City of God. Disciplined by the perturbations of the active life, Aeneas was purified so that he could achieve a final contemplative state. In more particular terms, they viewed the golden bough as a symbol of wisdom, and Aeneas's visit to the cave of Sibyl as a representation of the Platonic truth.[4]

Sidney viewed Aeneas, "so excellent a man in every way,"[5] as an epic hero who united active and contemplative ideals. "A vertuous man in all fortunes,"[6] Virgil's exemplary hero is a man who "governeth himselfe" in his familial and religious duties as well as on the battlefield. The "loftie image" of Aeneas provides an educative model both for his "outward government" and "his inward selfe."[7]

Spenser's treatment of heroism in *The Faerie Queene* insists upon this harmonious interrelationship between the inward and outward, the contemplative and active, the private and public. He shows the active life through the plot of the poem and the contemplative life through his "continued allegory." By unifying moral virtues and heroic deeds in his romance-epic, Spenser presented a possible solution to the philosophical conflict between contemplative and active ideals.[8]

The poet's inquiry into the nature of the hero and his quest is based on an understanding of fallen human nature. Because mankind lost Eden and virtue with the Fall, it is the exemplary hero's task to relearn the virtues in his struggle toward self-knowledge so he may regain lost paradise. Each of Spenser's heroes pursues his quest in such a way as to manifest an individual virtue, and at the same time define and exemplify its nature. Moreover, each quest dramatizes both the perils that impede the hero's progress and the spiritual and psychological conditions that provide the necessary aid in achieving the objective of his quest.

The pastoral episodes that constitute natural settings for the hero's contemplation, self-knowledge, and regeneration provide a means by which the poet defines the nature of individual heroic virtues. Spenser's concept of heroic virtue, then, is in large measure explored and defined through his use of the pastoral. The pastoral allows him to examine the consciousness and inward experience of each hero and thereby interpret the meaning of his quest.

The pastoral form in *The Faerie Queene* provided Spenser with a way of exploring and clarifying the relationships between nature and the order of grace, human nature, and sin and corruption.[9] The intention of the form itself is to explore and define these relationships, and because the form provides for imaginative richness, Spenser was particularly attracted to it. The guiding principle of his treatment of the pastoral is a greater understanding of man's nature, and he runs this principle through its many variations. Whether dramatizing and defining eternal life, man's original Edenic, or his fallen state, the poet exploits the many symbolic functions of the pastoral. Spenser examined its conditions and limitations as well as its versatility in his own elaborate and resourceful version of the genre. By nearly exhausting the possibilities and necessities of the form, he discovers the proper relationship between each titular hero and the pastoral world.

Spenser himself implicitly makes the rise of Red Cross Knight analogous to his own ascent as poet. He describes the Knight in his letter to Raleigh as a "clownishe younge man" who "rested him on the floore, unfitte through rusticity for a better place." Only when Gloriana assigns him to an adventurous quest does he rise from mere rusticity to heroic action.[10] Both Spenser and Red Cross Knight must achieve fame, glory, and wisdom through heroic effort, the Knight fulfilling his task appointed by Gloriana so that he will ultimately become the tutelary saint and patron of England, the poet fulfilling his task so that he will become the epic poet of England, a rival to Homer, Virgil, Ariosto, and Tasso.

After taking his pilgrimage and receiving spiritual instruction in the House of Holiness, Red Cross Knight meets an aged holy man, Contemplation. The Hermit addresses him as "thou man of earth" (1.10.52), punning on Red Cross's not-yet-revealed name, George, which derives from Greek *georgos*, meaning husbandman, and from *gaia*, earth. He relates to St. George that he had been discovered as an infant in "an heaped furrow" and brought up in "ploughmans state" (1. 10. 66). Spenser is telling us that the saintly knight is not of supernatural birth but a mortal man made of earth. Moreover, this rustic clown has ascended from his pastoral origins, his georgic beginnings, to heroic action and, beyond that, to heavenly contemplation. By exploring the development of Red Cross Knight through these formative states, Spenser clarifies the degrees or steps leading from the pastoral to the epic, which form a dialectic series in themselves. At the climax of Book 1, St. George is on the threshold of a further journey at the Mount of Contemplation, but the poet, like his Knight, must postpone heavenly contemplation, because he, too, must finish his appointed task.

At the beginning of his adventures Red Cross Knight confronts in the Cave of Error a dragon with her "cursed spawn of serpents small" (1. 1. 22). In this scene the poet uses pastoral imagery to describe the Knight and his situation:

> As gentle shepheard in sweete eventide,
> When ruddy Phebus gins to welke in west,

High on an hill, his flocke to vewen wide,
Markes which does byte their hasty supper best.

(1.1.23)

At first glance, the disparity in this epic simile between the
knight-errant and the gentle shepherd seems striking. Red
Cross is, after all, "full of fire and greedy hardiment" (1. 1.
14), ambitious for heroic action and fame. The imagery and
tone of the passage, however, suggest a bucolic contemplative
serenity, the twilight mood of Virgil's *Eclogues*. First, the poet
evokes familiarity through the actual, immediate world of experience, and by dispassionate observation he distances the
reader from the Knight as if he is to be seen from a higher level
of comprehension. Second, Spenser anticipates the later
recognition of Red Cross Knight's pastoral origins. Third, he
suggests that the Knight in the first of his many trials is inexperienced and naive, untried in the ways of the world, and
susceptible to deception.

He is "a gentle knight" and is like a "gentle shepherd"; the
adjective denotes both the chivalrous and the mild and kind.
Like the shepherd who looks after his flock, Red Cross Knight
is a protector of Una. Later, he becomes a type of the
Redeemer, and therefore both Christian Knight and
Shepherd.

In a realistic pastoral image, Error's serpents are compared
to gnats, which annoy and irritate the shepherd-knight but do
not injure him:

A cloud of cumbrous gnattes doe him molest,
All striving to infixe their feeble stinges,
That from their noyance he no where can rest.

(1.1.23)

The manly Knight, fit for "giusts and fierce encounters" (1. 1.
23), clad in the armor of God, is harassed by petty, feeble intellectual errors, which are numerous and mean: "But with his
clownish hands their tender wings/ He brusheth oft, and oft
doth mar their murmurings" (1. 1. 23). Rather than be
distracted by the offspring of Error, he must vanquish the Serpent that engendered them.

Though Red Cross in his "first adventure" (1. 1. 27) demonstrates strength and courage by cutting off the monster's "hatefull head" (1. 1. 24), he does not in his newly won self-assurance perceive that his victory was not a result of his own powers, but was brought about by his following Una's counsel of truth urging him to "add faith unto your force" (1. 1. 19). Because of his mistaken view of himself he is vulnerable in the next episode to Archimago's hypocrisy and deception by false pastoralism. Sleeping at Archimago's lowly hermitage with its "pastoral" props, cottage, forest, and simple meal, the Knight, in the spell of the conniving magician, dreams "of loves and lustfull play,/ That nigh his manly hart did melt away" (1. 1. 47).

From the Virgilian gate of "burnisht yvory" (1. 1. 40) these dreams are false and deluding. In an erotic dream Una seems to be brought to his bed by Venus and the Graces. Her beauty and seductive words sexually stir him. In spite of his initial defeat of Error, the Knight has been made passive by his own erroneous pride, and as if in unconscious collaboration with the dream, he is provoked by illusory sensual delights. Spenser describes the dream, however, with images of fresh pastoral loveliness:

> And eke the Graces seemed all to sing
> Hymen iö Hymen, dauncing all around,
> Whylst freshest Flora her with yvie crownd.

$$(1.1.48)$$

The *locus amoenus* of this dream is disarming in its delicacy and grace. Yet it is a false vision, and the poet hints at its deceptive ambiguity by his insistence upon the mere appearance of things: "Fayre Venus, seemde unto his bed to bring Her," and "the Graces seemed all to sing. . . " Una, in the Knight's waking state, is the "chastest flower" and "the daughter of a king"; now she is a "loose leman to vile service bound" (1. 1. 48). The surface of the dream seems innocent because of its pastoral charm. Instead, it is a beguiling parody of pastoral innocence, a meretricious imitation of the hymenal song played after the Knight of Holiness ultimately fulfills his assigned mission and becomes betrothed to the real Una, Truth.

This pastoral enclave within the action of Book 1 is an interlude that both deceptively offers the Knight an escape from virtuous deeds and reveals his own fallen nature: credulous, lustful, and proud. Though he rejects the false Una's seductive advances, he is completely deceived by a voyeuristic dream of his lady lying in the embrace of a lecherous squire. Hastily basing his judgment on his own dreams of lust, he is convinced of Una's infidelity and wantonness, and unchivalrously deserts her without explanation.

Once Red Cross is separated from Una, Truth, his spiritual state declines rapidly. The *areté* of this chivalric knight reveals his kinship with both Achilles and Turnus, who epitomize the old concept of martial heroism. Though at first Red Cross wins earthly combats against pagan knights and the dubious love of Duessa, he experiences guilt, melancholy, and the unforgivable sin of despair. His succumbing to temptation in the House of Pride, where he places himself in the service of Queen Lucifera, the loss of sexual innocence with Duessa-Fidessa, his imprisonment by Orgoglio, and his inability to refute Despair's persuasive but specious argument for suicide, all reveal Red Cross's sinful nature and his growing consciousness of his own guilt. He has learned, moreover, that the belief in his own deeds was no more than self-deceiving pride. Only Arthur, an instrument of heavenly grace, can save him from Orgoglio's enthrallment, and it is Una who rescues him from temptation in the Cave of Despair by reminding him of God's mercy and the saving power of grace.

The legend of Holiness, like the story of Aeneas, is full of suffering and melancholy. Red Cross Knight is a hero, like Aeneas, who must unite piety and arms, *sapientia et fortitude*, contemplation and action. Acting without self-knowledge, and without the inner fortitude of patience, winning physical combats only for personal fame and glory, such heroes can degenerate into Turnus or Sansfoy. Without truth Red Cross cannot be holy, and it is inevitable that he cannot win the external battles of arms because he cannot win the internal spiritual ones. His deeds are no longer heroic but sinful; he is not prompted by love of virtue but love of self. Red Cross, then, is not an active hero because he is not a contemplative hero.

As contemplative suffering man, Red Cross is guilt-ridden in the Cave of Despair. Here he experiences suicidal melancholy. Having been rescued by Una from surrendering to Despair, he is ready to acknowledge his sinfulness and his own insufficiency without grace. Una conducts him to the House of Holiness where he can recuperate physically, be healed of spiritual pride, and purified by Penance, Remorse, and Repentance, and receive instruction in Christian mercy. After the "sowle-diseased knight" (1. 10. 24) is purged of his sins through violent healing, and instructed in the "celestiall discipline" (1. 10. 18) of humility, love, and righteousness, this "man of earth" is led by an aged holy man to the Mount of Contemplation, where he is granted a glimpse of the New Jerusalem. Spenser compares the Mount of Contemplation to Mt. Sinai, the Mount of Olives, and finally Parnassus. He includes the home of the Muses because he wishes to suggest that the highest kind of poetry, as Piers declares in the "October" eclogue, is a divine vision that lifts man to heaven.[11] The holy man, Contemplation, prophecies that the Knight seeking the path of holiness will be called St. George, patron saint of England. But before he can enter the holy city as St. George and attain his promised place among the saints, he must finish

> ". . . that royal maides bequeathed care,
> Who did her cause into thy hand committ,
> Till from her cursed foe thou have her freely quitt."
>
> (1.10.63)

That is, he must postpone the contemplative joy of Heavenly Jerusalem until he has fought for Una and fulfilled his mission, uniting the ideals of hero and saint in physical and spiritual warfare on earth. He must resume his quest in this world and gain it through heroic struggle.

In order to liberate Una's parents, Adam and Eve, from the brazen tower in which they are imprisoned, Red Cross must slay the Dragon. In this crucial scene Spenser calls the reader's attention to a number of analogues from classical myth and Scripture. The Knight resembles Evander's Hercules, who struggles victoriously with Cacus the monster to free the enthralled Arcadians. More importantly, the three-day battle against the Dragon is a re-creation of Christ's harrowing Hell, His three-day descent through which Eden is restored and mankind freed from the bondage of sin. In addition, Spenser reminds the reader through symbolism of the crucifixion, the defeat of Satan, and the resurrection.

The scene of the battle between St. George and the Dragon is Eden, and therefore Spenser describes the setting with pastoral images. Eden is a symbolic landscape, and the images are schematically formal and hieratic. When, on the first day of battle, Red Cross is struck down by the Dragon, he falls into a spring. This spring is the sacramental Well of Life, a symbol of God's freely given grace, which washes man clean of the "guilt of sinfull crimes" (1. 11. 30). Although the Dragon believes he has vanquished his foe, the saintly Knight rises on the next morning restored by the waters of the spring. On the second day the Dragon badly wounds him, but the Knight severs one of the monster's claws and part of his huge tail. The outraged Dragon belches out smoke and flashing fire. Forced to back away from the scorching flames, Red Cross's "foreweried feeble feet" (1. 11. 45) slide in the mire and he falls, a second time, at the foot of a fruit tree, loaded with apples, symbols of sacrifice. This is the Tree of Life:

> There grew a goodly tree him faire beside,
> Loaden with fruit and apples rosy redd,
> As they in pure vermillion had been dide,
> Whereof great vertues over all were redd:
> For happy life to all which thereon fedd,
> And eke life to all everlasting did befall.
>
> (1.11.40)

Set alongside the tree of knowledge of good and evil that tempted mankind, this paradisal Tree of Life is a type of the cross. A stream of balm trickles from this tree, which heals deadly wounds, and Una bathes her injured hero through the night "with pretious balme" (1.. 11. 50). Red Cross rises fresh once more in a lovely pastoral dawn when "with mery note her loude salutes the mounting larke" (1. 11. 51). Rushing at the Knight, the Dragon intends to swallow him with open jaws. However, Red Cross, as chivalric Christ, pierces "his darksom hollow maw" (1. 11. 53) with his weapon and inflicts the deathblow. Three times the Dragon crashes to the ground, and finally expires in the Edenic garden.

It is in this garden that Red Cross Knight overcomes his fallen nature. The water from the Well of Life and the balm of the Tree of Life are symbols of the sacraments of baptism and communion, and in a larger sense they represent the power of freely given grace to save man from sin and restore his strength in spiritual conflict. What seems to be another pastoral enclave in the epic action turns out to be the climactic scene in the Legend of Holiness. The contemplative and active strains of the book converge in an epic battle within a pastoral landscape.

Eden, of course, is the *locus amoenus* of the biblical golden age. There are no shepherds here, except possibly Red Cross as a type of the Good Shepherd, and no lesser gods, Venus, Pan, or Cupid. But this pastoral place is a manifestation of God:

> Great God it planted in that blessed stedd
> With his Almighty hand, and did it call
> The Tree of Life . . .
>
> (1.11.46)

Typical of an Arcadian of Edenic *locus amoenus,* nature is heightened and idealized. Although it is within the order of nature, restored Eden is a new earth sacramentally united with heaven.[12] The spring, the fruit tree, and the mounting lark are creations of God's ordered, timeless, and sublime art. Here in Eden is a pastoral scene truly analogous to paradise.

Coming forward, Una praises God and thanks her "faithful knight" for the great conquest. When her father, the "aged syre" who is lord of Eden, orders the brazen gate to open and proclaims "joy and peace through all this state" (1.12.3), there is great rejoicing by those released from "eternall bondage" (1.12.4) to the Dragon as they honor their deliverer with laurel boughs, music, and dancing. Spenser describes the joyous scene with the pastoral imagery of dancing virgins "fresh as flowers in meadow greene" (1.12.6), and Una, crowned with a green garland, is compared to "fayre Diana, in fresh summers day" who "beholdes her nymphes enraung'd in shady wood" (1.12.7). Although the imagery of this scene recalls the Knight's erotic dream in Archimago's hermitage, chaste Diana in her garland replaces the harlot Flora crowned with ivy garland.[13] As they celebrate the Knight's victory and his betrothal to Una with trumpet music and feast, the poet emphasizes the golden age simplicity of their manner:

> Yet was their manner then but bare and playne;
> For th'antique world excesse and pryde did hate,
> Such proud luxurious pompe is swollen up but late.
>
> (1.12.14)

The royal court of Eden in its virtuous plainness resembles that of King Evander and his Arcadians in the *Aeneid*.

The epithalamium for Red Cross and Una is fitting for this concluding scene of Book 1. The sensuous imagery of flowers, wine, and perfume evokes the memory of Solomon's wedding hymn, the pastoral Song of Songs, and like the allegorical interpretation of that epithalamium, this betrothal scene represents the union of holiness and truth. The bride "without-ten spot" (1.12.22) also echoes the Song of Songs (4:7). Furthermore, as a type of the Redeemer, the Knight's betrothal to Una is like the marriage of Christ and His Church.[14] Spenser more explicitly elevates the meaning of the marriage festival when he blends the earthly music of hymeneal song with "the heavenly noise" of angels' voices, "Singing before th' Eternall Majesty" (1.12.39). This is the celestial music of Revelation (19:7), celebrating the marriage of the Lamb to come.

The marriage of Red Cross and Una cannot be made final in this concluding scene. The Knight must now go to the earthly city Cleopolis, and not the New Jerusalem, in order to finish his six-year service to the Fairy Queene. The pastoral joys of contemplation, peace, and harmony must be delayed. Even though he has slain the Dragon, Red Cross cannot accept the offer of Una's father, a Sabbath of "ease and everlasting rest"

(1.12.17). He must finish his appointed task in the fallen world and exercise his virtue in an active life of heroic struggle. Just as Aeneas does not tarry in Arcadia or the Elysian Fields, so Red Cross cannot remain in Eden or the Mount of Contemplation.

Until Red Cross overcomes his spiritual pride in the House of Holiness, he is hardly a paragon of virtue. He is more an archetypal sinner than exemplary hero and champion of Holiness. By exploring the theological and ethical limitations of conventional heroic virtue, Spenser dramatizes the inadequacy of classical heroism to an even greater extent than Virgil in the *Aeneid*, since the Renaissance poet evaluated classic premises from the point of view of Christian belief.

Through pastoral motifs, Spenser unfolds the story of Red Cross, his origins, task, temptation and fall, recovery, and final triumph. Brought up a rustic plowman, he is dedicated to Gloriana's task of freeing mankind from bondage to Satan and restoring Eden. He is, however, seduced and misled by the deceptive ease of his pastoral dream. Once Red Cross has succumbed to pride and carnality in amorous dalliance with Duessa in a *locus amoenus*, he is overcome by Orgoglio. Only after his rescue and religious training can Red Cross fight and defeat the Dragon in the Garden of Eden, and his victory and betrothal to Una are celebrated in a pastoral epithalamium. Although these pastoral motifs are not so explicit as the pastoral of Book 6, they function throughout the first book as important symbolic settings for the epic protagonist's quest, the places of temptation, dereliction, fall, education, and final spiritual triumph.

Sir Guyon, as champion of Temperance in Book 2, further exemplifies Spenser's criticism of the old heroic values. Because Temperance is by definition a virtue that consists primarily of a *not* doing, of a resistance to impulsive action, it is a kind of negative virtue.[15] Guyon must learn to restrain and subdue himself to the less active and unglamorous quest of self-control. What appears to be inaction and colorless passivity is a result of Guyon's inner struggle and his command over his passions through heroic renunciation.[16] The conflicts of Book 2 are primarily resolved, therefore, not by action but by resistance to action.

In Book 2 the pastoral settings in the Garden of Proserpine and the Bower of Bliss are in fact anti-pastoral; they are sinister and infernal places designed to deflect Guyon's quest and tempt him into sin by parodying the paradisal. Unlike the enclaves in the epic action of the *Aeneid*, which provide spiritual refreshment and restoration for the hero, these pastoral landscapes tempt the renunciatory hero either by enticing him into extreme passivity, ennui, and debilitation, or by inciting him into intemperate action caused by the very violence of his resistance and renunciation, thereby provoking action for the wrong reasons. Instead of *loci amoeni* that enable the hero to return to his virtuous deeds in the world, they are landscapes that test the hero, and where struggle, the resistance to temptation, must take place.

The Garden of Proserpine is an underground place of great melancholy, suffocating with darkness, silence, and deadly sorrow. While it is like the Garden of Eden, "goodly garnished/ With hearbs and fruits" (2.7.51), it is dead. The black garden is filled with funereal cypress, trees of bitter gall, poppy, and the hemlock that killed "Wise Socrates" (2.7.52), known for his temperance. The arbor has in its midst a silver seat where Proserpine, once goddess of the spring and now Queen of Hades, sometimes sits. A tree of golden apples, the evil fruit of avarice, discord, and death, stands by the silver seat. This tree is like both the golden apple tree of Hesperides and the Edenic tree that bore the forbidden fruit that tempted mankind and brought about the Fall. The branches of the fatal tree hang over Cocytus, and infernal river, and the damned soul of Tantalus wades in it: "Deepe was he drenched to the upmost chin" (2.7.58). A personification of avarice, Tantalus desperately reaches up for the evil fruit. Guyon perceives that he is "Ensample of mind intemperate" (2.7.60). Here, too, in this river is the soul of Pilate, who compulsively tries to wash both his hands in vain. He had chosen Mammon over God by delivering up "the Lord of Life to dye" (2.7.62). Mammon, Guyon's tempter, makes a final effort to persuade him to seize a golden apple or to rest slothfully on the silver stool, but the temptations prove futile, and he leads the Knight back to the upper world. Having spent three days in Mammon's cave without food or sleep, and having been continually exposed to Mammon's temptations to glory, honor, and riches, Guyon is overcome once he breathes the pure air, and collapses into a faint.

In both Books 1 and 2 the titular Knights arrive at the entrance of a paradisal garden for the climactic episode of their mission. Because the Bower of Bliss is a *hortus conclusus*, and a paradise of earthly delights, Spenser compares it to Eden: "Or Eden selfe, if ought Eden mote compayre" (2.12.52). Acrasia's Bower is a fallen Eden, however, not a sacred place that sacramentalizes nature but a profane place that perverts it. The Bower, like Armida's garden in Tasso's *Gerusalemme Liberata*, is the false paradise of Renaissance epic, an enchanted garden that perverts the golden age site and the earthly paradise.[17] Before Guyon confronts Acrasia ("incontinence"), he meets the habitués of the Bower, Genius, Dame Excess, and the sirens. The false Genius, who is "Pleasures porter" (2.12.48), greets the Knight of Temperance and offers him wine from his "mighty mazer bowle" (2.12.49). Unlike the god of birth and generation, this Genius is a "foe of life," a spirit of "guilefull semblants" (2.12.48). Guyon recognizes that he is a decadent spirit who leads men into lust through false-seeming and deceit, and he rebuffs him by overturning his bowl and breaking his conjuring rod. Pursuing the quest of Acrasia's bower, Guyon and his companion, the Palmer, pass through an earthly paradise. The Knight must look straight ahead and bridle his will so that he will not be distracted or tranquilized by the beauty of the pastoral landscape. They see a "comely dame," squeezing the "sappy liquor" (2.12.56) of grapes into a cup. Her fair garments are loose and in disarray, "that seemd unmeet for womanhed" (2.12.55). She offers Guyon wine from her golden cup just as she does when she greets all strangers. The Knight again refuses the proffered wine and, seizing the cup from her hand, he smashes it to the ground.

When Guyon beholds "Two naked damzelles" (2.12.63) bathing in a little lake, he is attracted by their beauty, and becomes tantalized by their attempts to provoke him sexually with their frolicking and contrived exhibitionism. While Guyon knows from the start that Acrasia's Bower is evil, the "wanton maidens" (2.12.66) are so enticing in their display of snowy limbs and lily paps that he begins to slacken:

> Whom such as Guyon saw, he drewe him neare,
> And somewhat gan relent his earnest pace;
> His stubborne brest gan secret pleasaunce to embrace.
>
> (2.12.65)

These bathing nymphs, laughing and blushing as they wrestle and leap from the water to flaunt their beautiful nude bodies, arouse the Knight of Temperance even further:

> Now when they spyde the knight to slack his pace,
> Them to behold, and in his sparkling face
> The secret signes of kindled lust appeare,
> Their wanton merriments they did encrease.
>
> (2.12.68)

The "faire spectacle" (2.12.67) in the water has the appearance of innocence and naturalness, but it is a calculated and artful performance that these coolly lascivious nymphs stage for its effect on the Knight. They intentionally provoke his prurience with studied bodily exposure: "And to him beckned to approch more neare,/ And shewd him many sights, that corage cold could reare" (2.12.68). The Palmer rebukes "those wandring eyes of his" and recalls him to duty:

> " . . . Now, Sir, well avise;
> For here the end of all our traveill is:
> Here wonnes Acrasia, whom we must surprise,
> Els she will slip away, and all our drift despise."
>
> (2.12.69)

Acrasia's Bower is similar in appearance to the *locus amoenus* of pastoral poetry, a golden world in which nature is created by art and looks like nature. In Arcadia or "sweet Parnasse" (2.12.52), a paradisal projection of the poet's mind, man is free to engage in recreative and contemplative ideals, and withdrawing from the fallen, brazen world, live a pleasurable life of virtuous and creative ease. In the Bower, however, recreation is not innocent play but rather a simulation of play that has designs on the passive viewer. The goal of contemplation here, moreover, is not detached stasis but kinesis, infantile fantasy or pornographic prurience.[18] Man is not free in the Bower; instead he loses his freedom by becoming enslaved to his sensual appetite and passions, and Acrasia's victims are symbols of man's intemperance and his ultimate degradation to the subhuman and bestial. Withdrawal to these gardens is not a philosophical retreat from the fallen world but admission to a poisoned, unregenerate world. *Otium* is not possible here, because fallen man cannot be temperate; he is continually tempted to perverse sensuality. Those who surrender to the voluptuous delights of the Bower have not virtuous and creative ease, but an idleness that is egotistical and debilitating.

That art intrudes upon nature in the Bower suggests the inherent moral weakness of the conventional version of the pastoral. The fictive art of fallen man cannot create an Eden but only simulate it in an illusory way. Spenser subverts the aesthetic ideal of epicurean self-sufficiency and idleness in the Bower by representing it as selfish, otiose, and parasitic. In the Bower art looks like nature, "That Natures worke by art can imitate" (2.12.42), but nature blends with art in such a bizarre way that they seem to imitate each other, and while in apparent harmony, are in mutual antagonism:[19]

> One would have thought . . .
> That Nature had for wantonnesse ensude
> Art, and that Art at Nature did repine;
> So striving each th' other to undermine
> Each did the others worke more beautify.
>
> (2.12.59)

The artificiality of nature[20] manifests itself in Spenser's detailed descriptions of "the most daintie paradise" (2.7.58). A gate to the enclosed garden is decorated with boughs and branches; the porch arched overhead is clasped by a vine seeming to entice a viewer with grapes that are compared to sapphire, ruby, and emerald; a trail of ivy is made of gold:

For the rich metall was so coloured,
That wight, who did not well avis'd it vew,
Would surely deeme it to bee yvie trewe.

(2.12.61)

The little lake in which the two nymphs bathe is fed by a fountain, and the bottom of the lake is "all pav'd with jaspar shining bright" (2.12.62).

Just as Acrasia's mannequins wish to misdirect Guyon's natural impulses with their artful enticements, so the false art of Acrasia's Bower aims to deceive man with the appearance of things. The grotesque combinations of the organic and the decorative, of life and art, are symptoms of the Bower's moral ambiguity. Moreover, the apparently volitional movements of branches that "dilate/ Their clasping armes, in wanton wreathings intricate" (2.12.53) and the ivy vine creeping "his lascivious armes adown" (2.12.61) create a menacing atmosphere of erotic restlessness. The metallic plants and vines suggest the sterility of the garden in the same way that the provocations to voyeurism and sexual itch lead to onanistic satisfactions and not procreative gratification.

One of the main features of this Bower of frigid eroticism is its excessive ornamentation. Because it is a place of intemperance, the beautifications are too intricate, crowded, and overburdened. The Bower is "too lavishly adorned" with "all the ornaments of Floraes pride" (2.12.50). Figures on the fountain epitomize the ambience:

Most goodly it with curious ymageree
Was overwrought, and shapes of naked boyes,
Of which some seemed with lively jollitee
To fly about playing their wanton toyes,
Whylest others did them selves embay in liquid joyes.

(2.12.60)

As if to arouse pederastic desire, a throng of naughty naked boys frolic on the carved fountain; and the adjective "curious" means carefully made and odd, but also suggests an impertinent desire to pry into secret things. The art of the Bower, for all its seductive sensuality, is banal and sinister, celebrating and exposing the sickness of idolatry.

Stealthily Guyon and the Palmer approach the place where the courtesan, Acrasia, reclines on a bed of roses with her latest lover, Verdant, "whose sleepie head she in her lap did soft dispose" (2.12.76). Without waking him, she is "greedily depasturing delight" (2.12.73) as she "sucks" his spirit with her eyes, kissing his lips. Guyon hears someone sing a "lovely lay": "Gather therefore the rose, whilest yet is prime" (2.12.75). The argument of this song is *carpe diem*, and while it expresses the moment of intense pleasure in experience, its hedonism is time-haunted and elegiac. As the virgin rose will soon fade and fall away, so mortal life passes, the voice sings. Therefore, gather the rose

> whilest yet is prime,
> For soone comes age, that will her pride deflore:
> Gather the rose of love, whilest yet is time,
> Whilest loving thou mayst loved be with equall crime.
>
> (2.12.75)

Though the pastoral imagery gives the song a kind of tranquil ease, its theme, and the reference to "equall crime," are melancholy, even somewhat despairing.

The young knight Verdant has surrendered to sensual intemperance and betrayed his pursuit of honor. His "warlike armes" (2.12.80), symbol of heroic action, hang uselessly upon a tree, and his shield is destroyed. Torpid, Verdant has in a sense yielded his masculinity also. Acrasia who leans over him awake has assumed the active and dominant role in their relationship.[21] If Guyon is to release Verdant, who is mankind, from bondage in the fallen Eden and overthrow those forces which cause man's fall, he must destroy the Bower, which is a corruption of the pastoral. Guyon and the Palmer trap the lovers in a Vulcan-like net, and bind Acrasia with chains. By freeing Verdant, Guyon symbolically undoes the effects of Mordaunt's death or man's first fall. Then the uncompromising Guyon destroys the Bower itself, with all its vicious beauty: "But all those pleasaunt bowres and pallace brave/ Guyon broke downe, with rigour pittilesse" (2.12.83).

In Books 3 and 4 Spenser's treatment of the relationship between epic and pastoral is complicated by the multiple interwoven pattern of the narrative and the several characters who represent chastity. However, in Britomart, the central character of both books, the poet provides a heroine who in her completeness as warrior and woman integrates the heroic and pastoral. As warrior she is descended from ancient Trojan blood, has a "hevenly destiny" (3.3.57). Dressed in martial armour of the Saxon queen Angela, she must "atchieve an hard emprize" (3.3.53). Merlin's prophecy to her, like that of Anchises to Aeneas, foretells the future of her royal descendants. In canto 4 Spenser compares the martial Britoness to other epic heroines, Homer's Penthesilea, the biblical Deborah, and Virgil's Camilla. On her heroic quest, the armed virgin rejects the lustful Malecasta, wounds the knight Marinell in combat, and in the culminating episode of the Legend of Chastity assumes Arthur's role as savior by freeing defenseless Amoret from her terrible enthrallment to Busirane. Here she is praised for possessing "huge heroicke magnanimity" (3.9.19).

However, the pastoral is the means by which Spenser defines the virtues of womanhood, which must be protected by this active heroism. In order for Britomart to become a heroine, she must first learn to be a complete woman.[22] That is, she must understand the urges of her own sexual nature and learn its virtuous procreative purpose. The heroic and pastoral are united when she accepts the responsibilities of her spiritual nature and lends her aid to chastity. Her womanly and heroic quest is to make "her seeke an unknowne paramour,/ From the worlds end, through many a bitter stowre" and then to raise "Most famous fruites of matrimoniall bowre" (3.3.3). The paradisal *hortus conclusus* of her virginity will blossom, and become a fruitful bower of married chastity. This pastoral bower of generation will be perfected after Britomart finds her husband, Artegall, marries him, and bears children. Only after the pastoral ideals of womanhood have been realized can their heroic line fulfill British history and providential will.

Because Britomart is a complete woman and a heroine of chastity, she unites and balances two complementary aspects of chastity, chaste love and chaste virginity.[23] These complementary aspects are represented by the twin daughters of the maiden-mother Chrysogenee, Amoret and Belphoebe.

Amoret is brought to the Garden of Adonis as an infant by Venus and is brought up by Psyche. In the Garden of Adonis, at the center of Legend of Chastity, Spenser envisions a pastoral enclave of chaste love, marriage, and maternity. Like Britomart's fruitful marriage bower, the Garden of Adonis symbolizes the chaste heroine's potential for personal, sexual fulfillment.

The Garden of Adonis clearly symbolizes the reality of which the Bower of Bliss is a perverted imitation. In the *locus amoenus* tradition, both have their Genius, eternal spring, and lovers. There is "continuall spring" in the Garden, but there is also "harvest there/ Continuall, both meete at one time" (3.6.42), the harvest suggesting the natural fruitfulness of the Garden. While the Bower intimates what is false, imitative, and sterile, the Garden represents the real, natural, and fertile. In contrast to the libertine porter, "Old Genius" is a god of birth and generation, who lets in and out "all that to come into the world desire," and "a thousand naked babes attend/ About him day and night" (3.6.32). The Garden presents the cyclical process of conception, birth, growth, decay, death, and rebirth through which all life passes in the natural order. Here in the Garden is the creation of pre-formed beings that gradually come to existence in orderly succession. Unlike the Bower's regressive fantasies, it is a golden age of free natural generation. God commands living things to "increase and multiply" (3.6.34) and the Garden as a place of creative *eros* symbolizes the fulfillment of His command.

The presence of Time, however, shows that the Garden is within the realm of mutability. Time's scythe mows "the flowring herbes and goodly things" (3.6.39). While the Bower tries to fight time and death through lifeless art and the plaintive urgings of *carpe diem*, the Garden attains a genuine perpetuity through the acknowledgment that all living things must pass, but will return in due time.[24] Time is a necessary condition for the development of forms.

The Garden of Adonis is like the unfallen Eden. Sensuality and physical love are as innocent as in paradise:

Franckly each paramour his leman knowes,
Each bird his mate, ne any does envie
Their goodly meriment and gay felicity.
(3.6.41)

Spenser's erotic imagery informs his descriptions of the Garden. The stately Mount of Venus standing in the midst of paradise is the *mons veneris*, focus of sexual pleasure, representing the reproductive forces of nature.[25] Sexual passion is not perverted as it is in the Bower, but is natural, healthy, and virtuous, part of the providential scheme.

The Venus-Adonis myth, of which the Acrasia-Verdant relationship is a parody, asserts the divinity of the Garden. The sexual union of Venus and Adonis is a symbol of the eternal generative process pervading the whole physical universe.[26] A dying god, Adonis is subject to mortality, but he transcends the destruction of time by being annually reborn along with all the living things that renew themselves with the sun.[27]

Ascending the scale of being, the poet provides a second myth, the allegory of faithful lovers, Cupid and Psyche. The myth of Psyche symbolizes the trials and ultimate purification of the soul. Love is spiritual as well as erotic. "After long troubles" Psyche now lives with Cupid in "steadfast love and happy state" (3.6.50), and their union suggests wedded love. They have a daughter, Pleasure, who, unlike the perverted, sterile pleasures of the Bower, which are their own end, represents the morally innocent pleasure of sexual love that has generation, the proper use of created nature, for its end.

Nature in the Garden of Adonis is innocent and perfect, in a golden age of goodness and pleasure. Nature and time are two major concepts with which the pastoral poet is concerned, and Spenser's treatment of the Garden exemplifies his exploration of both. A pastoral enclave in the epic action, the Garden of Adonis functions as an antithesis both of the Bower of Bliss and of the entire fallen world of self-love, lust, sadism, rape, incest, and sodomy, the perversions of *eros* in Book 3. It is a paradigm of the true creativity of nature and love.

The temple of Venus in Book 4 combines the pastoral with the court of love setting, and presents the social implications of love and courtship, for here nature and society are united. In the Temple of Venus, Amoret is seen against a background of the social aspects of love.[28] It is here at the foot of Venus's altar that the knight Scudamour discovers her and wins her hand. In the Temple, Venus represents specifically human love, whereas in the Garden of Adonis she symbolizes the generative power of love.

The Temple is "seated in an island strong,/ Abounding all with delices most rare" (4.10.6). At the Temple the garden "seem'd a second paradise . . . So lavishly enrich't with Natures threasure" (4.10.23), and all the various flowers and trees in their ordered plenitude suggest "Th' Elysian Fields" (4.10.23). Yet this *locus amoenus*, unlike the Garden of Adonis, is characterized by the ambiguous presence of art, which supplies "all that Nature did omit" (4.10.21). The bridge to the island, for example, is built with "curious corbes and pendants graven fair," and its porches rising on stately pillars are "fram'd after the Doricke guise" (4.10.6). In the midst of lawns, springs, and delightful bowers "to solace lovers trewe," there are "False labyrinths" that daze the eye and amaze "Nature selfe' (4.10.24). The progress to the center of the Temple is sometimes artfully devious, and although the winding paths in the garden are delightfully mystifying, they threaten insecure lovers with the hazards of love and courtship.

With his Shield of Cupid, Scudamour encounters Doubt, Delay, and Danger, personifications drawn from erotic allegory who represent the anxieties of courtly romance. Yet "thousand payres of lovers," free from the labyrinth of fears, roam the walks and alleys of the garden enjoying "sweet loves content" (4.10.26). Apart from these lovers are famous pairs "tyde/ In bands of friendship," Hercules and Hylas, David and Jonathan, Orestes and Pylades, heroes whose devotion is grounded in "chaste virtue" (4.10.26) and whose loves never decay.

The figure of Concord at the Temple brings together both happy lovers and troubled, wretched ones, for Concord is a cosmic principle that unites all. After the lovers sing a hymn to Venus in the Temple, Scudamour finds Amoret, attended by personified ideals of passive femininity, Courtesy, Cheerfulness, Modesty, and Obedience, seated in the lap of Womanhood.

Because Amoret has been sheltered in the innocent and idyllic Garden of Adonis, and trained in the creative ideals of passive womanhood, she is unprepared for the destructive forces of unchaste sexuality in the world. Married to Sir Scudamour, she is traumatized by her moral and physical fears in the House of Busirane. Britomart, the Knight of Chastity, must achieve the quest meant for Scudamour, whose erotic desire prevents him from assaulting the House and freeing the imprisoned Amoret. Only the chaste heroine can pass through the wall of fire and release Amoret from Busirane's sadistically erotic pleasures.

On the tapestries that line the walls are figures of myth who represent obsessive love, evil passion, and degeneracy, which "in thousand monstrous formes doth oft appear" (3.11.51). Cupid in the House of Busirane incarnates tyrannical, lawless, and cruel love. In the processional wedding masque he is a "Winged God" armed with arrows, followed by a courtly retinue including "Reproach, Repentaunce, Shame" (3.12.24), who carry instruments of torment, sharp stings, whips, and burning iron-brands.

Britomart's heroic deeds in intervening for Scudamour, passing through the dreadful flames, delivering Amoret, and chaining Busirane demonstrate both her "huge heroicke magnanimity" (3.11.19) and her alliance with the Garden of Adonis. In rescuing Amoret, who represents marriage and generation, Britomart has rescued her own potential for fruitful chastity, and deepened her understanding of the meaning of her quest for Artegall.

While the Garden of Adonis is the setting for Amoret's up-bringing, the forest wilderness is the site of her twin sister Belphoebe's education. The Garden of Adonis is Venus's earth ly paradise; the forest is Diana's paradisal bower. Enclosed by mountains and mighty woods is a "fair pavillion, scarcely to be seene," Belphoebe's *locus amoenus*, "an earthly paradize" (3.5.40). Spenser's description of this pastoral enclave deep in the woods emphasizes its natural freedom of action but also its restraint:

And like a stately theater it made
Spreading it selfe into a spacious plaine;

And in the midst a little river plaide
Emongst the pumy stones, which seemd to plaine
With gentle murmure that his cours they did restraine.

(3.5.39)

This element of restraint suggests Belphoebe's virginity, and as she is trained by Diana and her nymphs in the discipline of the chaste, she has become a woman of restrained will and abstinence as well as heroic action.

Belphoebe's role in the narrative action reveals the most noble characteristics of chaste virginity. She rescues the wounded Timias and takes him to her paradisal pavillion in the wood, where she nurses him back to health with restorative herbs. In this episode she shows her pity and tenderness. She shows her "Heroick mind" (3.5.55) and deeds, however, when in the fourth canto she kills the monstrous Lust who, invading her Arcadian wilderness, has captured her frail twin sister. That she, and not Britomart, is the only person able to destroy Lust suggests that it cannot be a temptation for her.

However, when she sees the cured Timias kissing Amoret after she has been saved from Lust, Belphoebe's noble heart is filled with disdain and indignation. Although she does finally forgive the repentant Timias, her special destiny is not fruitful marriage but a life of abstinence and active virtue. Thus she fuses pastoral Diana, the archetypal virgin huntress, and the heroic Gloriana, the virgin queen.

The story of Florimell in Books 3 and 4 illustrates a form of chastity that is helpless, fearful, and passive. Although Florimell's passivity seems to be in marked contrast to the heroic action of the Knight of Chastity, Britomart necessarily shares Florimell's vulnerability in her very sexuality. Beginning with her escape from the "griesly foster," Florimell's misadventures are characterized by threat and flight. Escaping from Arthur, from the Hag's son, from a hyena, from the old fisher, and from Proteus, Florimell is always in flight from pursuing lust. But she is also searching for Marinell, as Britomart searches for Artegall. Just as Amoret, imprisoned by a wall of flame, is rescued from Busirane by Britomart, so Florimell, imprisoned by a wall of waves, is rescued from Proteus by Marinell,[29] who is a guest at the wedding of the Thames and Medway.

The wedding of the Thames and Medway occupies a climactic position in Book 4. A pastoral symbol of order and concord, it unites lovers and friends as well as rivers. The meetings of Britomart and Artegall, Amoret and Scudamour, and Florimell and Marinell make possible the processional masque of generative creativity.

A "solemne feast" is held "In honour of the spousalls . . . Betwixt the Medway and the Thames" (4.11.8). In attendance are Neptune and his queen Amphitrite, Triton, Nereus, and all the other divinities of oceans and rivers. They pass in procession, and their pageant represents nature's inexhaustible life and ordered freedom.

Throughout the description of the wedding procession, the poet shows the relationship between nature and history, pastoral and heroic. In his roll call of wedding guests there are "old heroes" and "famous founders of puissant nations" (4.11.15), including "mightie Albion," son of Neptune and "father of the bold/ Warlike people which the Britaine Islands hold" (4.11.15). Among the famous rivers is "Divine Scamander, purpled yet with blood/ Of Greeks and Trojans, which therein did die" (4.11.20). The Thames is crowned with "towres and castels" of "famous Troynovant," whose very name evokes the heroic link between Aeneas's Troy and historical Britain. The river Eden is "stainde with bloud of many a band/ Of Scots and English both, that tyned on his strand" (4.11.36); the "baleful Oure" is "late stained with English blood" (4.11.44). All these places have heroic associations, and recall historical memories of disorder and epic struggle. Yet the mutable world of history is merged with the continual flow and concord of nature, becoming part of the succession of lovely, peaceful pastoral landscapes.

The emblematic figure of the pastoral Medway as the bride "with flowres bescattered" and wearing "A chapelet of sundry flowers" (4.11.46) unites the heroines of chastity, Britomart, Amoret, and Florimell, who have found their husbands, and who represent virtuous love and human generation as part of God's providence. In this epithalamium, the flowing currents of the wedding processional have blended all these figures, divine, human, and natural, as the unifying power of love integrates and orders the mutable realms of Proteus and history.

Whereas the pastoral epithalamium that concludes Book 4 leads back to the harmony and unity of the prelapsarian world, Book 5 immediately leads away from it to the fallen world of history.[30] Significantly, this book is the only one in which there is no pastoral episode. Spenser begins the Legend of Justice by referring to the loss of the Golden Age, and this great classical myth of the Fall prepares the way for his exploration of the "stonie" world of strife. In order for the Knight of Justice to restore peace, virtue, and goodness of "Saturnes ancient reign" (5. prologue. 1), he must rectify the injustice of the historical and political world by heroic action.

If in Red Cross and Guyon the poet criticizes the old *ethos* of the active hero, and attempts to define the nature of true heroism, he characterizes in Artegall, the titular knight of Book 5, a man who has much in common with the heroes of the classical epic poetry. Whereas the other virtues treated in the poem are private and inward, justice is public and political, and therefore more rigorously conforms to the classical ideal of the heroic. Sir Artegall is a hero whose love of virtue prompts his deeds, demonstrating valor in warfare and other physical acts. In "his heroicke grace and honorable geste" (3.2.24) Artegall is like the Homeric hero, and that he has won "Achilles armes" (3.2.24) makes this similarity explicit. Moreover, as a good governor he exemplifies leadership and concern for the public welfare and order of the commonwealth. In his many confrontations with evil, his actions show him to have wisdom and fortitude. Yet the fallen world is such that, for all his active heroism, he is ultimately shamed, scandalized, and in effect defeated.

In this bitter and melancholy book, we are taken directly into the poet's and our own iron age, a world of empirical reality. By allegorizing actual historical events in the climactic episodes of the book, Spenser emphasizes the reality of Artegall's world. As an instrument of justice, Artegall must act in a world of self-interested ambition, coercion, and brutality. With his iron man, Talus, who rigidly executes the laws, Artegall must administer public justice by impersonally punishing the guilty. Artegall's motto, *Salvagesse sans Finesse*, is an indication that his is a rough justice.[31] Both he and his iron policeman must use terror and force in order to combat injustice in the iron world. Whatever the episode, the themes are violence, communism, rebellion, war, themes largely social and political, and Artegall has no respite from his prosecution of justice. Because there is no freedom and ease in his life, there can be no *otium*, and the lack of pastoral enclaves in the book suggests that he cannot find even temporary relief from his wearying quest and struggle, and therefore he has no contemplative restoration.

After Artegall liberates Irena from the tyrant Grantorto in the concluding canto of the book, he attempts to mete out justice by punishing traitors and establishing an orderly reign in Irena's kingdom, the tasks assigned by Gloriana. He is recalled to Gloriana's court, however, before he can complete his mission. Returning ingloriously from his uncompleted task, he is met by two wicked hags, Envy and Detraction, who heap abuse and slander upon him by accusing him of excessive cruelty in his struggles against rebellion. In an ironic perversion of a pastoral image, the poet describes these hags:

Who when they nigh approaching had espyde
Sir Artegall, return'd from his late quest,
They both arose, and at him loudly cryde,
As it had bene two shepheards curres had scryde
A ravenous wolfe amongst the scattered flocks.

(5.12.38)

The aesthetic ideal of courtesy in Book 6 provides relief from the harsh moral confrontations with the iron world in Book 5. However, while the Arcadian episode constitutes the thematic center of the sixth book, it is only a pastoral enclave within it. The book as a whole is free of the structural complexities of the earlier books, and has fewer historical allusions than Book 5, but it does share with Artegall's adventures a narration of events that are violent and evil. Malice, malevolence, envy, and slander pervade the book in the guise of recreant knights, haughty ladies of the court, cannibals, and brigands.

Moreover, the symbol of slander, the Blatant Beast, links this book to Book 5.

Calidore's heroic quest is to capture and muzzle the Blatant Beast, which has been enlisted by Envy and Detraction to slander Artegall and Gloriana's Court. On his quest, however, Calidore visits Arcadia and faces a crucial dilemma there. He is offered a choice of worlds, the heroic and pastoral. If he prefers an idyllic life among the shepherds, he elects a way of life free from ambition and he no longer need pursue the elusive Blatant Beast, nor engage actively in a world of courtly vanity, warfare, and coercion. If he chooses Arcadia, however, he must step down from his high place of knighthood, reversing the Virgilian progression from pastoral to heroic. In withdrawing, he escapes from the world's turmoil and woes, risking self-indulgent ease and possibly derelict sloth. Can he remain in the paradise within when the unregenerate world without calls for heroic action?

In Calidore's dilemma we see the symbolic confrontation of two views of life, contemplative and active, and two poetic worlds, pastoral and epic. In poetry generally, the heroic and the pastoral are in continual interaction, logically implying each other. The incursions of the heroic within pastoral poetry tend to undermine the fragile pastoral myth of self-sufficiency and contentment. In the epics of Virgil and Spenser, on the other hand, the poets gravitate toward the pastoral as if disappointed by the world of heroic action, needing the relief of pastoral contemplation. The mutual resistance of these elements may be destructive, as one reveals the insufficiency of the other to deal with the whole of life. While the epic is so comprehensive as to permit pastoral enclaves, these idyllic episodes frequently function in what may seem a subversive way; Evander's and Melibee's Arcadias tend to undermine the epic premises of ambition, glory, and fame.

The pastoral enclave in Book 6 at first appears to assimilate and convert the heroic, in that the epic hero, Calidore, becomes a shepherd. Calidore finds the home of courtesy among shepherds and poets, in a pastoral world of innocence, simplicity, and gentleness. Courtesy is a modest, unheroic virtue; it is "defynd . . . not in outward shows, but inward thoughts" (prologue. 5). Just as pastoral poetry was classed as a subservient genre, one of the lower manifestations of poetry, so courtesy grows "on a lowly stalke" (prologue. 4). Though courtesy derives its name from the court, Calidore finds it best expressed and enacted away from the "forgerie" of the court, in a pastoral community undefiled by the Blatant Beast he pursues.

Beginning with the pastoral poetry of Theocritus and Virgil, courtesy constitutes one of the natural virtues of every ideal shepherd. Courtesy, "the poetry of conduct"—to use C. S. Lewis's definition—[31] is a natural gift, and manifests itself in humility, sincerity, and fellow feeling. In Book 6, characters such as Tristram, the Salvage Man, and Pastorella apparently represent the courtesy that can be found in those who have no social rank or worldly position. Yet we discover, after all, that they are nobly born. Calidore learns that Tristram, ranger of the forest green, is the son of the former King of Cornwall. The Salvage Man, a lonely dweller of the woods who does not know how to speak, becomes the protector of Serena and proves that he must be of gentle blood. Pastorella is not really a shepherdess at all but the daughter of Sir Bellamoure and Lady Claribell. Gentle birth, then, predisposes a person to virtue. While courtesy grows on a lowly stalk, it adorns Queen Elizabeth's court, "where courtesies excell" (prologue. 7).

In Melibee, however, we have a genuine example of a character whose courtesy is not linked to gentle birth. The simple bucolic meal shared by Melibee and Calidore recalls the banquet of Evander and Aeneas, and the shepherd's articulation of pastoral ideals resembles the Arcadian King's moral lessons. Melibee lives a plain life in the country, taught by nature to be content with what he has. There is no ambition here, and therefore no envy. The shepherds live an innocent life of freedom, contentment, and peace. In his youth Melibee disdained the lowly shepherd's life and, being ambitious, he left home to seek the "roiall court" (6.9.24). He vainly spent his youth in court, and through his experiences there he learned about ambition and discourtesy. He recognized, moreover, that the pastoral was not a place but a state of mind: " 'It is the mynd that maketh good or ill,/ That maketh wretch or happie, rich or poor' " (6.9.60). The shepherd tells the courtier that life in Arcadia is a result of choice. He himself has chosen to hang up his arms and retire from knighthood to live "this simple sort of life" (6.9.33). Calidore, in love with Pastorella, seeks permission to remain in Arcadia.

Melibee's pastoral virtues and Pastorella's beauty lead the Knight into enjoyment of rural society. At first he makes an error in this community of shepherds by offering money to Melibee for food and shelter, but the good old shepherd courteously declines, telling him that his "bounteous proffer" (6.9.33) is inappropriate for their simple, frugal life.[32] Furthermore, Calidore courts Pastorella in an inappropriate courtly manner. Brought up under "base shepheards wings" she never saw "knightly service" and does not care for his "courteous guize" (6.9.35). When he is rejected by her, he drops his "loftie looke," doffs his "bright armes," and dresses himself in "shepheards weed" (6.9.36). He goes with Pastorella every day to the fields and keeps "her sheepe with diligent attent,/ Watching to drive the ravenous wolfe away" (6.9.37).

Calidore's romantic rival is Coridon, a genuine rustic. Coridon's name derives from Virgil's second *Eclogue*, in which the rejected shepherd complains that his simple gifts, when compared to those of his rival, are inadequate. Spenser's Coridon brings his rural gifts to Pastorella:

> . . . little sparrows, stolen from their nest,
> Or wanton squirrels, in the woods far sought,
> Or other daintie thing for her . . .
>
>   (6.9.40)

He recognizes, however, that Pastorella prefers Calidore, "this newcome shepheard" (6. 9. 40), and does not regard his presents. Calidore shows his generous spirit, his "courteous inclination" (6. 9. 42), when during a shepherds' dance he puts the inept Coridon in his own place to dance with Pastorella, and sets her garland, intended for him, upon Coridon's head.

At the beginning of canto 10 the narrator reminds us that his hero has neglected his quest and vow. The attractions of the retired, contemplative life and his love of Pastorella make Calidore forget his heroic pursuit of the Blatant Beast:

> Who now does follow the foule Blatant Beast,
> Whilest Calidore does follow that faire mayd,
> Unmyndfull of his vow, and high beheast
> Which by the Faery Queene was on him layd,
> That he should never leave, nor be delayd
> From chacing him, till he had it attchieved?
>
> (6.10.1)

Living "amongst the rusticke sort," Calidore has abandoned his "former quest, so full of toile and paine" (6. 10. 2), his new quest being to woo Pastorella and gain her love. Though Calidore is guilty of dereliction of duty, the narrator, who himself wore shepherd's weeds, knows this imagined land of contentment and contemplation, and expresses his sympathy with Calidore's love of *otium*:

> No certes mote he greatly blamed be,
> From high step to stoup unto so low.
> For who had tasted one (as oft did he)
> The happy peace which there did overflow. . .
>
> (6.10.3)

As Dido turned Aeneas aside from heroic duty, so Pastorella causes Calidore to betray his high purpose. Pastorella, however, is an incarnation of the loveliness and simplicity of pastoral life, and it is that life which attracts the Knight of Courtesy.

In the vision of Mount Acidale, Spenser intensifies the precarious segregation of epic and pastoral. Calidore hears "the merry sound/ Of a shrill pipe" (6. 10. 10) on the spacious plain of Acidale and discovers "An hundred naked maidens lilly white,/ All raunged in a ring, and dauncing in delight" (6. 10. 11). They form a circle around three beautiful ladies, and in the center of this group is

> Another damzelle, as a precious gemme
> Amidst a ring most richly enchased,
> That with her goodly presence all the rest much graced.
>
> (6.10.12)

The circular dance becomes an epiphany of cosmic order as
the poet compares it to the stars, which "move in order excellent" (6. 10. 13). These maidens circling around the country
lass, Rosalind, are the Graces, patrons of courtesy. Rosalind,
not Gloriana, is at the center of the ring because these maidens
are free from the compulsion to act in feudal service, and their
dance, created by inspired poetic imagination, is a perfect expression of order and spontaneity.[33] Their world is pastoral, not
heroic. Spenser's imaginative persona, Colin Clout, who is rapt
in his own vision, makes the music to which they dance without
self-consciousness:

> He pypt apace, whilest they him daunst about.
> Unto thy love, that made thee low to lout;
> Thy love is present there with thee in place,
> Thy love is there advaunst to be another Grace.

(6.10.16)

As Colin, Spenser now fully participates in the poem. Piping
for the Graces, he creates a vision of their beautiful dance. His
vision of innocence is a moment of crystallization in the book
that symbolizes courtesy in its absolute form, and it represents
the inspired creation of the golden world of poetry for the
whole poem. On Mount Acidale grace takes over from nature.
Throughout this description of the piping shepherd and dancing maidens, the poet expresses and enacts ideas of grace in all
their human and divine dimensions.[34] Grace has the meaning
of musical embellishment as in Colin's piping; it also means
charm and poise of movement as revealed in the maidens'
dance. It means considerateness and responsiveness, exemplified by Calidore's acts of courtesy. The Graces, of course,
are three sister goddesses who are givers of charm and beauty.
Grace has a theological meaning, the unmerited divine gift
given man for his regeneration and sanctification. Colin's song,
inspired by the Graces, is a heavenly gift, and his inspiration is
the aesthetic counterpart of God-given grace.

In this scene, Spenser elevates *lusus* and the recreative mode
of pastoral poetry to a contemplative vision in which faith and
art meet and dance. The antithesis between nature and art in
pastoral poetry is transcended in the vision on Mount Acidale

by grace and inspiration. In Spenser's poetic realization, art itself is nature, and both reach their perfection in grace. The pastoral vision is elevated to the unearthly beauty of the dance of the universe.

Calidore, whose name means "beautiful gift," has the grace to see, if only for the moment, the dancing maidens. He breaks in upon Colin's contemplative vision and the creation of his poetry: "resolving, what it was, to know,/ Out of the woods he rose, and toward them did go" (6. 10. 17). The dancers immediately vanish. Because Calidore belongs to the iron world of the epic, he cannot make the golden world of Arcadia or Mount Acidale his. He experiences both as an outsider, and contemplates the pastoral world with the pensive yearning of one who is not of it. Calidore cannot enjoy Colin's vision with the poet's freedom because the *ecstasis* of seeing it would draw him into contemplative *otium* not proper to a wayfaring knight who has a quest to finish.[35] He has succumbed for the moment to the innocence and contentment of pastoral life, but by rather clumsily intruding into the vision of its perfection he has shattered a fragile condition of consciousness. Ashamed of his "luckless breach" (6. 10. 29) he asks the shepherd-poet to pardon him.

At this late point in Book 6, it would seem that pastoral contemplation, in its affirmation of a golden world, is superior to heroic action. Discussing the pastoral episodes at the end of Book 6, Donald Cheney remarks:

> That these episodes happen to conclude the completed portion of the poem has seemed eminently fitting to those readers who take lively pleasure in paradox. The point at which the patron of Courtesy forsakes the court seems a wholly appropriate ending to an action which began in Book I with the repudiation of pastoral for the loftier strains of epic; that Calidore should encounter here the rejected mask of Spenser, Colin Clout, only underscores the irony of this return.[36]

Although continuing *otium* is unavailable to the heroic knight, it is a state he wishes for. This peace and order suggest permanence, yet the fragile vision on Mount Acidale represents instability and precariousness. The transitory vision is as fragile as the pastoral myth itself, and the dissolution of that vision foreshadows the later raid and ruin of Arcadia.

And again, forces inside Arcadia menace and oppose its harmony. One day a tiger attacks Pastorella:

> A tigre forth out of the wood did rise
> That with fell clawes full of fierce gourmandize,
> And greedy mouth, wide gaping like hell gate,
> Did runne at Pastorell her to surprize.
>
> (6.10.34)

Coridon runs in haste to rescue her, but when he sees the tiger, "though cowherd feare he fled away as fast" (6. 10. 35). Because of his cowardly failure to protect Pastorella, she must be saved by Sir Calidore. The Knight-shepherd, having "no weapon, but his shephards hook" (6. 10 36), fights the tiger and kills it. In this he is like Hercules, who rescued the Arcadians by killing Cacus the monster. In the rivalry between the Knight of Courtesy and the true rustic, Sir Calidore wins the love of Pastorella as he reveals his superiority in generosity, graciousness, and courageous stregth. She rejects his rival, confirming her earlier antipathy to Coridon, who if "fit to keepe sheepe, unfit for loves content" (6. 10. 37). The attack of the tiger and Calidore's heroism, moreover, is an anticipation of the later raid of the Brigands and Calidore's desperate rescue.

To gauge the full bearing of the outside world on the pastoral, one must understand the relationship between the incident on Mount Acidale and the Brigands' raid of Arcadia. Pastorella has accepted Calidore's love, but after a period of happiness together the pastoral enclosure is destroyed by the ravages of the outside world. When Calidore returns from a hunt one day he discovers that

> A lawelesse people, Brigants hight of yore,
> That never usde to live by plough nor spade,
> But fed on spoile and booty, which they made
> Upon their neighbors which did nigh them border,
> The dwelling of these shepheards did invade,
> And spoyld their houses, and them selves did murder,
> And drove away their flocks, and other much disorder.
>
> (6.10.39)

With this massacre and the captivity of Pastorella, the lawless brutality of the iron world claims dominion over the idyllic order of Arcadia. Arcadian happiness, like the vision of Graces on Mount Acidale, must be fragile and brief. Furthermore, the poet illuminates what is wrong with Calidore's desertion of duty; Pastorella proves vulnerable to those malevolent forces he has ignored and forgotten when retiring from a life of heroic action. Calidore begins to realize that the pastoral world is subject to the violence and brutality from which he thought he had escaped.

The ruthless Brigands, who no longer gain a living by plow or spade, commercialize the booty they seize by selling their victims into slavery. Because the captain of the Brigands has fallen in love with his captive, Pastorella, he will not let her be sold to merchants. The Brigands quarrel with him, and during a fight Coridon stealthily escapes. Melibee and the other shepherds, however, are killed, and Pastorella is held under guard by the Brigands, who have killed their captain. After Calidore has discovered the ruins of his paradise and the shepherds gone, he searches the countryside:

> He sought the woods; but no man could see there;
> He sought the plaines; but could no tydings heare:
> The woods did nought but ecchoes vaine rebound;
> The playnes all waste and emptie did appeare;
> Where wont the shepheards oft their pypes resound,
> And feed an hundred flocks, there now not one he found.
>
> (6.11.26)

He meets Coridon, who tells him the "woefull tale" (6. 11. 30), believing that Pastorella, with the shepherds, has been killed. Coridon is afraid to return to the Brigands' lair, his heart

> through fear was late fordonne
> Would not for ought be drawne to former drede,
> But by all meanes the daunger knowne did shonne.
>
> (6.11.35)

However, he finally agrees to accompany Calidore. Both take their shepherds' hooks, "but Calidore had, underneath, him armed privily" (11. 36). Taking his arms, Calidore resumes his role of knight. He has the training and skill of a knight, and he means to act as a knight, not as a shepherd, to rescue Pastorella. Calidore finds her in the Brigands' cave, and fights for her. Even in the description of his heroic combat, however, the poet makes a rural comparison:

> How many flyes in whottest sommers day
> Do seize upon some beast, whose flesh is bare,
> That all the place with swarmed do overlay,
> And with their little stings right felly fare;
> So many theeves about him swarming are,
> All which do him assayle on every side,
> And sore oppresse, ne any him doth spare:
> But he doth with his raging brond divide
> Their thickest troups, and round about him scattreth wide.
>
> (6.11.48)

This pastoral simile, like so many others in the poem, contributes to the sense of pastoral nature as an ideal throughout the book. The homeliness of the description provides a realistic counterpoint to the bookish romance of the captivity episode. Furthermore, the figure of Calidore as a bull brushing away summer flies suggests his tremendous power over the petty, sordid thieves.

After this victory, Calidore restores to Coridon the sheep the Brigands had stolen. Through this act, Arcadia is in a sense restored. Bur Coridon replaces Melibee, the pastoral philosopher, as leader. The cloddish and cowardly rustic now represents the pastoral community, and the ideas Arcadia as a place of contemplation and wisdom no longer exists. Pastorella, who embodies what was charming and lovely in Arcadia, will no longer be there, for she is taken by the Knight to the Castle Belgard, the home of her true parents.

The tension between the ideals of the pastoral and epic, the contemplative and active lives, reaches its limits as the brutality of the iron world invades and pillages a golden world enclosed and apparently self-sufficient. But the "lowly quiet life" (6. 9. 35) of Melibee could not defend itself against the ravage of reality. Sir Calidore comes to the realization that his pursuit and capture of the Blatant Beast is necessary, for the Beast has in effect brought its destruction to a pastoral refuge. Resuming the heroic quest, Calidore gives up a paradise that was never really his and is now a paradise lost. His experience, however, with Melibee and Colin Clout was not in the last analysis a dereliction of duty, for Arcadia provided him, as it provided Aeneas, with a personal involvement in the pastoral and a greater understanding of a paradise within, so that the meaning and value of his quest are illuminated.[37] Arcadia as a physical place has been destroyed; all that remains of it, as Melibee told Calidore, is in the mind.

Calidore finally tracks down the beast, and in an epic struggle overpowers it. Binding its jaws with an iron muzzle, he leads it by a chain throughout the land, and

> all the people, where so he did go,
> Out of their townes did round about him throng,
> To see him leade that beast in bondage strong,
> And seeing it, much wondered at the sight;
> And all such persons as he earst did wrong
> Rejoyced much to see his captive plight.
>
> (6.12.37)

Though Calidore has muzzled the Beast of Slander at last, its captivity is not permanent. It breaks its bonds, menaces humanity, and cannot be captured again: "So now he raungeth through the worlde againe,/ And rageth sore in each degree and state" (6. 12. 40). Calidore's quest was not futile, but his success was incomplete. He has muzzled the Beast for himself and for Gloriana's court, but not for all humanity.[38] Slander is rampant once more, and future generations must have its heroes to recapture it.

At the conclusion of the book, the narrator tells us that Slander spares no one, not even the Poet:

> Ne spareth he most learned wits to rate
> Ne spareth he the most gentle poets rime,
> But rends without regard of person or of time.
>
> (6.12.40)

The Blatant Beast is a monster that uses his "blasphemous tong" (6. 12. 34) to destroy the courteous, the poetic, the heroic, and the visionary.[39] Arcadia cannot survive if the Beast triumphs nor can the gentle poet, Colin Clout, and his vision of the Graces.

In the final fragment of *The Faerie Queene*, the "Cantos of Mutabilitie," Spenser provides in miniature form a continuum of pastoral, epic, and visionary poetry. The pastoral and epic develop through conflict toward a harmonious resolution in the visionary. The myth of Arlo Hill constitutes the pastoral episode; the myth of Mutability's rebellion and trial, the heroic; and the "unperfite" last canto, the visionary conclusion.

Arlo is a metaphor for a fallen Eden, and therefore contributes to the central story of Mutability's rebellion against heaven. Set in a pastoral framework, this mythological tale at first seems to be no more than a whimsical digression. In diminishing the moral power of the pastoral, the poet demonstrates its inadequacy, once nature has fallen to the hostile forces of the experiential world, to deal seriously with contemplative themes of nature, time, and death. Within this pastoral enclave, however, Spenser draws thematic and narrative parallels, on a small scale, with the larger epic action of the Cantos. Faunus's spying Diana's nakedness, for instance, parodically counterpoints Mutability's presumptuous rebellion against the gods of heaven.[40] As Cynthia, goddess of the moon, is Mutability's first victim, so Diana, another name for the moon goddess, is Faunus's. Furthermore, Spenser makes reference to Satan's temptation of Eve in the Garden of Eden when Faunus successfully tempts the nymph Molanna with "Queene-apple, and red cherries from the tree"[41] (7. 6. 43). Finally, just as Mutability corrupts the earth with sin and death, so Faunus is responsible for Diana's curse on idyllic Arlo Hill so that this *locus amoenus* becomes infected with wolves, robbers, and rebellious, lawless Irishmen.

Just before the high court of Nature convenes at Arlo Hill to hold the trial of Mutability against Jove, the poet departs from the main narrative to tell a mythological tale of Arlo and its pastoral surroundings. Arlo Hill is "the highest head" of "old father Mole" (7. 6. 39), the Ballyhoura hills near the poet's estate of Kilcolman. In the character of Colin Clout, he had praised these mountains with "shepheards quill" (7. 6. 36).

The narrator prefaces his tale of Faunus and Molanna by indicating that a humble style would be more appropriate to his pastoral subject:

> And, were it not ill fitting for this file,
> To sing of hilles and woods, mongst warres and knights,
> I would abate the sternenesse of my stile,
> Mongst these sterne stounds to mingle soft delights.
>
> (7.6.37)

The description of Arlo as it was before the fall emphasizes the Arcadian nature of the *locus amoenus*. Arlo was so beautiful and fertile that Diana chose it:

> She chose this Arlo; where shee did resort
> With all her nymphes enranged on a rowe,
> With whom the woody gods did oft consort:
> For with the nymphes the satyres love to play and sport
>
> (7.6.39)

The pastoral landscape, with its cool shade, fresh flowing fountains, hills and dales, becomes both humanized and divinized by the appearance of the nymphs and satyrs, who come to this earthly paradise to play and love in an ordered, harmonious, and apparently timeless golden age. The "Foolish god Faunus" (7. 6. 42), however, brings about chaos because of his presumption. He corrupts Molanna, a river nymph, bribing her with apples and cherries, to let him hide where he can secretly watch Diana bathing in her nakedness. When Faunus, playing the Peeping Tom, sees Diana bathing her lovely limbs,

> He could him not containe in silent rest;
> But breaking forth in laughter, loud profest
> His foolish thought.
>
> (7.6.46)

Unworthy of divinity, Faunus is called a mere "Babbler" (7. 6. 46). This kind of colloquial language, and the poet's rustic simile comparing Diana to a "huswife," illustrates Spenser's humbler pastoral style:

> Like as an huswife, that with busie care
> Thinks of her dairie to make wondrous gaine,

> Finding where-as some wicked beast unware
> That breakes into her dayr' house, there doth draine
> Her creaming pannes, and frustrate all her paine.
>
> (7.6.48)

The homely images of the dairy and creaming pans create a deliberately anti-heroic atmosphere. This lower style expresses the humble reality of Mutability's terrestrial existence.

While the sinful presumption of Faunus corresponds to that of Mutability and Satan, he acts out a burlesque version of sin, and suffers a merely farcical restribution. Now that Faunus is in Diana's custody, she and her nymphs

> . . . mocke and scorne him, and him foul miscall;
> Some by the nose him pluckt, some by the taile,
> And by his goatish beard some did haile.
>
> (7.6.49)

With his horns, tail, and goatish beard, Faunus is a devil-buffoon. Clad in deerskin, he resembles both Acteon and Falstaff, chased by Diana and her hounds. We see "silly Faunus" (7. 6. 49) last in his grotesque costume, speeding through Arlo and pursued by howling hounds, so "That all the woods and dales, where he did flie,/ Did ring again, and loud reecho to the skie" (7. 6. 52).

Diana, however, is still "full of foul indignation" (7. 6. 54) and abandons the brooks and mountains of lovely Arlo, laying a "heavy happless curse" (7. 6. 55) on the region. In the description of Diana's curse, the poet uses the recurring thematic image of a pastoral enclave being assaulted by the hostile forces of the surrounding territory:

> . . . that wolves, there she was wont to space,
> Should harbor'd be, and all those woods deface,
> And thieves should rob and spoile that coast around.
>
> (7.6.55)

Because Arlo is Ireland as well as Eden or Arcadia, his final lines in the canto,

> Since which, those woods, and all that goodly chase
> Doth to this day with wolves and thieves abound:

Which too-too true that lands in-dwellers have found,

(7.6.55)

divest the pastoral landscape of mythology and imaginative play, placing it squarely in reality, the "too-too true" world of history and politics, an iron world existing outside of Faery Land.

Spenser invests his epic protagonist, Mutability, with some of the virtues of the human heroic. The Titaness is an active individualist who is in quest of personal glory; she has energy, enterprise, and resolution. These virtues, however, are corrupted by her willful pride and assertion of self-sufficiency. Defying the power of the gods, she tries to prove that heaven itself is mutable, and attempts to extend her dominion over it. She is not satisfied with her reign over earthly affairs, and desires universal power. A proud contentious rebel, she reveals her *hybris* in her drive for honor and glory, for absolute power in earth and heaven.

Before Dame Nature and all the gods, she pleads her case by declaring that she reigns over earth. She argues that water, air, weather, and fire constitute demonstrable proof of her claim. She seeks to verify her rights further with witnesses, a procession of times and seasons. Order, Nature's sergeant, summons them, and his role suggests that while the times and seasons do demonstrate motion and change, their succession also shows the order, recurrence, and stability of the created world.

In this allegorical pageant, personifications of the seasons and months make their appearance in a processional calendar like *The Shepheardes Calender* itself. Each personification suggests human activities, and many have associations with man's close relationship to the generative cycle of nature. These are georgic images of rustic toil, process, bounty, and attained fulfillment. Sturdy March grasps a spade in his hand and strews seeds on earth, filling "her womb with fruitful nourishment" (7. 7. 32); June has "his plough-yrons" (7. 7. 35), July his scythe and sickle; August is crowned with ears of corn; September marches in with knife-hook, heavily laden "with the spoyle of harvests riches" (7. 7. 38); October treads wine vats; November with sweaty brow has been fattening hogs. Last of the months, February sits in his wagon, and has by his side "his plough and harnesse fit to till the ground" (7. 7. 42). In this last month it is implicit that the end anticipates a beginning, a time for March to return in the eternal cycle and sow once more the seeds of life. The postlapsarian world does not have the happiness of perpetual spring of Eden, but the richness, variety, and beauty of the earth are results of mutability and the Fall.

Chill December does not mind the winter cold because he celebrates with "merry feasting" and "great bonfires" his "Saviours birth" (7. 7. 41). In this month the poet suggests that a divine power transcends mutability, yet in human incarnation participates in the natural order of things.

Day and Night and the Hours follow in the procession, moving in a circle and taking turns to watch heaven's gate. Last in the procession of time is Death, but Life "like a fair lusty boy" (7. 7. 46) walks ahead of him. This whole procession seems to vindicate Mutability's claim about change and motion in the nature of things, yet paradoxically it asserts the coherence and stability of the world. Nature, like Adonis in the Garden, is subject to mortality, "Yet is eterne in mutabilitie,/ And by succession made perpetuall" (3. 6. 47).

Nature's cosmic judgment is that mutability appears to rule everything, but what seems to be change is in fact an evolutionary "dilation" of things that, according to Providential plan, "worke to their own perfection" (7. 7. 58). Further, Nature declares that a time will come when none will see change: "But time shall come that all shall changed bee,/ And from thence forth none no more change shall see" (7. 7. 59). After Nature utters her brief and enigmatic judgment, she and all the assembled gods on Arlo Hill vanish as suddenly as the Graces on Mount Acidale.

In the "unperfite" last canto of Book 7, and in the last stanza of the whole poem, Spenser turns from his role of epic narrator and joins his mortal audience. He contemplates what Nature has said about time "when no more change shall be,/ But stedfast rest of all things" (7. 8. 2). In an act of visionary power he sees "the pillours of eternity" (7. 8. 2) and the day of eternal rest. The vision he beholds is a paradise beyond the paradise of the pastoral, and beyond the reach of poetry itself. By elevating the terms of Nature's judgment to a higher level of contemplation, he expresses the longing of his soul for a divine order:

> But thence-forth all shall rest eternally
> With Him that is the God of Sabbaoth night;
> O that great Sabbaoth God graunt me that Sabaoths sight!
>
> (7.8.2)

God is both Lord of Hosts and Lord of the Sabbath; He is both the active and epical God of armies and the contemplative God of eternal rest.

This vision of eternity has been glimpsed before in the poem, when Red Cross beheld the New Jerusalem. The Knight had to postpone contemplative joy until he finished his heroic struggle on earth. The poet, like Red Cross, has a vision of the eternal, and he also must finish his quest. But the poem, a memorial to mutability in its seeming incompleteness,[42] is completed in fact by this vision of a divine order that brings all time and history, as well as his poem and life, to a close.

4

Milton's Pastoral Poetry

MILTON knew as an inexperienced young poet that he must play the oaten reed before he was ready to take the trumpet of heroic poetry in hand. Sharing the general assumption that the epic was the definitive poem for its age, he would have to prepare himself arduously before writing it. The epic was to be written late in life, as Virgil and Spenser demonstrated, because the genre demanded universal learning, lengthy writing experience, and a matured talent. Milton, of course, conceived the role of the epic poet in terms of this tradition. By temperament and calling, moreover, he gravitated toward the moral purpose, patriotic themes, and heroic actions of epic poetry. His Latin Gunpowder Plot poems, written at eighteen, were Milton's attempt to write in the heroic mode before he was ready. Phineas Fletcher, the Spenserian who influenced these brief pseudo-epics, had written of Virgil and Spenser in *The Purple Island*:

> Two shepherds most I love with just adoring;
> That Mantuan swain who changed his slender reed
> To trumpet's martial voice and loud roaring,
> From Corydon to Turnus derring-deed;
>   And next our home-bred Colin's sweetest firing;
>   Their steps not following close, but far admiring.
> To lackey one of these is all my pride's aspiring.
>
> (6.5)[1]

However, it was neither Corydon nor Colin but the great epics that provided Milton's inspiration for writing a poem "Doctrinal and exemplary to a Nation."[2] Restraining his youthful impatience by writing pastorals as a kind of preparation for the epic, his poems reveal an opposition between a self-disciplined poetic training and his frustrated amibition to write the epic.

The temptation for young Milton, then, was to write the heroic poem prematurely, and in so doing risk failing on a huge scale. That he resisted this temptation reflects his humility and self-knowledge, and the resistance itself gives his pastoral poetry much of its emotional tension and complexity.

"On the Morning of Christ's Nativity"

A poem celebrating the incarnation of the Hero-Redeemer, the Nativity Ode follows its models, the golden age eclogues of Virgil and Spenser, in many ways. All three poems belong to the pastoral tradition, each one in turn expanding and enriching it. Virgil united pastoral and epic verse in his fourth *Eclogue*; Spenser, in the "Aprill" eclogue, integrated pastoral with ode and hymn; Milton encompassed these diverse poetic modes in his own Nativity Ode. Because of the generically hybrid, composite nature of the poem, Milton plays a variety of roles. Identifying himself as John Milton and carefully including the date of composition, 1629, he calls our attention to the literal, historical poet, his youthful age, and contemporary time. But he also assumes several personae: the shepherd singing of the Nativity and pastoral life; the priest reenacting the Incarnation through hymn and liturgy; the bard glorifying the epic victory and triumph of Christ, the Redeeming Hero; and, finally, the inspired *vates* prophecying the millennium.

Milton's use of various personae and his careful deployment of generic elements, particularly of pastoral and epic, constitute an important part of the dialectical movement of the poem, which is based upon a continuous interaction of oppositions: pagan and Christian, body and spirit, time and eternity. This thematic and generic interaction develops through conflict and resolution toward harmony.

Milton shows his sense of genre by counterpointing Arcadian elements with heroic and visionary themes. In the eighth stanza he creates an idyllic vignette, an enclave of "Shepherds on the Lawn"[3] who seem to live in Arcadia or the English countryside rather than Judaea[4] These shepherds, "simply chatting in a rustic row," enjoy a life of idle and innocent ease, unaware of the great cosmic events around their pastoral enclosure. Their god is Arcadian Pan, guardian of the flocks; they do not know that "mighty *Pan*" is reborn as Christ, the Good Shepherd. They occupy their thoughts instead with simple pastoral concerns, "their loves, or else their sheep." Milton's poetic style in this stanza suggests the rustic diction of these simple herdsmen. In contrast to the lofty and ornate language in which he describes his celestial vision, the poet's tone and diction are modulated and become plain, homely, and frequently monosyllabic, befitting the low matter of the pastoral, the shepherds' ordinary lives and "silly thoughts." Since they are ignorant of what has just happened, the sudden revelation of the music of the spheres makes apparent the disparity between the world of ordinary time and the supranatural events that transform both nature and time.

The poet again returns to classical pastoral imagery after his prophetic account of the cessation of the oracles and the Last Judgment, and changes his tone and imagery in his description of the flight of the nymphs and local deities. The twentieth stanza constitutes a kind of miniature pastoral elegy:

> The lonely mountains o'er
> And the resounding shore,
>   A voice of weeping heard, and loud lament;
> From haunted spring and dale
> Edg'd with poplar pale,
>   The parting Genius is with sighing sent;
> With flow'r-inwov'n tresses torn
> The Nymphs in twilight shade of tangled thickets mourn.

Spirits who have traditionally inspired pastoral poetry are banished from the *locus amoenus* of the poet's consciousness, and Milton discloses an ambivalent regret and nostalgia for this fragile Arcadian world. These plaintive spirits, unlike the brutal gods of ancient Palestine, are sympathetically described as lovely and humane. Arcadia, with its mountains, springs, and flowers, is being emptied of vitality, color, and music. As in the traditional pastoral elegy, melancholy nature echoes the grief of its inhabitants. Mournfully, the landscape reverberates with the sound of weeping and sighing, as the old pagan harmony between the human mind and vernal nature is disrupted. The departure of the nymphs recalls the desertion of Arlo Hill in Spenser's "Cantos of Mutabilitie." The landscape that had been animated by nature-spirits has become divested of its imaginative power. The beauty of Arcadia fades into "poplar pale" and "twilight shade," a ghostly place reflecting the shepherd-poet's own hesitation to see it dissolve.

The pastoral elegy typically laments the disruptive intrusion of *eros* and death into the Arcadian enclave. There is an implied consolation, however, in this elegiac scene in the Nativity Ode, for with the incarnation of the God of Love and everlasting Life, the harmonious relationship between man, nature, and God has been elevated to a level of grace beyond the possibility of change. While Virgil's pastoral elegy in *Eclogue* 5 consoles the mourning shepherd by elevating Daphnis to Olympus, Milton's pastoral elegy offers the consolation of the Son of God, who descended to this experiential world of time and nature.

The figure of Pan functions as an important link in the poem between Arcadian and Christian pastoral. Arcadian shepherds worship pagan Pan, symbolized by his goat's head and cloven hoofs, who unites man and beast. This goat-man played the music of unredeemed nature on his seven reeds as he frisked with nymphs. Milton's referrence to Pan in the eighth stanza recalls the traditional legend, reported by Plutarch and retold in the gloss to Spenser's "Maye" eclogue, that at the time of Christ's nativity, a voice was heard shouting across the calm sea, "Great Pan is dead!"[5] The birth of God has caused the death of gods. Christ's birth brought about Pan's death because Christ replaced him. Elaborating on the identification, E. K. writes:

> *Great Pan* is Christ, the very God of all shepheards, which calleth himself the greate and good shepherd. The name is more rightly (me thinkes) applyed to him, for Pan signifieth all, or omnipotent, which is onely the Lord Jesus.

Besides, E. K. says that a traditional interpretation of Pan's demise is that

> Pan, though of some be understood the great Satanas, whose kingdome at that time was by Christ conquered, the gates of hell broken up, and death by death delivered to eternall death, (for at that time . . . all oracles surceased, and enchanted spirits, that were wont to delude the people, thenceforth held theyr peace).

Instead of the union of man and beast, we have in the Nativity Ode the union of God and man. The diabolical goat-man is dead; the heavenly God-man is born. The shepherd-god has given way to the Good Shepherd. Whereas the shrill music of the pan-pipe caused panic in the listener's heart, the music of crystal spheres and angelic symphony lifts up man's soul. Heaven and earth are "in happier union" as the golden age is established through a new covenant between man and God.

In the Arcadian stanzas of the poem, Milton presents a critical confrontation between pastoral fiction and Christian truth in which the pagan myth disintegrates. In the Christian pastoral we have another confrontation between fiction and reality; it is the meeting between Milton as shepherd-poet and the Word of God. Here, however, the historical and spiritual reality of the Nativity scene supports the poet's pastoral fiction. In the enclave of the manger, Milton finds his place of initiation, where his own talent as a poet is brought into confrontation with the Christian pastoral tradition. As Milton wrote of the Nativity Ode in his Elegy 6, he fashions his "simple strains" on his "native pipes." Assuming the role of shepherd who runs before the Magi, the poet offers his "humble olde" in the rude manger and lays it lowly at the Christ Child's feet.

Unlike the Arcadian shepherds, who had been occupied with mundane thoughts, this divinely inspired shepherd both hears and re-creates the cosmic music in pastoral song. Although nature in the pagan pastoral is presented as warm, sensual, and fertile, the Christian shepherd's landscape, that of the Winter Solstice, is cold and bleak. In contrast to the flowers and springs of the Arcadian numphs, or the "*Memphian* Grove or Green" with its "unshow'r'd Grass," the birth of Christ takes place in "the Winter wild." Nature doffs her "gaudy trim" and hides her "guilty front with innocent snow," and the only light and warmth the shepherd feels is not from the physical sun but the spiritual Son.[6].

Just as in one of the major paradoxes of Christianity, which says the humble shall be exalted, so the simple strains of the shepherd's native pipes can exalt the simple humanity of Mother and Child. The shepherd's almost naive description and familiar balladlike rhythm of the first six lines of the hymn evoke the mood of a simple nativity carol, but the swelling, Spenserian final line anticipates a tone grander and more exalted. The hymn begins and concludes in a crib for beasts, but while it is merely a "rude manger" at the beginning, it is transformed by grace and inspiration into "the Courtly Stable" in the last scene. As the "blest Virgin" lays "her Babe to rest," the visitors are not simply shepherds of Bethlehem or the Wise Men, but "Bright-harness'd Angels" waiting in heavely expectation to serve the King.

Milton draws from the Christian pastoral tradition, moreover, which equates shepherd and priest. He celebrates the timeless moment when Logos becomes Man in a liturgical poem of public praise. The Nativity Ode in both the prelude and hymn constitutes a formal offering to God through the ceremonial reenactment of incarnation and vicarious suffering,

> Wherein the Son of Heav'n's eternal King,
> Of wedded Maid, and Virgin Mother born,
> Our great redemption from above did bring.

In his incantatory evocation of Christian doctrines, the glory of God, "Trinal Unity," original sin, incarnation, and redemption, the poet imaginatively assumes the office of priest to carry out his ritualized Christmas service. He orchestrates the service, moreover, with angelic choirs and symphony, described in musical imagery and onomatopeia. This sensuous richness of language and imagery contributes to the spectacle of public worship. The elaborately ornate personificatons of Peace dividing the clouds with her myrtle wand, and of Mercy descending from above, "Thron'd in Celestial sheen,/ With radiant feet the tissued clouds down steering," are emblems and scenic designs derived from the court masque. Ruled by "Trinal Unity," personifications of Mercy, Justice, and Truth develop the theme of incarnation.

The celebrant's devotion to the Nativity and Passion gains a singular power from its brevity and foreshortening:

> The Babe lies yet in smiling Infancy,
> That on the bitter cross
> Must redeem our loss . . .
>
> (16)

Superimposed upon the smiling baby Jesus is the future figure of Christ, the Suffering Redeemer. As in the cycle of the ecclesiastical year, the poem moves very quickly from the Birth of Christ to His Passion and Death.

Just as Pan prefigures Christ as Good Shepherd in the pastoral portion of the Nativity Ode, so the infant Hercules in the twenty-fifth stanza symbolically anticipates Christ as divine man and hero-deliverer:

> . . . Nor *Typhon* huge ending in snaky twine:
> Our Babe, to show his Godhead true,
> Can in his swaddling bands control the damned crew.

The pagan infant god strangles the serpent in his cradle, whereas Christ, a meek baby, is so spiritually powerful that he can conquer the pagan, demonic world. Moreover, Christ's silencing the oracle, routing the pagan gods, and defeating the dragon reveal Him as exemplary hero who delivers mankind from the enemy.

Milton's primary concern is with the incarnation of the Hero-Redeemer as the central event in history. The historical and heroic elements in the poem operate together, because for Milton, as for other great Renaissance poets, the external world of historical movements and events, and heroic action, are inseparable.

This sense of history is revealed in the poet's attention to the particular time of Christ's birth during the *Pax Romana* of Caesar Augustus. That the sole historical incarnation took place when "No War, or Battle's sound/ Was heard the World around" indicates that the destructive activities of the fallen world had been suspended, and worldly kings "sat still," awaiting the birth of the King of Heaven. As for the mystery cults that flourished during this period, the poet suggests through images of pagan gods the prototypical nature of their symbolism:

> . . . And mooned *Ashtaroth,*
> Heav'n's Queen and Mother both,
> > Now sits not girt with Tapers' holy shrine,
> The Libyc *Hammon* shrinks his horn,
> In vain the *Tyrian* Maids their wounded *Thammuz* mourn.
>
> (20)

The figures of wounded Thammuz, the weeping maidens, and "Heav'n's Queen and Mother" are all historical as well as mythic prefigurations of Christianity. In Thammuz-Adonis we have the particulars of a dying-god myth and nature cult that are but imperfect types of Christianity and historical influences on it.

The world was at peace and "The Trumpet spake not." Just before the golden age to come, however, the trumpet of God "must thunder through the deep." The poet tonally and onomatopoetically re-creates the martial trumpet to express Christ's prophecy of the Last Judgment. In silencing the false oracles, routing the heathen gods, and vanquishing the Satanic Dragon in warfare, Christ becomes the epic hero of the providential history of mankind. The Ode treats Christ as the transcendent paragon of heroic action, and the poet glorifies His virtuous deed and victory in epical tone and language, thereby broadening the range of his poem.

The poet's role, however, that best expresses the harmonious reconciliation of thematic and generic oppositions is that of the inspired prophet, or *vates*. One model for Milton's vatic role, of course, is Virgil's golden age *Eclogue* in which the poet announces that he will "sing a somewhat loftier strain" and then uses a lyrical and apocalyptic style to prophesy the return of the original Golden Age. Another major model is the Messianic prophet of the Bible, and in the prelude Milton's reference to "the holy sages" and to Isaiah's image of the coal-bearing seraph identifies the poet's role and the oracular character of his inspiration. He inteprets the meaning of history, not as epic poet who glorifies heroic deeds in time, but as a *vates* in an ecstatic vision of the future and the heavenly Jerusalem.

Inevitably, therefore, Milton drew upon Virgil's fourth *Eclogue* for his celebration of the Nativity. One of Spenser's followers, Michael Drayton, wrote in "To the Reader of his Pastorals":

> the Blessing which came on them to the testimoniall Majestie of the Christian name, out of SIBYLS Moniments, cited before Christ's Birth, must ever make VIRGIL venerable with me: and in the Angels Song to Shepheards at our Saviors Nativitie Pastorall Poesie seems consecrated.[7]

Here Drayton identifies Virgil's prophetic *Eclogue* with Christ's nativity as examples of sacred pastoral. The thematic, generic, and stylistic parallels between Virgil's fourth *Eclogue* and Milton's Nativity Ode are many. Both poems announce the birth of the divine child in history and the coming of the golden age; they unite pastoral, heroic, and prophetic modes; and they use an elevated vatic tone and style. A major difference, however, between the way in which Virgil and Milton view the golden age is that the Roman poet sees it as a return to the old Golden Age, while the Christian poet interprets history as linear, and therefore his golden age occurs in eschatological time.[8] As a Christian, Milton rejected Virgil's pagan concept of cyclical time by insisting upon a course of temporal events including the sacrifice of the Son of God, leading to the Last Judgment. For man to hear the celestial music of the golden age he must be cleansed of sin, and he cannot hear it until the harmony between mankind and God is restored in a new covenant. In the thematically pivotal sixteenth stanza, the poem shifts radically in tone, expressing the sudden, tragic, yet necessary intrusion of time and history in his vision: "But wisest Fate says no,/ This must not yet be so . . . ." Only through the "bitter cross" and the "trump of doom" can there be a real restoration of harmony. The crucifixion and Last Judgment lie between man and the golden age.[9]

Christ's routing of the pagan gods is symbolic of the victory of Christian truth over the illusions of pagan belief, including those regarding nature and time. For Virgil, nature responds to the birth of the child with the exuberant growth of an earthly paradise. Following his epic and prophetic interpretation of history, Virgil returns to the pastoral setting with its ploughman, rams, and meadows, and while this landscape is natural, it is sensuous nature intensified and heightened. In Milton's Ode, on the other hand, the poet personifies nature to suggest her fallen moral character. Ashamed that "her Maker's eyes" will behold her "sinful blame" and "foul deformities," she hides "her guilty front." Although she manifested her postlapsarian erotic sensuality by wantoning with the Sun, "her lusty Paramour," she now attempts to change. In contrast to the extravagant fertility of nature in Virgil's eclogue, Milton's imperfect Nature must "doff her gaudy trim" and cover herself with "The Saintly Veil of Maiden white." The Christian poet rejects the pagan concept of nature as sinless, just as he rejects the pagan cyclical concept of time and history.[10]

Although Virgil's fourth *Eclogue* is the model for both Spenser's "Aprill" eclogue and the Nativity Ode, Spenser's treatment of his golden age is predominantly pastoral, whereas Milton develops his theme mainly in a heroic and visionary way. Spenser does address Calliope, the epic Muse, and he attempts, like Milton after him, to integrate history with the pastoral. For both, the pastoral is a vehicle for exploring the meaning of nature in the golden age. Stylistically, Milton's poem shows indebtedness to the "Aprill" eclogue in its use both of simple rustic diction — though Spenser's "forswonck and forswatt" is more extreme — and of personifications of nature. This direct influence is obvious in the seventh stanza of the Nativity Ode:

> And though the shady gloom
> Had given day her room,
>   The Sun himself withheld his wonted speed,
> And his his head for shame,
> As his inferior flame,
>   The new-enlight'n'd world no more should need;

> He saw a greater Sun appear
> Than his bright Throne, or burning Axletree could bear.

In Spenser's fourteenth stanza we find:

> "I saw Phoebus thrust out his golden hedde,
>   Upon her go gaze:
> But when he sawe how broade her beames did spread,
>   It did him amaze.
> He blusht to see another sunne belowe,
> Ne durst again his fyrye face out showe:
>   Let him, if he dare,
>   His brightnesse compare
> With hers, to have the overthrowe."

The two stanzas have marked similarities: both personify the sun, contrast its inferior beauty and power to the subjects of the poems, Christ and Eliza, and describe these subjects as greater suns. Yet there is a diffeence, too. Spenser's sun maintains his god's name, Phoebus; Milton's sun has been divested of divine status. While Spenser abandons his sun, Milton traces his degeneration later in the poem where we see him in the twenty-sixth stanza domesticated and reduced to an infantile condition, in his bed "Curtain'd with cloudy red," pillowing "his chin upon an Orient wave."

Spenser's golden age eclogue, despite its epic gestures, is primarily "recreative." The poet's hymn of praise to the Virgin Queen, while patriotic and even religious in meaning, is a poem of playful fantasy and invention. Furthermore, it is a timeless season in Spenser's eclogue, abundant with "Daffadowndillies,/ And cowslips, and kingcups, and loved lillies," and not a "Winter wild" as it is in Milton's Ode. Nature in "Aprill" is not fallen; instead, it is ordered and made permanent by art. In contrast to Milton's banished moaning nymphs, Spenser's join a pastoral procession as "Ladyes of the Lake."

Both Eliza and Christ reconcile the heroic and pastoral. Spenser's Eliza is a ruler as well as shepherd's goddess. She is elevated from shepherdess to one of the Graces. In Milton's poem God Himself descends to earth to become man, the Shepherd-Hero. As Grace and goddess of the shepherds, Eliza is symbol of pastoral song and myth. As Son of God, Christ incarnates the Word and the music of the spheres.

The Nativity Ode gave only three lines to the Passion, and Milton later attempted to develop that theme in poem that would be its Easter companion piece. Vida had written an epic, the *Christiad*, on the life of Christ, and Milton, rather than blowing "Cremona's Trump," played "softer airs" that were "more apt for mournful things." In this unfinished work, "The Passion," he tried to extend the heroic element in the Nativity Ode by implicitly comparing Christ's suffering to the labors of Hercules: "Most perfect *Hero*, tried in heaviest plight/ Of labors huge and hard, too hard for human weight." Milton's own laborious effort, however, proved too difficult. He confessed the subject "to be above the years he had, when he wrote it, and nothing satisfied with what was begun, left it unfinisht."

In the seventh "Prolusion," Milton writes explicitly about such premature efforts and the necessity for preparation:

> because I have learned from books and from opinions of the most learned men this, that in the orator as in the poet nothing commonplace or mediocre can be allowed, and he that wishes deservedly to be considered an orator ought to be equipped and perfected with a certain encompassing support of all the arts and of all science. Since my age does not permit this, I have preferred up to the present, while providing myself with these supports, to strive earnestly after that true reputation by long and severe toil, rather than to snatch a false reputation by a hurried and premature mode of expression.[11]

His "long and severe toil," then, coincided with his serving a literary apprenticeship to learn the craft of poetry. Preparation for a "true reputation" meant that he had to postpone heroic works by continuing to write pastoral poetry rather than snatching "a false reputation." Significantly, Milton says he found himself as a poet through contemplation in the English countryside, where he enjoyed pastoral *otium*:

> I myself invoke the glades and streams and beloved elms of the farms, under which during the summer just gone by (if it be permitted to mention the secrets of the goddesses) I recall to mind with pleasant memories that I enjoyed the highest favor of the Muses, where amid fields and remote woodlands I have seemed to myself to have been able to grow up as it were in seclusion.[12]

Like Virgil's Tityrus enjoying his pastoral ease in seclusion, lying under the spreading trees, young Milton in the bucolic language around Horton played the oaten reed.

Pastoral poems, from Virgil to Spenser, reflect the mind of the poet in meditation as he is caught in the conflict of various attitudes and values, and they show how that mind grows in exploring these opposing perspectives, creating a pattern of experience that is an interpretation of life. The pastoral poet may experiment with different modes of perception in an imaginative way. "L'Allegro" and "Il Penseroso" exemplify this experimentation with poetic sensibility and creativity.

"L'Allegro" and "Il Penseroso"

These twin poems reflect the golden age of youth, in which a poet is free from the necessities of life and compulsion by others. Milton's youthful golden age is pastoral, and the poet conceives of life in terms of the recreative and contemplative. The poems are devoted to "secure delight," liberty, and pleasure.

Milton's persona, or imaginative identity, in these reflective poems is that of the withdrawn poet who contemplates his own image and the moods of his psyche in the mental landscape he creates. This reflection on the intellect and sensibility adapts perceptions, imaginings, and memories, including those of his reading experience.

As a study of the young poet's literary sensibility, the companion poems reveal Milton's indebtedness to his English predecessors. Through the use of literary allusions, echoes, and stylistic imitations, the apprentice poet demonstrates an understanding of, and deference to, the literary tradition of which he is part. Furthermore, in accord with his theme of the pleasures of the imagination, Milton's references to Chaucer,

Shakespeare, and Jonson help define the nature of the poet's imaginative experience as he strolls through a mental landscape of his own creating. The pastoral debate itself, with its catalogue of pleasures and its invitation, is derived from a traditional genre made familiar by Marlowe's "Passionate Shepherd" and Raleigh's reply. The final couplets of "L'Allegro" and "Il Penseroso," of course, clearly echo Marlowe's popular lyric. In exploring his poetic identity, Milton in effect traces his own literary genealogy as he does those of Euphrosyne and Melancholy. Modulating his poetic style with versatility, he re-creates the stylistic characteristics of his poem's antecedents, among them Elizabethan songs, madrigals, and masques, and Spenserian romance in which evocative poetry suggests "more is meant than meets the ear."

Exploring the creative imagination, the poet gives attention as well to the unconscious mind; the experience of dreams is a rich reservoir of images, a source of inspiration for the creative process. In "L'Allegro" he concludes his evocation of the imaginative world of romance and masque: "Such sights as youthful Poets dream/ On Summer eves by haunted stream." The prelude of "Il Penseroso" banishes "hovering dreams" that delude the mind, yet later in the poem the persona welcomes "some strange mysterious dream" that enriches the poet's mind as he sleeps in "close covert" by a murmuring brook.

In the traditional form of a pastoral debate, these companion poems share conventions with both Virgil's singing matches and Spenser's moral debates. Milton's personae engage in a poetic contest, emphasized through parallel sequences, so that, like the alternate songs of the *Eclogues*, the second singer must imitate and surpass his rival. Just as Coridon sings the praises of Alexis, and Thyrsis of Phyllis, L'Allegro and Il Penseroso praise their particular Muses, Mirth and Melancholy, as their divine mistresses. Milton, the poet, proposes the challenge for himself; life with the Muse is the pledge; the reader is the judge.

The apparent antithesis of the pastoral debate, however, is really a coming, or playing, together. The pleasures of

"L'Allegro" and "Il Penseroso" are compatible in that they are both pleasures of the human imagination. Although at first they may appear to be in diametrical opposition, the poet rejects a simplistic either/or state of mind.[13] Instead, these parallel poems celebrate the experiencing consciousness, which is free to explore the creative possibilities of both modes of perception without having to deny either one its pleasure or value. That is, "L'Allegro" and "Il Penseroso" must be taken together as a single work that comprehends the multiplicity and variety of human experience.

As in Spenser's *Calender*, which is patterned after the cycle of the twelve-month year and encompasses the diversity of human experience, Milton's "L'Allegro" and "Il Penseroso" trace the cyclical pattern of the twenty-four-hour day, constituting a microcosm of man's life.[14] The companion poems are structured in a hierarchical as well as sequential order. They progress in steps from the poet's youthful holiday world to the studious life of the intellect, and his "old experience" of mature religious contemplation, lifting him finally to the "Prophetic strain."

In the ten-line prelude of each poem, the poet rejects and ritually banishes the contrasting mood. The "loathed Melancholy" that the poet banishes does not give pleasure or inspire artistic creativity; rather, it is a despondent, pathological, and emotionally paralyzing melancholy, like the irrational depression of Cornelius Gallus in Virgil's tenth *Eclogue* or Colin's self-destructive introversion in the plaintive eclogues of the *Calender*. That is, this melancholy is a travesty of what is praised in "Il Penseroso,"[15] and the inflated rhetoric and phantasmagoric imagery in the prelude describe the symbolic landscape of a psychological hell, with the three-headed watchdog, darkness, raven, and "low-brow'd Rocks." Similarly, the "vain deluding joys" banished at the beginning of "Il Penseroso" are not the pleasures of the cheerful man. They are, instead, deceptive illusions of the "idle brain," not productive because ungoverned by the rational mind.

After the prelude, each persona invokes his presiding deity. Describing the parentage of Mirth and Melancholy, Milton improvises his own myths to express the spontaneity and freedom of his imaginative faculties. The divinities, personified abstractions, and spirits of place that gather in the poems humanize both time and space. Incarnations of ideas, they show how the human imagination, through myth and poetry, vitalizes and animates the ordinary world. The tone of Milton's myth-making is buoyant and, as in Spenser's recreative "Aprill," the poet creates his own mythological genealogy with fantasy and freedom. His myth of West Wind meeting Aurora "once a-Maying" has the delicate, fresh sensuousness of an English pastoral masque:

> There on Beds of Violets blue,
> And fresh-blown Roses washt in dew,
> Fill'd her with thee a daughter fair,
> So buxom, blithe, and debonair.

(21-24)

L'Allegro says explicitly what he wants: "And if I give thee honor due,/ Mirth, admit me of thy crew." In the act of giving this goddess her honor, he becomes a cheerful man. The poem itself effects what it speaks about. Through its variations on the theme of Mirth, the persona honors her by enjoying her pleasures as he catalogues them.

Both central figures, Mirth and Melancholy, are idealized abstractions, and therefore in themselves there is only slight individualization. Analyzing them, however, the poet explores their component parts with greater particularity. Each goddess appears with her train of companions. "The Mountain Nymph, sweet Liberty" whom Mirth leads in her right hand emphasizes the importance of unconstrained freedom if the mind is truly to enjoy the pleasures of Mirth. The personification of "Laughter holding both his sides" illustrates the poet's ability to bring an idea to life and sensuous human form in one compressed line. Peace, Quiet, Spare Fast, and silence follow Melancholy with her "ev'n step, and musing gait." The *otium*, or "retired Leisure," of Arcadia frees the pensive man to contemplate. Just as Liberty is Mirth's chief companion, so the "Cherub Contemplation" soaring "on golden wing,/ Guiding the fiery-wheeled throne" is Melancholy's. This visionary image taken from Ezekiel explains why Melancholy, the "pensive Nun," looks with "rapt soul" at the skies, and it anticipates, moreover, the thematic climax of both poems where the poet himself is dissolved into ecstacies in a moment of transcendent happiness as he experiences mystical contemplation.

The human actors in the pastoral landscape are a realization in tangible form of the poetic mind at work. The plowman, milkmaid, mower, and shepherd, however, are not particularized, but Milton concisely describes the outlines of his idealized and generalized figures. Like Spenser's procession of personified Months in the "Mutabilitie Cantos," they are georgic images of rustic activity symbolizing fruitful nature to which man himself belongs.

When the persona observes Corydon and Thyrsis at their savory dinner, Phyllis hastily leaving her bower to bind sheaves with Thestylis, or youths and maids "Dancing in the Checkr'd shade," he does not participate in those activities himself but stands apart as creator-spectator, the shepherd who tells his tale. He is like Colin Clout envisioning the dancers and music on Mount Acidale. Perhaps all these events that Milton describes are "as youthful Poets dream."[16] Although many of L'Allegro's pleasures are active and communal, the pastoral singer himself is solitary and detached. He describes activity, but it is the activity of imagining and creating that Milton as cheerful man enjoys. "L'Allegro" is a recreative poem in that the cheerful man enjoys *otium*, freedom from "eating cares" in a pastoral landscape that complements the creation of poetry, which is play. This play is possible in a "Sunshine Holiday" of the mind, and though the poet does not hay or dance, he does tell stories, not only of Faery Mab or Puck, but the narrative of his own imaginative experience with "heart-easing" Mirth.

As in most pastoral poetry, the landscape serves as a subjective symbol as well as objective reality. In contrast to the prelude of "L'Allegro" which describes a lurid, nightmarish region of the "horrid shapes," the landscape of the poems proper are idyllic and ordered, a *locus amoenus* in which nature is seen through art. Although the poet describes the cycle of a day, there is a sense of timelessness about his private, imagined

Arcadia. Moreover, his prosodic shift from the somewhat sprawling and irregular prelude to the peripatetic rhythm and tetrameter couplets of the poems has the effect of artfully trimming and articulating the lines and series of scenes so that they follow each other in orderly succession. These imagined scenes are objectified by the poet through his sensuously precise descriptions, but the emphasis is as much upon the poet's imagining eye as upon the objective scene:[17] "Straight mine eye hath caught new pleasures/ Whilst the Landscape round it measures . . . . " That is, the scenes of a cottage chimney smoking between two aged oaks, or the shepherds telling tales at night while they drink spicy nut-brown ale, for all their graphic vividness, are more imagined than observed. The landscape images of "Il Penseroso," however, are even more internalized. The pensive man's solitary strolling in the woods, listening to the nightingale, and gazing at "the wand'ring Moon" all express the pleasures of introspection and reverie. Even the sensuous particularity of the "minute-drops off the Eaves" with its close intensified seeing and hearing, is part of the pensive man's interior landscape. The movement of these scenes flows in an associative rather than logical way.[18] Furthermore, Milton has changed the rather brisk rhythms of "L'Allegro" to verse paragraphs that are slower and more spacious and encompassing, supporting a mood of pensive reverie.[19]

The subjective symbolic landscape of "L'Allegro" has, in spite of its cheer and mirth, intimations of melancholy. At times, Milton's persona must subdue the sadness he feels: "Then to come in spite of sorrow/ And at my window bid good-morrow . . . . " The poignant phrase "in spite of sorrow" gives an expressive tension and a kind of ambiguity to his earlier violent dismissal of melancholy, and his attraction to mirth and scenes of communal cheer. When he asks to be lapped in soft Lydian airs, he reveals that he has felt "eating Cares," and implies that he can ward off despondency only in a never-ending moment of pleasurable oblivion.[20] His withdrawal, solitude, and suppression of sorrow anticipate the conditional, indecisive couplet that concludes the poem. *If* Mirth can give these delights, only then will he live with her. The "if" ex-

presses a supposition and not a fact, for he is not certain that
Mirth can actually provide happiness, and even when he attempts to invoke her spirit and catalogue her delights, he is
touched by moments of doubt and sadness.

The symbolic myth of Orpheus at the conclusion of
"L'Allegro" develops and deepens this melancholy ambiguity:

> That *Orpheus'* self may heave his head
> From golden slumber on a bed
> Of heapt *Elysian* flow'rs, and hear
> Such strains as would have won the ear
> Of *Pluto*, to have quite set free
> His half-regain'd *Eurydice*.
> These delights if thou canst give
> Mirth, with thee I mean to live.
>
> (145-52)

Although the passage, with its fragrant flowery bed and soft
melodic strains, is sweet in epicurean pleasures, the tone is
languid and wistful. The music Orpheus hears is given to him
from "The hidden soul of harmony." Because his magical art
represents the union of man and nature, and could therefore
possibly redeem a soul from death, this music inspires the hope
that he can bring his lost wife back from Hades.[21] These
musical strains, the would-be cheerful man says, would have
won the ear of Pluto. Eurydice, however, was only
"half-regain'd." As in Book 4 of Virgil's *Georgics*, Orpheus
does temporarily regain his wife from death through the power
of music, but he loses her a second, more painful time, forever.
So Milton's persona half-regains Mirth, and then loses her at
the end of the poem to melancholy. Mirth is as vulnerable and
precarious as the pastoral myth. In "Il Penseroso," on the other
hand, Orpheus is not passive but actively makes the music
himself. This music is not a delightfully voluptuous Lydian air
but melancholy, and it "made Hell grant what Love did seek."
The poet, then, creates music so melancholy that it draws
"Iron tears down *Pluto's* cheek." The music of noble melancholy, or "Il Penseroso," has more supernatural power because
it confronts tragic experience. As his brief meditation on tragic
and epic poetry suggests, the pensive man's philosophical ac-

ceptance of sorrow frees him from the anxieties that a man, in desiring mirth, attempts to avoid. The poet-mystic descends and is purified, then ascends from Hades as a symbol of the internal quest of the human spirit.

Whereas the movement of "L'Allegro" is horizontal through humanized space, Il Penseroso's progress is vertical, as the poet rises toward a greater understanding of his ultimate purpose. In his pursuit of wisdom, the pensive man looks upward and ascends gradually, guided by the "Cherub Contemplation" who "soars on golden wing." The "high lonely Tow'r" functions at the center of the poem as the beginning of contemplative vision. Philosophers and poets of the past, exalted spirits of Elysium, are conjured as the pensive man climbs upwards. [22] His study of Hermes and Plato opens up "vast Regions" where "The immortal mind" may leave behind the flesh and the pleasures of sensation. References to both Orpheus and Musaeus, the mythical bard of Virgil's Elysium, suggest the soul's liberation from nature, time, and death. Unlike the pastoral community of "L'Allegro," the spiritual community of "Il Penseroso" is comprised of those who dedicated themselves to a life contemplating the divine. The pensive man, moreover, hears

> . . . sweet music breathe
> Above, about, or underneath,
> Sent by some spirit to mortals good
>
> (151-53)

and this music lifts him to the high-roofed church filled with the resonant harmonies of "pealing Organ" and "the full voic'd Choir below." Here his consciousness is altered and expanded. Devotional contemplation has led him to mystical union, and he is dissolved into ecstasies.

Before the poet can experience the eternal, he has to clear a space for himself in the fallen world of compulsion and necessity. This imagined space, or enclosure, is the place from which his desire for contemplation springs. Arcadia provides the initial step, but the poet must abandon it and rise beyond his golden world of images. The enclosure of "Il Penseroso" is other than the circumscribed pastoral place of "secure delight"; the "studious Cloister's pale" and the "Mossy Cell" are eremitic enclosures in which man may contemplate the divine in nature, in which introspection is fulfilled by looking outward. Milton's pensive man, like Spenser's contemplative hermits in *The Faerie Queene*,

> . . . may sit and rightly spell
> Of every Star that Heavn' doth shew,
> And every Herb that sips the dew.

(169-71)

Reconciling grace and nature, he may know the transcendent unity of being by contemplating the interrelatedness of stars high in heaven and the lowly things of earth. Only by looking toward heaven can man, both L'Allegro and Il Penseroso, become balanced in the present. The Renaissance contest between enjoyment and cognition is resolved as Milton progresses from pleasure, to inquiry, and ultimately to vision. "L'Allegro" and "Il Penseroso" describe in linear ascent the true aspirant's development from his pastoral art, a "long and severe toil" studying works devoted to the contemplation of things eternal, to his maturity and "old experience," which culminates in inspiration, "something like Prophetic strain."

Arcades

Milton's courtly entertainment *Arcades* uses pastoral motifs and setting to represent the ideals of social virtue and contemplative wisdom. In the masque the poet invalidates the old pagan Arcadia by creating a Christian Arcades. This new Arcadia, symbolized by the home of the Countess of Derby, for whom the masque was written and performed, is a site of the golden age.

The Harefield estate in Middlesex, where the celebration took place, becomes in *Arcades* a symbolic representation of the idyllic *locus amoenus* to which Arcadian nymphs, shepherds, and poets make their pilgrimage. Milton allegorized his subject as a rural queen and the estate at Harefield as a pastoral world of the imagination. The poet creates a fiction that uses the literal presence of the Countess and the objective reality of Harefield, its actual lane of elm trees, so that "this night's glad solemnity" becomes the masque itself.

Although *Arcades* looks forward to the fuller, more complex use of the pastoral in the masque presented at Ludlow Castle, it looks back to the pastoral themes of both the Nativity Ode and the companion poems. The innocent shepherds' solemn quest for the Countess parallels the search of the Magi for the infant Christ; the soliloquy of the Genius of the Wood which describes the heavenly music of the spheres echoes the angelic choir and symphony of the golden age Ode; the flight from Arcadia, and the progress from recreative play to contemplative wisdom, from the pagan world of nature to the Christian order of grace,[23] are thematic movements resembling "L'Allegro" and "Il Penseroso."

Milton's pastoralizing of the Countess and his mythic elevation of her from rustic queen to shepherds' goddess in a holiday world resembles Spenser's blazon in the "Aprill" eclogue. When Queen Elizabeth visited the house at Harefield in 1602, she was, like the Countess of Derby in *Arcades*, honored by masquers. The similarities between Spenser's Elisa and Milton's Countess are striking and significant. In her allegorical roles, the Countess personifies many of the same ideas as the Queen in Spenser's poem. As sylvan Muse, she represents poetic inspiration, and her presence in the local English countryside transforms the old Arcadia and makes it new and perfect; as a Virgo-Astraea figure she symbolizes the idea of the golden age restored by a divine social order. *Arcades* as pastoral panegyric insists upon the reciprocity between the artistic and social orders.

This brief masque consists of three songs and a recitative in heroic couplets. The theme and slight plot are developed through these verses. The action of the masque begins when a group of young Arcadian shepherds and nymphs who have been looking for their Arcadian queen appear. They are "some Noble persons of her family . . . in pastoral habit, moving toward the seat of State." Having journeyed on a quest, they discover that their "solemn search hath end." At the goal of

their journey they express wonder and reverence at the
Countess's radiance and divinity. Discovering how she exceeds
her fame, they compare her favorably with pagan deities,
Latona, Cybele, and Juno. They are amazed to find that "this
clime," England, holds "a deity so unparallel'd."

The Genius of the Wood appears and tells the "gentle
swains" and "Fair silver-buskin'd Nymphs" that he knows they
are visitors from "famous *Arcady*" who are on a quest. He offers
to guide them through the pastoral landscape, and should they
follow him, he will bring them right to the glittering seat of
State on which the goddess-queen sits. He then identifies
himself as "the pow'r/ Of this fair Wood" who has received his
benign magical arts "by lot from *Jove*." It is his function to take
care of the grove, to nurse, heal, and bless the woods and
plants of Harefield, a "hallow'd ground." In the deep of the
night when his duties are done, he listens with rapt enchant-
ment to "the celestial *Sirens'* harmony." His description of this
heavenly music of the spheres operates as a climax to his
speech, and provides the Platonic-Christian framework for the
whole masque. This music cannot be heard by those "Of
human mold with gross unpurged ear." The music sings to the
Fates, lulling "the daughters of *Necessity*," so that those who
are pure can hear it, freed from compulsion and able to enjoy
otium in their contemplation of things eternal. Now that the
Genius himself has found his "great Mistress" and adores her
with "low reverence," he is able to listen to harmonies of
heaven. Moreover, he tells the Arcadian pilgrims that if his
"inferior hand or voice could hit/ Inimitable sounds," he
would exalt her "peerless height." Seeing the relationship be-
teen her royal virtue and celestial harmony, the Genius of the
Wood expreses the union of music and the virtuous social
order of Harefield.

As in Spenser's "Aprill" eclogue where Hobbinol sings to the
"daynte Nymphs" to forsake their bowers and "hether looke/
At my request" to sing the praises of "fayre Elisa," so Milton's
Genius urges the nymphs and shepherds to leave mythic Arcadia and follow him to the Christian and English Arcadia of
Harefield. The Genius sings the second song, "O're the smooth
enamell'd green," as he leads them toward the Countess. "No

print of step hath been" suggests that Harefield-Arcadia is a place not bound by mere physical nature; it is an ideal landscape in which grace has redeemed both nature and art. They progress up the great avenue of thick elms at Harefield, the Queen's walk "Under the shady roof/ Of branching Elm Starproof." The imagery here echoes Spenser's description of the "shadie Grove" in Book 1 of *The Faerie Queene*:

> Whose loftie trees, yclad with sommers pride,
> Did spread so broad, that heavens light did hide
> Not perceable with power of any starr.
>
> (1.1.7)

But this landscape is not the Wood of Error, for the Countess herself radiates a heavenly light. The Genius tells his Arcadian guests that "Such a rural Queen/ All Arcadia hath not seen."

The concluding choric song, "Nymphs and Shepherds dance no more," exhorts the other nymphs and shepherds to abandon mutable Arcadia. The landscape of the old Greek Arcadia is described a sandy and stony, sterile compared to the "better soil" of Harefield. Dancing and tripping, the pastoral activities of the old Arcadia are light-hearted and recreative; however, the "twilight ranks" in Pan's Arcadian mountains suggest the gloomy passing of the old pagan order. The recreative sense of play, which the make-believe pastoral disguises and which the music and song of this festive celebration evoke, leads the nymphs and shepherds to a contemplation of timeless heavenly music, and then to the ultimate contemplation of virtue and wisdom at the seat of the Countess. The pilgrims are assured that the Countess is nobler than Syrinx, Pan's mistress and personification of the old Arcadian music. Whereas Syrinx symbolizes the sensuous melody of pastoral song, the inspiring music of Harefield is the celestial harmony of the golden age. The Arcadian pilgrims will "have greater grace/ To serve the Lady of this place." The word *grace* by its simultaneous reference to natural beauty, music, and spiritual virtue, defines the divine order in society at Harefield. The pilgrims have been guided from the physical landscape of their mythic pagan home and, elevated to Christian grace, from make-believe to belief. The concluding couplet of the song repeats: "Such a rural Queen/

All *Arcadia* hath not seen." This final refrain expresses in pastoral imagery the central thematic compliment of the whole masque.

A Mask Presented at Ludlow Castle

Not since his unfinished "The Passion" had Milton used heroic themes and characters. In "L'Allegro," "Il Penseroso," and *Arcades*, he had abandoned the heroic to play his pastoral song in the golden world of Arcadia. Progressing from pastoral recreation to divine contemplation, he had by-passed the heroic in these poems of pastoral *otium*. *A Mask*, however, explores and defines the relation between the pastoral and heroic. Within the context of the masque Milton discovers a necessary intermediate step in a dialectical movement: between the orders of nature and grace there is Virtue's dramatic struggle with Vice; between Arcadian play and divine contemplation there must be morally heroic action.

The poet's use of pastoral setting, conventions, and attitudes in the *Mask* exemplifies his complex exploration of the pastoral. As in *Arcades*, the *Mask* resists the pastoral even as it exploits it. The setting of the woods, for example, in which the Lady is lost, suggests a moral ambiguity. What seems to be a place of retirement from the confusion of life is a place of mazes where the Lady becomes bewildered and fearful. "Each and every alley green" perplexes the lost traveler with its confusing labyrinth of passages. The woods offer shade for rest and cooling fruit for hunger, but in those woods there are temptations to the body and soul. The herdsmen who celebrate their rural festivities by praising "the bounteous Pan" may in fact be dangerous, drunken men. An Attendant Spirit can descend into the woods as a good shepherd to guide the lost and weary traveler homeward, but Comus also can emerge from the darkness, a false shepherd intent on misleading the lost pilgrim to sin and death of the soul. Comus pretends to the innocent mirth of the pastoral when he says that his wild rout is like "pert Fairies and dapper Elves" and when he uses fresh pastoral images of "Wood-Nymphs deckt with Daisies trim," but this feigning is exposed as his tone abruptly shifts to the incantation to the sinister Cotytto, "Goddess of Nocturnal sport," who presides over obscene ritual orgies at midnight. The apparent honesty, goodness, and courtesy of the shepherd is deceit, "well-placed words of glozing courtesy," and his "low/ But loyal cottage" is a palace of pride. In Comus we see how the traditional pastoral premises of self-sufficiency, liberty, and epicurean delight are perverted into egotism, license, and brutalizing incontinence.

Through Milton's use of the pastoral, however, he defines and embodies the heroic virtue of chasity. His exemplary heroine, the Lady, must protect the *hortus conclusus* of her virginity. She must assent to her spiritual nature, but at the same time learn the claims of her physical nature. For if she is to ascend "higher than the Sphery chime," she must be willing to confront and withstand the temptations of this fallen world, which is a testing-ground for the human soul. Instead of escaping temptation and trial, then, the true servant of virtue must be ready to combat evil. That is, Milton's moral hero cannot retreat into a pastoral enclave for a fugitive and cloistered virtue, but must exercise obedience, reason, and patience in an unregenerate world fraught with misfortunes and the perils of evil. In *A Mask*, the Lady, who is the aspiring servant and the heroine of chastity, must exercise her virtue to redeem her physical nature through confrontation and combat with her adversary.

The Elder Brother's personification of chastity, as a "quiver'd Nymph" who is "clad in complete steel" recalls the image of Spenser's Britomart, the martial virgin armed with spear and shield, appareled in her "goodly armour" (3.3.59). Beneath their knight's armor, however, both Britomart and the Lady are young women, vulnerable by their human nature to temptation. The Lady, like Britomart, must understand the nature of her womanhood as she becomes heroine of chastity. Just as Britomart on her quest rejects Malecasta and vanquishes Busirane, so the Lady must struggle with the unchaste Comus in order to defeat him.

When Dr. Johnson observed that Milton's *Mask* is "a drama in the epick style,"[24] he noted that in spite of traditional pastoral setting, motifs, and images, the work has affinities with both drama and epic. It is dramatic in its unified action and also in the conflict between the Lady and Comus, which through dialogue and action reveals their individualized characters. Moreover, as the protagonist, the Lady develops in the unfolding plot, from an innocent untried by experience, who, initiated by ritual entry into the labyrinth of the self, becomes a mature young woman. She has gained through her ordeal a greater self-knowledge, a recognition of the daimonic, and a stronger faith in the divine order.

Only when the Lady acknowledges Comus's presence in her physical nature, experiences his temptations, and actively exercises her reason, temperance, and fortitude of patience, does she grow to be a true servant of virtue. Although more physically passive than active, the Lady conquers the temptations of the flesh because she has the character of a renunciatory hero which, according to Hallett Smith, is comprised of "wisdom, prudence, and self-control."[25] Her victory over Comus parallels Guyon's triumph over Acrasia in the Bower of Bliss. Moreover, the symbolic meaning of the Lady's victorious combat with Comus is enriched by the fact that this masque was presented at Ludlow Castle on Michelmas Night, which celebrates the warrior Angel who vanquished Satan, and who guides Christian souls, consoling them in their trials, leading them toward eternal light. The Lady also prefigures Christ of *Paradise Regained* in his heroic renunciation of Satan's temptations.

The allegorical setting of the masque consists of the dreary wood, the enchanted palace of Comus, and Ludlow Town and castle. Whereas in the traditional pastoral nature reflects the shepherd's conscious mind, the nature of the dark wood in *A Mask* reflects the Lady's unconscious mind. That Milton's pastoral takes place at night and not in the usual Arcadian sunshine holiday suggests that the world of Comus is nonrational and unconscious. The Lady's interior journey takes her through these three scenes: a dangerous wild wood, a symbol of human subrational consciousness, where the god of instinctive appetite, Comus, and the supernatural Spirit contest for the Lady; the palace of Comus, the seat of temptation and evil and Ludlow, the virtuous society of the Lady's human father and the heavenly home of her divine Father.

"Within the navel of this hideous Wood" Comus dwells, and for the Lady to be separated from her brothers and lose her way in the primitive darkness of the "leafy labyrinth" is to expose herself to the "tangl'd wood" and mazes of the human psyche. This is the labyrinth within the unconscious where the virgin Ariadne faced the minotaur before she found her way to freedom. From his mountain watch the Attendant Spirit looks down into this "bottom glade" where by night Comus and "his monstrous rout are heard to howl/ Like stabl'd wolves." Assuming the role of *pastor bonus*, the Attendant Spirit protects his innocent, vulnerable flock from the assault of predatory wolves. Before descending to this ominous world of Spenserian romance, resembling the Wood of Error, he has taken on "the Weeds and likeness of a Swain." In an implied comparison with Orpheus,

> Who with his soft Pipe and smooth-dittied Song
> Well knows to still the wild winds when they roar,
> And hush the waving woods,
>
> (86-88)

the Attendant Spirit defines his mythic role of shepherd as poet-musician who has the magical art to control and subdue savage nature.

In the tradition of the anti-masque, Comus and his "rout of Monsters, headed like sundry sorts of Wild Beasts" enter, "making a riotous and unruly noise." After the Attendant Spirit's finely controlled recitative about the hierarchical order of the universe, the lurching rhythms of the unrestrained antic dance inverts that order, and the men and women who have been transformed into beasts represent the unnatural degradation of humanity by incontinence. With defiance and bravado, Comus falsely claims that he and his consorts "are of purer fire" and "Imitate the Starry Choir." The bestial appearance and frenzied cavorting, however, manifest disordered movement and sublunary corruption. If the cosmos itself is a universal dance, and the concept of the dance inherent in the masque form itself symbolizes order and harmony, then the "barbarous

dissonance" of the anti-masque, the monsters' dissolute revelry and tipsy dance in the wild wood symbolize the subrational impulse to anarchy, a ritual returning them to primeval chaos. Although the song of Comus asserts the spontaneity and freedom of their apparently care-free lives, his followers, by regressing to a subhuman state, have lost their free will and become enslaved by their own irrational passions.

Comus and his followers "knit hands, and beat the ground,/ In a light fantastic round." When the Lady enters, they break off their dance. Comus's speech is now formal and subdued as he hears "the different pace,/ Of some chaste footing near about this ground." Perceiving that some virgin is "benighted in these woods," he declares confidently:

> I shall ere long
> Be well stock't with as fair a herd as graz'd
> About my Mother *Circe*.
>
> (151-53)

A herdsman of lost degraded souls, Comus assumes the guise of a "harmless villager" to deceive the Lady, and acts out a parody of the pastoral ideal. His are the vices of the worldly, selfish *pastor malus*, a shepherd who like Spenser's Palinode in the "Maye" eclogue that Milton admired, abuses his role to gratify himself with the erotic pleasures of physical nature.

In the Lady's soliloquy, Milton critically examines and counterbalances contrary pastoral attitudes. The Lady, wandering "the perplex'd paths of this drear wood," reveals ambivalent feelings about the countryside. The landscape operates as a psychological symbol of both her fear and hope; the wild wood is a world in which "Good and evill . . . grow up together almost inseparably."[26] She sees the woods as the place of "bounteous Pan," and hearing the rustic sounds of "jocund Flute or gamesome Pipe," fears that it stirs up herdsmen's primitive emotions so that they wantonly dance in a harvest festival "for their teeming Flocks and granges full." This pastoral world, with its intemperate physical vitality and sexual energy, threatens the innocent Lady because it lacks reasonableness, order, and virtue.[27] Moreover, she fears that she will "meet the rudeness and swill'd insolence" of those "late

Wassailers" who have been celebrating the rituals of the shepherd's god. Lost "in the blind mazes of this tangl'd wood," she feels apprehension and vulnerability. At the same time, she remembers the "spreading favor of these pines" where she has rested, and innocently hopes that her brothers, from whom she has been separated, will return bringing her "berries, or such cooling fruit/ As the kind hospitable woods provide."[28] She thinks of dusk as "gray-hooded Ev'n . . . in Palmer's weed," and her religious personification suggests her hope that nature will protect her in her own pilgrimage through the woods. This other view of nature is that it is benign and generous, conforming to a higher moral order. The "silver lining" that she sees in a "sable cloud" intensifies her ambivalence.

Hoping to attract her brothers' attention, the solitary Lady sings an echo song. This song of Echo and Narcissus, with its delicate pastoralism, is a kind of love complaint, revealing the Lady's own plight. She is "the love-lorn Nightingale" singing her mournful song in the silver-gleaming darkness of the wood. It is the nymph Echo, however, who is most important in the song; she is both a traditional pastoral figure and a metaphor for the relationship between heavenly harmony and human music.[29] The final two lines of the song are long, resonant, and explicitly thematic:

> *Tell me but where,*
> *Sweet Queen of Parley, Daughter of the Sphere,*
> *So mayst thou be translated to the skies,*
> *And give resounding grace to all Heav'n's Harmonies.*

(240-43)

Because "grace" is Echo's, it resounds, but the theological meaning of the word, although unspecific, suggests that there is an order of heavenly grace, and its graceful music transcends physical nature and the dithyrambic rhythms of the antimasque.[30]

That Comus, son of Circe and priest of "dark-veil'd Cotytto," is emotionally affected by the innocent and soulful beauty of the Lady's plaintive song suggests his own complex ambiguity. Comparing her song to those of his mother and the sirens, he recognizes that the sensual music of nature lulls the senses to sleep, and drives its listeners to "sweet madness," but this music of the virtuous soul makes him feel "sober certainty of waking bliss." Here is sensuality haunted by intimations of spiritual beauty; Comus, for a moment, is tempted into goodness by the Lady. Almost chastened by this experience of innocence, he feels contradictory emotions. Returning to his egotistical hedonism, however, he declares that he shall possess her and make her his queen.

Echo, of course, does not answer the Lady's pastoral song; ironically, it is Comus, disguised as a shepherd, who does. Because the Lady is inexperienced and unsuspecting, she is easily deceived by Comus, who plays upon her trust in "fair pretense" and "well-plac'd words of glozing courtesy." Playing the harmless shepherd and Shropshire villager, his assurance that he knows "each lane and every alley green,/ Dingle or bushy dell" has the beguiling charm of a Spenserian pastoralist or Shakespeare's Puck. He tells her that he has seen her brothers, and evokes a rural English setting:

> Two such I saw, what time the labor'd Ox
> In his loose traces from the furrow came,
> And the swink't hedger at his Supper sat.
>
> (291-93)

Invited to his "low and loyal cottage," the Lady accepts, and calling him "good Shepherd," she naively and ironically affirms the conventional pastoral perspective, the myth of the shepherd's honesty, innocence, and courtesy:

> Shepherd, I take thy word,
> And trust thy honest offer'd courtesy,
> Which oft is sooner found in lowly sheds
> With smoky rafters, than in tap'stry Halls
> And Courts of Princes.
>
> (321-24)

The Lady and Comus depart just as the two brothers enter, searching for their sister. Whereas the Elder Brother romanticizes their "gentle taper" in the dark woods as their "star of *Arcady*" whose "streaming light" will lead them to their sister, the Second Brother hopes for the solace of more homely and naturalistic things, cheerful sounds of flocks in their pens, pastoral reed, whistle, or village cock. The Elder Brother presumptuously insists upon the absolute safety of their sister; the Second Brother fears for her exposure to physical dangers.[31] Worrying about her discomfort in "the chill dew, amongst rude burs and thistles," he is alarmed by the possibility that even while they speak, she is "within the direful grasp/ Of Savage hunger or of Savage heat." The older boy in an off-hand way accuses him of being "over-exquisite," of feeling anxiety about "uncertain evils" that are "false alarms of Fear" and bitterly self-deluding. That the Elder Brother loquaciously appeals to the authority of books rather than experiential knowledge of the real world reveals his inadequate understanding of virtue, which he sees as self-sufficient. The Second Brother, on the other hand, is preoccupied with the potential aggression and eroticism of nature:

> But beauty, like the fair Hesperian Tree,
> Laden with blooming gold, had need the guard
> Of dragon watch with unenchanted eye,
> To save her blossoms and defend her fruit
> From the rash hand of bold Incontinence.
>
> (393-97)

Rejecting his brother's naturalistic view of the Lady's danger, the Elder Brother is calmly assured that, because their sister is chaste, she "is clad in complete steel." Each brother, however, is only partially right in his understanding.[32] The one perceives the reality of external, physical danger, but he does not see that there are greater moral and supernatural dangers to which the Lady is exposed; the other, who is too facile and dogmatic in his ideological convictions, overlooks the actuality of his sister's predicament, but he does have some understandig of the mystical virtues of chastity and "the unpolluted temple of the mind."

The Attendant Spirit enters, disguised as the shepherd Thyrsis. The younger brother identifies him as his "father's Shepherd," and the Elder Brother sees him as an Arcadian shepherd-poet rather than a shepherd-priest in a fallen, experiential world:

Thyrsis? Whose artful strains have oft delay'd
   The huddling brook to hear his madrigal,
   And sweeten'd every musk rose of the dale.

                                                        (493-95)

Thyrsis replies that he was "wrapt in a pleasing fit of melancholy" and meditating on his "rural minstrelsy" when he heard the "barbarous dissonance" amidst the wilderness, and then heard the Lady's Echo song. Taking up the Lady's image of the "lovelorn Nightingale," he sees her symbolically as a "poor hapless Nightingale," portentously evoking memories of the Ovidian tale of mournful Philomela, raped by Tereus. He informs the brothers of their sister's perilous situation with "that damn'd wizard hid in sly disguise." Appalled by this fact, the Second Brother angrily asks, "Is this the confidence/ You gave me, Brother?" The Elder Brother, however, persists in his abstract, doctrinaire view that "Virtue may be assail'd but never hurt." He abruptly changes his tone, however, to boast about his forthcoming feats of martial heroism:

   . . . I'll find him out,
   And force him to restore his purchase back,
   Or drag him by the curls to a foul death,
   Curs'd as his life.

                                                        (606-9)

Thyrsis tells him that although he loves his chivalric heroism, his "bold Emprise," swords alone will do little good in saving the Lady. He explains about a magic herb called haemony, which has the virtue to counter Comus's black magic and undo his enchantments. This haemony, like the moly that Hermes gave to Ulysses to protect him against Circe's seduction and magic, has supernatural powers. Thyrsis's description of haemony emphasizes its pastoral origins: "a certain Shepherd Lad" who was well skilled in healing plants and herbs had shown it to him. Although it "bore a bright golden flow'r . . .in another Country," in this soil it is a "small unsightly root" with darkish and prickly leaf. To make it work its "divine effect . . .the dull Swain/ Treads on it daily with his clouted shoon." Haemony, then, is a simple herb, and like that "lowly stalke" of Spenser's, courtesy, which is planted in "the sacred noursery of virtue," grows humbly in a pastoral world of innocence and humility.

Comus, of course, does not take the Lady to a "lowly shed" at all, but to his stately palace and the sophisticated world of the court. Chained up in his palace, the Lady sees both the pleasures of court life and the rabble of "ugly-headed monsters." These theatrically actualized properties and figures make strikingly clear the relationship between the primitive wild wood, Comus's libertine philosophy of nature, courtly luxury, and the grotesque degeneration of incontinent, "easy-hearted man."

In this central, most dramatic scene of the masque, the Lady must combat the illusions of the pastoral and reject Comus's temptation to sensual intemperance. Her moral debate will allow her consciously and rationally to understand the human meaning of nature in a strenuous way, and in her experiential trial with Comus "purify" herself by learning to recognize the true relationship between man and nature. But the Lady is literally chained by Comus because the young woman is physically weaker. More important, she has been lost in the wild woods and experienced the subrational darkness of her own being. Having confronted her lower nature, the instincts and grosser passions embodied in Comus, her flesh, not sinful in itself, has become immobilized.[33] Although her mind is free to counter the seductive arguments of sensual appetite with moral ideals, she does not, because of her paralyzing ambivalence, have the power to liberate herself from her physical bondage in the chair of Comus. In this intellectual struggle with him, her faith in reason and virtue grows, but whe cannot save herself; discovering that her reason and moral conduct are insufficient, she must rely on supernatural grace.

Comus begins the pastoral debate with a *carpe diem* argument, which recalls the Bower of Bliss episode and emphasizes the Lady's youth and physical beauty:

> . . . See, here be all the pleasures
> That fancy can beget on youthful thoughts,
> When the fresh blood grows lively, and returns
> Brisk as the April buds in Primrose-season.

> (668-71)

Taking up this seasonal flower imagery later, he warns her that if she does not enjoy sensual nature and lets time slip, she will, "like a neglected rose," wither "on the stalk with languish't head." Comus's world of nature is time-haunted and decaying, and his urging her to enjoy the immediate moment is inherently melancholy. Then he accuses her of misusing her beauty by betraying nature, which is meant, he says, "For gentle usage and soft delicacy." His language becomes hardened, however, as he develops his commercial-legal figure:

> But you invert the cov'nants of her trust,
> And harshly deal like an ill borrower
> With that which you receiv'd on other terms.
>
> (682-84)

When the Lady responds to his arguments by saying that only good men can give good things, and bad things are "not delicious/ To a well-govern'd and wise appetite." Comus attempts a facile evasion by distorting what she has said, taunting her for praising "lean and sallow Abstinence." In his second speech, Comus exuberantly praises the vitality and plenitude of nature:

> Wherefore did Nature pour her bounties forth
> With such a full and unwithdrawing hand,
> Covering the earth with odors, fruits, and flocks,
> Thronging the Seas with spawn innumerable.
>
> (710-13)

Everywhere, he says, there is a riot of superabundance. On the earth and in the sea there is health, erotic fulfillment, and fertility. Although appealing to nature's generosity, Comus exposes his own parasitic epicureanism: "But all to please and sate the curious taste?" Comus's temptation to free and easy sensual pleasures exemplifies, for Milton, the dangers of the pagan and pastoral *otia*. The underlying epicureanism of this ideal of self-sufficiency is exploitative and self-indulgent. Moreover, in the sensuous particularization of the spinning worms' "green shops," Comus banalizes the world of nature by using the materialistic terms of the marketplace. Similarly, calling beauty "nature's coin," which "must be current," he reveals the acquisitiveness of his callous hedonism. In spite of his appeal to nature's fertility, then, his self-centered arguments and overburdened language are evidence that his world is not the Garden of Adonis but the Bower of Bliss. Resembling both "pleasures Porter" with cup and conjuring rod, and the Circean Acrasia, Comus leads men by illusions into intemperance and sin.

Answering Comus's specious argument, the Lady speaks of nature as a "good cateress' who provides

> . . . only to the good
> That live according to her sober laws
> And holy dictate of spare Temperance.

(764-67)

Temperance, not intemperance, then, belongs to a humane order of nature. In nature man learns restraint, conservation, and proportion. When the Lady says the blessings of nature are meant to be dispensed in "unsuperfluous even proportion" to just men and not to swinish gluttons, her tone of austere anger resembles Spenser's good shepherds in his Mantuanesque moral debates. A "swinish gluttony" that "Ne'er looks to Heav'n amidst his gorgeous feast" expresses her view that man's relation to nature must include the order of heaven, for grace perfects nature and makes it sacramental. Similarly, her references to "the Sun-clad power of Chastity" and "the sage/ And serious doctrine of Virginity" attest to her belief in the necessary union of nature and grace. For the Lady, then, the knowledge of nature must involve experience at the level of grace.

Boldly assaulting the "necromancer's hall," the Lady's brothers attempt to rescue her. Although they have been warned by Thyrsis to rush on Comus with "brandish't blade," break his cup, and seize his wand, they fail to do the last, and Comus escapes. Unlike Spenser's Guyon and Palmer, who hold Acrasia fast, the boys, because they inadequately understand mankind's condition, cannot bind the "false enchanter" or reverse his phallic rod. The Attendant Spirit, therefore, must use other means by which to liberate the Lady "fixt and motionless" in the chair. He has learned of the river nymph,

Sabrina, through Meliboeus, "The soothest Shepherd that ere pip't on plains."

Before his invocation of Sabrina, whom Spenser had celebrated in the second book of *The Faerie Queene*, the Attendant Spirit praises the poet under the name of Meliboeus, just as Spenser had praised Chaucer-Tityrus. The "Old Swain," of course, knew not only the myth of Sabrina, but also the stories of the loyal virgin, Una, wandering through the perilous wood; the Knight of Temperance overcoming the temptress Acrasia; and Britomart, the virgin-warrior, after the Masque of Cupid, rescuing Amoret from black magic in Busirane's palace.

The Attendant Spirit's description of Sabrina as spirit of the Severn, moreover, recalls Spenser's wedding of the Thames and Medway in that both unite history with the pastoral. In the story of Sabrina, based on Geoffrey of Monmouth's *Historia Britonum*, he describes her heroic lineage. As symbol of British and Welsh patriotism, Sabrina is given epic stature. Saved from "her enraged stepdam *Guendolen*," Sabrina is taken by "water Nymphs" to the bottom of the Severn, where she undergoes "a quick immortal change" and is "Made Goddess of the River." Her metamorphosis merges history and nature, epic and pastoral. The river nymph visits herds, and with her magical powers helps "all urchin blasts, and ill-luck signs." At their festivals the shepherds

> Carol her goodness loud in rustic lays,
> And throw sweet garland wreathes into her stream
> Of pansies, pinks, and gaudy Daffodils.
>
> (849-51)

The symbolic figure of Sabrina parallels the Lady in several ways: both are guiltless maidens who experience terrible trials, and a time of death-in-life, and finally undergo "a quick immortal change." Moreover, just as Sabrina is descended from Brutus, the Trojan founder of Britain, so the Lady is the "fair offspring" of "A noble Peer of mickle trust and power" who governs "An old and haughty Nation proud in Arms." Of such heroic lineage, Sabrina has the power to save, and the Lady, rejecting temptation in her struggle with Comus, becomes heroine of chastity. Both Sabrina and the Lady are figures who belong to a pastoral landscape of innocence, but the Lady represents moral heroism, and Sabrina, whose magical operations have heroic effect, is a contemplative symbol of grace.

With Sabrina's supernatural aid, the Lady is finally freed from the "marble venom'd seat." The Attendant Spirit urges her to flee the palace now that Heaven lends them grace. "A faithful guide," he leads her to "holier ground," her "Father's residence." The Lady emerges from private withdrawal to communal life, and from innocence to the wisdom of experience. There at Ludlow Town and castle, Arcadian shepherds celebrate the social union "With Jigs and rural dance." "The Country-Dancers," unlike Comus and his rout, engage in innocent mirth and revelry. The swains at Ludlow, however, end their playful recreation when the Spirit commands: *"Back Shepherds, back, enough your play,/ Till next Sun-shine holiday."* Presenting the three children to their father and mother, the Spirit formally announces the moral and educational import of their experience:

> *Here behold so goodly grown*
> *Three fair branches of your own,*
> *Heav'n hath timely tri'd their youth,*
> *Their faith, their patience, and their truth,*
> *And sent them here through hard assays*
> *Witha crown of deathless Praise,*
> > *To triumph in victorious dance*
> *O'er sensual Folly and Intemperance.*

(968-75)

By returning to the symbol of "the crown that Virtue gives" in the prologue, the Attendant Spirit emphasizes the moral structure of the masque. So, too, does the concluding courtly dance, which the masque performers and Edgertons join. The gradual progression from the anti-masque, to revels, to the ordered and ceremonious dance symbolizes a hierarchical universe.

In the epilogue the Attendant Spirit returns to "the broad fields of sky" and the Gardens of Hesperus. This paradisal garden, where the Graces sing around the golden tree in an eternal summer, suggests Spenser's Garden of Adonis and is a celestial *locus amoenus*. These Graces, described by the Attendant Spirit, correspond to those shown in the design of the Medal of Tornabuoni: Castitas—Pulchritudo—Amor.[34] The Platonic definition of Beauty, "Beauty is Love combined with Chastity," is reflected in the dialectic of Milton's masque and his transcendent synthesis. Above both country and courtly dances, there is a contemplative vision of heavenly revelry and masque dancing:

> Along the crisped shades and bow'rs
> Revels the spruce and jocund Spring,
> The Graces and the rosy-bosom'd Hours,
> Thither all their bounties bring.

> (984-87)

The hierarchical order of the final Ludlow scene ascends from the country dance, to the announcement and emblematic dance of moral triumph, to the visionary epilogue. The poet recapitulates in this dialectical movement pastoral recreation, heroic action, and finally a contemplation, born of experience and wisdom, of a heavenly Arcadia.

Here in the golden age, celestial lovers, Venus and Adonis, symbolize natural sexual instinct, erotic fulfillment, and the perpetual generation of life. Yet the symbolic image of the sadly sitting "*Assyrian* Queen" and her wounded lover suggest a spiritual imperfection. The Spirit ascends in a process of refinement to a higher form of love in the emblem of Cupid and Psyche. Psyche, like the Lady, wandered long and had trials before she found love. Representing purification by trial and misfortune, Psyche, the human soul, unites with Heavenly Eros. She becomes "his eternal Bride,/ And from her fair unspotted side" bears "Two blissful twins," Youth and Joy. This is a miniature epithalamium celebrating the consecrated love of married couples and family. Suggested in the images of fruitful gardens and gods is the theme of regenerate and regenerative nature. In contrast to the false *voluptas* or incontinence of Comus, the pleasures of the Graces and the two pairs of celestial lovers in the heavenly Garden symbolize a Neoplatonic conception of noble *voluptas*.[35]

The Attendant Spirit's final lines return to the concept of the true servent of virtue, who by due steps aspire to heaven:

> Mortals that would follow me,
> Love virtue, she alone is free,
> She can teach ye how to climb
> Higher than the Sphery chime.

(1017-21)

The Attendant Spirit, like Milton, is the shepherd-poet who knows that in the postlapsarian world we need art, a moral skill that instructs as well as pleases man. The Ludlow Castle masque, exploring the relation between nature and grace, implicitly defines the efficacy of art in terms of both. The Spirit knows, moreover, that man's virtue and skill are not enough, that he needs inspiration and divine grace: "Or if Virtue feeble were,/ Heav'n itself would stoop to her."

Lycidas

In a letter to Diodati, written about two months before *Lycidas*, Milton tells his friend:

> What besides God has resolved concerning me I know not, but this at least: He has instilled into me, if into any one, a vehement love of the beautiful. Not with so much labour, as the fables have it, is Ceres said to have sought her daughter Prosperina as it is my habit day and night to seek for this idea of the beautiful, as for a certain image of supreme beauty, through all the forms and faces of things (for many are the shapes of things divine) and to follow it as it leads me on by some sure traces which I seem to recognize.[36]

The letter, which affirms the idealistic poet's God-given love of beauty, also suggests in the allusion to mournful Ceres his own sense of loss and yearning as he seeks the Platonic idea and image of the beautiful. At the same time that he describes his devotion to the aesthetic, he suggests in the pastoral image of Proserpina, traditionally associated with the loss of eternal spring, the brief life of man. The allusion elegiacally modulates

his earnest tone of affirmation. His developing aesthetic principle includes an awareness of death, an awareness that becomes
greatly intensified in his pastoral elegy, *Lycidas*.

This elegy reflects a kind of crisis for Milton in the relation
between pastoral fiction and actuality. The arbitrary fact of
Edward King's premature death compelled him to consider his
own mortality. It was not merely the fact of death, however,
that made him uneasy; he feared that if he took his time in
preparing himself for the epic, an early death could thwart the
fulfillment of his great aspirations. As Harold Bloom has
remarked, "The great pastoral elegies, indeed all major elegies
for poets, do not express grief but center upon their composer's
creative anxieties."[37]

If the pastoral had validity and value for Milton, it was
because it explored the relation of poetry to the world of fact,
and therefore acknowledged the principle of death in the
universe. This awareness of the effect of death on poetry, and
of the death of poetry itself, demanded that he consider his
own poetic ambitions. The pastoral tradition provided him
with the freedom to be at once personal and impersonal in his
depicting the actual and ideal, the brazen and golden worlds.
A major tension and dissonance in *Lycidas* develops from the
confrontation between the impersonal, idealized form of the
pastoral elegy and contingent reality. The "digressions" in the
poem, as Jon S. Lawry has pointed out, persistently "enforce
actuality" upon the traditionalized ideas of the form,
"threatening to destroy as actuality had destroyed Edward
King."[38]

But Milton draws from the pastoral elegiac tradition, which
idealized the poet's expression of sorrow and attempted to
assuage it by exalting the memory of the subject. Emphasizing
his own participation in this continuity of artistic purpose, he
drew from many precedents, borrowing the elaborate conventions from the *consolationes* of Theocritus, Moschus, Virgil, and
Spenser. His subsuming under his pastoral form such formal
elements as the role of shepherds, invocation to the Muses, the
mourning of nature, questioning of the nymphs, and procession of mourners, helps express the universality of death and
the timelessness of mourning, and formalizes his own grief.

The achievement of the poem, however, is neither pedantic imitation nor a patchwork of literary recollections from his great elegiac predecessors, but a highly individualized transformation of these impersonal, traditional elements. At once using and subverting these conventions, Milton's pastoral elegy constitutes a singular realization of the possibilities and necessities of the genre.

Of course, there are marked similarities, generic and thematic, between *Lycidas* and Spenser's "November" eclogue. Both pastoral elegies are drawn from Virgil's fifth *Eclogue*, and like that poem begin in sorrow and conclude with joyful consolation. Both are Christian elegies and show the ultimate victory over nature. Lycidas, like Dido, is assured of resurrection. In both elegies, moreover, the persona's contemplation of paradise consoles his grief, bringing him to an *ecstasis* of mystical understanding. Yet the differences between the two pastoral elegies are striking. "November" is less personal in its strict formality; *Lycidas* is intensely personal, and the evolving meditative thought eventuates in a free, exploratory style, violent tonal shifts, and structural irregularity. Spenser's eclogue is narrow in range; Milton's elegy is broadly inclusive, integrating disparate aspects of human experience.

In *Lycidas* the poet creates a meditative argument in which the structural and stylistic dynamics reflect the persona's troubled state of consciousness as he attempts, in his grief, to comprehend violence, injustice, and death in the world. The dispersion of themes, structural asymmetry, and prosodic irregularity in the poem corroborate the troubled introspection of the shepherd-poet confronting a morally and physically disintegrating world. Just as there is a tension between the generic paradigm and the empirical world of reality, there is a tension within the poem between its formal structure, suggesting an ordered artificial golden world that is permanent, and those extreme shifts in tone and disordering digressions which resist and undermine the formal framework, emphasizing an evolving process rather than artifact. After the prelude, the three movements that constitute the main body of the poem[39] dramatize the shepherd-poet's continual struggle with the obtruding reality that both disrupts the formal structure of his song and threatens those familiar pastoral consolations which he tentatively accepts, and then must reject as an inadequate fiction. Paradoxically, the external traditional form expresses the pastoral ideal of freedom; the arbitrariness and necessity of the real world, on the other hand, are expressed by a freedom from form.

Milton brings together the symbols of poetry, death, and immortality in the opening lines: "Yet once more, O ye Laurels, and once more/ Ye Myrtles brown, with Ivy never sere . . ." The poet's laurel represents his glory and fame; the myrtle is a dark reminder of death and the continual necessity for mourning. These plants are evergreens, however, and therefore also symbolic of immortality, which transcends both earthly fame and physical death. With these symbolic plants, then, the poet prefigures the larger thematic pattern of the whole poem: the pastoral ideal of song, its destruction by death, and finally, a new song borne by faith in the immortal soul. Here, however, because the persona feels that he lacks inward ripeness, he is reluctant to lament the death of his friend. Just as Lycidas's death was premature, so must he his own effort. Although the Arcadian world in which the two shepherds enjoyed their idyllic pleasure was free from constraint, the fallen world is subject to time and death. The persona, therefore, must pluck the berries before they are ripe:

> And with forc'd fingers rude,
> Shatter your leaves before the mellowing year.
> Bitter constraint, and sad occasion dear,
> Compels me to disturb your season due:
> For *Lycidas* is dead, dead ere his prime.

(4-8)

Lycidas himself was plucked violently from his life, and the "uncouth Swain" who grieves for him has no choice but to force and shatter, singing his lament before his own maturity, "ere his prime." The relationship between poetry and death becomes a central thematic concern.

Lycidas was dedicated, like the persona, to poetry: "he knew/ Himself to sing, and build the lofty rhyme." Invoking the "Sisters of the sacred well," he expresses the hope, as Virgil did for Gallus, that "some gentle Muse" will mourn him as he now mourns the loss of Lycidas. The images of his own urn and shroud suggest that he is preoccupied with the fragility of life. Developing this close personal identification with the dead shepherd, he describes their pastoral life together: "nurst upon the self-same hill,/ Fed the same flock." The two shepherd-poets resemble Virgil's shepherds, "ambo fluentes aetatibus, Arcades ambo" (both in the bloom of life, Arcadians both).

The mourning shepherd takes a journey back to their origins, returning to a mythical golden age of innocence and spontaneity, free from "Bitter constraint." This longing to regress, however, reveals his present state of sadness and perplexity. Not yet being able to comprehend the tragedy with which he is presently confronted, and uncertain as to what the future holds, he regresses to an illusory land of innocent recreation. But he now has the knowledge that death is also in Arcadia — *Et in Arcadia Ego*. This idealized memory of a golden age ironically suggests a sense of permanence, for it is a pastoral world in which values are secure, and where the poet seems unthreatened by any kind of change. The Arcadian landscape symbolizes their earlier innocence, happiness, and playful creativity. Without self-consciousness or premeditation, the two shepherd friends played their oaten flutes, and "Rough *Satyrs* danc'd, and *Fauns* with clov'n heel/ From the glad sound would not be absent long . . ." The dancing fauns, like those in Virgil's sixth *Eclogue*, represent a union of pastoral *otium* and classical mythology with the spirit of *lusus*, and harmony between the poet and an idealized natural world.

Peace in Arcadia is brutally interrupted, however, and the *locus amoenus* is transformed into a wasteland. Singing of death in Arcadia is foreboding, for the elegiac tone is incongruous with the assumed idealism of the pastoral world. To mourn the death of Lycidas, who embodies this idealism, is to bring about the collapse of the pastoral fiction and therefore the ruin of the idyllic landscape of the poem. Images of canker, taint-worm, and frost invade the golden world, symbolizing the change and decay of fallen nature. The thyme is wild and "the gadding Vine op'ergrown"; the *locus amoenus* has become violated as roses and flowers in "their gay wardrobe" lose their color and life. With disaster in the Edenic garden, nature is corrupted and bears death. Contagious disease and death plague the sheepfold and pasture as well as garden, and "weanling Herds that graze" are afflicted with a killing sickness. The power of generation is gone, and with it hope of continuity in nature. Although the persona tries to interpret the blight and death as a sign of nature's mourning Lycidas's death, he also comes to the more realistic recognition that nature itself is not free from change and death. What had been a regression into a mythical paradisal time suddenly becomes a time of paradise lost.

With Lycidas's death and the ruin of the landscape, the pastoral can no longer maintain its dream state. Dependent on the real world, private *otium* yields to universal disorder. Although the shepherd-poet asks the nymphs why they did not protect their "lov'd *Lycidas*," he admits that neither they nor their "old *Bards*" could prevent his death "when the remorseless deep" closed over his head. Just as the pastoral Muses were not there to help Virgil's Gallus, the spirits of poetry were absent when Lycidas sank to his death. Recognizing that his belief in the power of poetry to save life is illusory, "Aye me, I fondly dream!" he surrenders his naive trust in it. Even if the Nymphs had been there, they would have been impotent before the remorselessly indifferent forces of nature, which neither know nor care about man's fond dreams. The Epic Muse could not save "her enchanting son," Orpheus, who, as Spenser tells us in the "October" eclogue, had the civilizing power to restrain the lusts of lawless youth. But Orpheus himself was slain and dismembered by the irrational forces of man's nature, a rout of hostile Bacchantes. Although this archetypal poet was divinely inspired and knew the secrets of Creation, his music failed to save him and failed to redeem the soul of his wife from the lower world. The image of his decapitated head, his "gory visage," drifting down the swift stream, returns to the theme of death by water and expresses the idea of the disintegrating world.

Other questions are asked regarding the value of poetry in a world of death and natural disorder. The shepherd must consider his own destiny and examine his predicament as a poet, both his ambition to be immortal and his actual mortality in a fallen world. Although the persona identifies the poetic voca- tion with the pastoral state, he implies that the "uncessant care" needed to pursue that vocation is in opposition to the traditional pastoral view of poetry in terms of leisure, ease, and play.[40] Because Arcadia is in ruins, and paradise lost, the seriously dedicated poet who tends "the homely slighted Shepherd's trade" requires self-descipline and renunciation, the scorning of delights and the living of "laborious days." The persona implicitly contrasts the "gentle Muse" of pastoral poetry and "the thankless Muse" of epic poetry. If the shepherd aspires to write on heroic themes, he must accept the ascetic regimen of the epic poet. But the easy gratification of the senses and poetic success, symbolized by sporting "with *Amaryllis* in the shade,/ Or with the tangles of *Neaera's* hair," are alien to the laborious days he foresees for himself. Like the "faciles Nymphae" or the "lasciva puella" of Virgil's third *Eclogue*, Amaryllis and Neaera represent the thoughtless recreation of a sensual Arcadia. In contrast to the pastoral, the epic arouses the poet's aspirations to a dedicated life and fame:

> *Fame* is the spur that the clear spirit doth raise
> (That last infirmity of Noble mind)
> To scorn delights and live laborious days.
>
> (70-72)

This passage about fame, however, is itself questioned; fame is an infirmity, and the poet recalls that all poetic endeavor, par- ticularly disciplined poetic ambition, is futile when there are such injustices in the world as Lycidas's premature death. What a terrible reward for those poets dedicated to the homely slighted Shepherd's trade if the poet's "thin-spun life" is split arbitrarily by the constraining shears of "the blind *Fury*." In a passage Virgilian in its elevated tone, the god of inspiration, Phoebus Apollo, interrupts and tells him: "*Fame* is no plant that grows on mortal soil." For the first time in the poem, the theme of immortality is explicitly introduced. This lofty assurance "of so much fame in heav'n" is then suspended, to recur in the third section of the poem, which redefines and develops the meaning of both fame and heaven in Christian terms. Although the persona cannot yet have a full understanding of these ideals, he does see that he must relinquish the pastoral, rendered inadequate by reality, and progress, as in Piers's speech in "October," to the worthier moral purpose of the heroic mode.

Having heard a "strain" of a "higher mood," the shepherd-poet descends from the epic, returning to the humbler pastoral strain: "But now my Oat proceeds." The gods of the sea and wind defend themselves against his charge of responsibility for the drowning of Lycidas. The whole pastoral world, on land and water, was innocent of his death but ineffectual in preventing it. That Lycidas's ship had foundered in a calm sea suggests to him that human life is subject to meaningless disasters for which no one is responsible. He questions, therefore, the values of any serious purpose in such a universe.

This passage operates as a transition between the first section on poetry and death in nature, and the second section, which addresses itself to moral disorder in the fallen world. Here Milton explores the meaning of shepherd as moral pastor. Whereas the symbolic imagery of the preceding section is drawn from pagan pastoralism, here it is Christian and ecclesiastical. Yet "the faithful Herdman's art" does not preclude the meaning of shepherd as poet. Aspiring to become a heroic poet, the shepherd must fulfill the role of pastor in order to enlighten man morally and remedy the corrupt society in which he lives. Postlapsarian nature needs art to correct and order it. The art of the faithful shepherd, then, unites poet and pastor in a truly dedicated life.

St. Peter's lament for the "young swain," Lycidas, who showed such promise as a *pastor bonus*, is followed by a prophetic indictment of a corrupt clergy who have failed to feed the hungry sheep of England. In contrast, Lycidas, like Spenser's Piers, represents the true shepherd unwaveringly devoted to the welfare of his flock. St. Peter's attack on the opportunistic, self-interested bishops is in the vein of the Renaissance humanists and Spenser's moral eclogues. The invective against the vices of the *pastor malus* resembles particularly the "Maye" eclogue, which Milton praised in his *Animadversions*.

Blind mouths! that scarce themselves know how to hold
A sheep-hook, or have learn'd aught else the least
That to the faithful Herdman's art belongs!

(119-21)

The danger of the hungry flock's innocence is that the sheep
are blind to worldly corruption, and therefore peculiary
vulnerable to the "grim wolf," those "false prophets" of whom
Saint Matthew warned that they come in sheep's clothing, but
"inwardly are ravening wolves."

St. Peter's closing and climactic prophecy about the "two-
handed engine" is at the opposite pole from the earlier Arcadian idyll, and this mounting indignation against moral
disorder has a primitive and apocalyptic power that creates a
crisis for the whole pastoral framework of the poem. The sudden shift from St. Peter's suspended fury to the muted and
fragile beauty of the flower passage, with its elegiac consolation, relaxes the tension but also reveals ironically that the
shepherd-poet is not willing to see the experiential implications
of divine retribution; deflecting the poem's impulse toward aggression, he retreats to pretended innocence or assumed ignorance, dwelling on beautiful but surmised flowers. The
physical pastoral world, however, cannot be redeemed by
either false pastors or false consolations.[41]

As *homo artifex*, the shepherd regresses to the imagined Arcadia of his illusory dreams as he describes, with the same
elaborate, self-conscious artifice of the flower passage in
Spenser's "Aprill," the flowers mourning the death of Lycidas:

> The glowing Violet,
> The Musk-rose, and the well-attir'd Woodbine,
> With Cowslips wan that hang the pensive head,
> And every flower that sad embroidery wears;
> Bid *Amaranthus* all his beauty shed,
> And Daffadillies fill their cups with tears,
> To strew the Laureate Hearse where *Lycid* lies.

(145-51)

Humanizing these flowers, his imagination strains to restore
the harmony between man and nature. By evoking this illusion, he temporarily denies the reality of that relationship in

the fallen world. But he subverts this false consolation and generic formulation by revealing that nature is really indifferent to human fate, and the flower-bedecked hearse he describes does not in fact exist. Lycidas, of course, is not ensconced within the confines of a dry, fragrant bier; he is "perhaps under the whelming tide" at the "bottom of the monstrous world," a prey to sea creatures as unconscious and amoral as flowers, who feast on his flesh and bones. The persona must recognize, then, that he had indulged his "frail thoughts" to "dally with false surmise." Because violence, suffering, and death are too intolerable to contemplate, he protects himself from reality with comforting delusion. That death is invested with peculiar terror reveals man's alienation from nature. The pastoral consolation of nature's mourning, with its sentimental pathos and unreality, fails to comprehend the complexity and depth of truth, and cannot, therefore, sufficiently console.

This confinement within the pastoral ideal, as narrow as the imagined hearse, is opposed to the broad geographical seascape of the world; that is, the "Laureate Hearse" is contrasted with the "shores and sounding Seas" far away, where Lycidas's "bones are hurl'd." In opposition to the world of fact is the enclosure of a "little ease." With Arcadia in ruins, however, the shepherd-poet's vision goes northward "beyond the stormy Hebrides," and like the Angel on St. Michael's Mount at Land's End, the poet looks south toward Namancos and Bayona, but then suddenly and passionately turns home, to England, to heaven: "Look homeward Angel now, and melt with ruth."

Milton's England, like Virgil's *patria* in his *Eclogues*,[42] is unusual in pastoral poetry because it refers to a specific place not Arcadian and implies nonpastoral values such as national pride, justice, and history. This understanding of England is prophetic and the view of history eschatological. The guardian Angel of England must look at England's moral sickness, spread by false shepherds whose selfishness and worldliness St. Peter had vehemently denounced.

The persona's vision of pastoral innocence has been contrasted throughout the poem with his experience of the fallen world. But now he unites these two opposing views by transcending them with his eschatological fervor, in a revelation of a Christian paradise. Home, for the shepherd and the Angel, is heaven. Although Phoebus had spoken of fame in heaven, he did not explain. St. Peter, in his thunderous wrath, made the shepherd-poet aware of both evil and divine justice. "The great vision" of Michael, the Christian patron of mariners, navigates him homeward. Transcending physical nature, Christ "that walk'd the waves" leads him from death to life, mortality to divinity, from the pastoral world of nature to a Christian pastoral heaven. As a result of the uncouth swain's experience he has lost his Arcadian innocence, moved through and beyond experience, to a new stage of consciousness, an angelic understanding.

In the mystical resolution of the poem, the woeful shepherds are told to weep no more: "For *Lycidas* your sorrow is not dead,/ Sunk though he be beneath the wat'ry floor . . . ." Christ, the Good Shepherd, who has the supernatural power to walk the waves, raises Lycidas from the sea to the streams of his heavenly home. Water in the physical world was the place of his death; in heaven it is the principle of baptismal anointment and rebirth. In this transfiguring rebirth, Lycidas becomes both a Christian saint and, as an Arcadian shepherd, "Genius of the shore."[43]

The pastoral landscape in heaven, with its groves and streams, is the *locus amoenus* in which true, lasting freedom and *otium* exist. Milton's Christian pastoral, like Virgil's Elysian Fields, is lovelier than Arcadia, for it is an eternal and sacred place of contemplative joy. The pastoral song of physical love, represented by Amaryllis and Neaera, is transformed and perfected into heavenly love. Looking back at the "worthy bidden guest," which echoes St. Matthew's account of the nuptial feast, the "unexpressive nuptial song" is the celestial epithalamium sung at the marriage of the Lamb. This pastoral wedding song reasserts the joy, love, and creativity that had been destroyed in the fallen world, and the recreation of the Saints is to sing in full choir the Word of God.

While still keeping within the pastoral form and convention, Milton has in fact both subverted and transcended the limits of the pastoral. In the earlier sections of the elegy he used pastoral to explore the relation of poetry to the world of fact; now he uses it to explore the world of vision.

In the narrative ottava rima that concludes the poem, Milton steps out of his persona's mind. Just as the uncouth swain freed himself from his troubled introspective meditation and sees himself more clearly and wholly, the reader now views him in the third person, and the whole poem is cast into a new, eternal perspective.[44] The shepherd-poet no longer yearns to regress into an Arcadian dream of the past. Having discovered man's proper place in the cosmic order, he sings in an act of self-transcendence in the "still morn." Having descended into the depths of sorrow, confusion, and anger, his spirit has ascended, after tragic experience, purified and enriched. At sunset the Virgilian shadows fall, but he rises in the dawn with greater purpose, ready to perform heroic deeds and sing new songs: "Tomorrow to fresh woods, and pastures new."

The evolving meditation of the persona and poem reenacts the Virgilian progression. Through the elegy, the shepherd-poet advances in a dialectical pattern: he remembers and relives Arcadian innocence and play; reject the inadequacy of the pastoral fiction to comprehend reality; dedicates himself to the heroic, spurred by his ambition for fame and glory; and rises, finally, to a contemplation of a pastoral heaven, which Arcadia had incompletely foreshadowed, of enlightened innocence and eternal joy.

Paradise Lost (I)

M<small>ILTON</small> turned his mind toward the heroic poem after his youthful period of pastoral poetry had reached its climax with *Lycidas*. He promises in "Mansus" a national epic based on the legendary history of Britain, announcing his intention to write on an Arthurian subject. His reference to Arthur "etiam terris bella momentum" (waging his wars beneath the earth) suggests that his projected *Arthuriad* was to be a heroic, patriotic poem that would narrate Arthur's heroic warfare against the heathen. Just as Virgil's *Aeneid* had glorified the Romans, his national Christian epic was to glorify the English people serving Christ and King.[1] In his "Epitaphium Damonis," a pastoral elegy on the death of his friend Charles Diodati, Milton's persona, Thyrsis, echoing Virgil's seventh *Eclogue*, promises to hang the oaten pipe of pastoral poetry on a pine tree: "O, mihi tum si vita supersit, / Tu procul anosa pendebis, fistula, pinu . . ." (And then, O my pipe, if life is granted me, you shall be left dangling on some old pine tree far away and quite forgotten by me). Then he describes his proposed subject as including a history of the Britons, from the approach of the Trojan fleet under Brutus to the times of Arthur. He deliberately follows the Virgilian progression, from apprenticeship in pastoral poetry to the heroic mode, which Sidney praised as "not onlie a kinde, but the best and most accomplished kinde of Poetry."[2]

Although Milton speaks in *The Reason of Church Government* of looking for a king or knight who "might be chosen. . .

to lay the pattern of a Christian Heroe,[3] he later abandoned Arthur as possible epic hero, and by the time he wrote *Paradise Lost* he had given up his search. Only the Son could be "the pattern of a Christian Heroe."

Milton's epic does not glorify a martial, national hero of legendary history of a nation, and therefore it is a very different kind of epic from the *Arthuriad* of his earlier ambitions. *Paradise Lost* is a classical epic on a Christian theme, the fall and redemption of man, in which the poet narrates the providential history of mankind.

Milton and the Epic Tradition

Because *Paradise Lost* is an epic poem, Milton had to deal with the traditional theme of heroic action. A Christian poet, he was to reject the classical conception of the hero and define true heroic action founded on the Christian ideal of obedience and suffering patience,[4] of which Christ is the exemplar. Milton discovered a greater heroism than in the models established by either classical epic or medieval and Renaissance romance. Aspiring to celebrate Christian heroism, he explains his rejection of pagan heroism in the prologue to Book 9:

> . . . Sad task, yet argument
> Not less but more Heroic than the wrath
> Of stern *Achilles* on his Foe pursu'd
> Thrice Fugitive about *Troy* Wall; or rage
> Of *Turnus* for *Lavinia* disespous'd
> Or *Neptune's* ire of *Juno's*, that so long
> Perplex'd the *Greek* and *Cytherea's* Son.
>
> (13-19)

Reviewing the themes of the *Iliad*, the *Aeneid*, and the *Odyssey*, the poet defines and dismisses the nature of traditional heroism and "Heroic Song" (9. 25).

Milton saw the highest function of poetry as "Teaching over the whole book of sanctity and vertu, through all the instances of example."[5] Therefore he intends to "soar/ Above th' Aonian

Mount" (1. 14-15), both surpassing his classical predecessors and undermining their conception of heroic knowledge and action. The "wrath of stern *Achilles*" and the "rage of *Turnus*" represent a pagan heroism celebrated in the classical epic and measured by arms and a passion for battle:

> Not sedulous by Nature to indite
> Wars, hitherto the only Argument
> Heroic deem'd . . .
>
> (9.27-29)

The reckless egoism and passion of Achilles and Turnus find their outlet inevitably in brutalizing deeds of war. Similarly, the "fabl'd Knights" of the chivalric romance who fight "In Battles feign'd" (9. 30-31) represent a degenerate heroism. That these false heroes are described with their "tinsel Trappings" (9.36) emphasizes their dependence on physical, external strength; "tilting Furniture, emblazon'd Shields" (9. 34) suggest the shallowness and inadequacy of the chivalric conception of heroism based on personal glory and honor. Against these perversions of heroic action which, Milton says, have been given a "Heroic name" (9. 40), Milton redefines true heroic virtue as internal and contemplative, "the better fortitude/ Of Patience and Heroic Martyrdom" (9. 31-32). Christian heroism is built not on classical or chivalric *areté* but on obedience to God. The fallen Adam in the final book of the poem emerges as the human exemplar of the Christian virtues of humility, obedience, and love.[6] The "one greater Man" (1. 4), however, is Christ. Adam's concept of the true hero, therefore, is not the active warrior but the contemplative ideas of the Suffering Servant:

> that suffering for Truth's sake
> Is fortitude to highest victory,
> And to the faithful Death the Gate of Life.
>
> (12.569-71)

In his rejection of the hero in epic and chivalric romance, Milton reveals what Harold Bloom calls "misprision" or "poetic misreading"[7] of both Virgil and Spenser. By substituting raging Turnus for pious Aeneas, and by avoiding the moral and religious ideas in Spenserian romance, most particularly in the legend of Holiness, Milton revises his predecessors' handling of heroism in order to discredit the earlier tradition and displace the established models.

In Satan the poet creates a character who embodies all the qualities of the Homeric hero. Satan, like Achilles and Turnus, exemplifies the military virtues of the pagan epic tradition. He has, moreover, their ferocity and lust for revenge. Motivated by an egotistic desire for glory, Satan demonstrates daring enterprise, Odyssean guile, and dauntless courage in warfare. The poet reinforces the affinity between Satan and the classical heroes through parallels with Homeric and Virgilian epic. He shows, however, that this concept of heroism is spurious and deficient, incompatible with the concept of Christian virtue. That Satan, a classical epic hero, is the antagonist of the Creator demonstrates Milton's repudiation of the traditional epic ideas of martial heroism. Whereas Christian heroic virtue is defined in terms of loving service to God, Satan's rebellion against God illustrates a conception of heroic action that is in opposition to the ideals of obedience, sanctity, and martyrdom.

Virgil's Aeneas, unlike Achilles and Turnus, prefigures Milton's concept of the hero. Dedicated to ancestors, family, and nation, pious Aeneas acts selflessly at the call of duty, in harmony with the will of Providence. The heroism of Aeneas is different from that of wrathful Achilles or raging Turnus; he exemplifies "the better fortitude of patience." As he serves divine purpose his *virtus, pietas,* humble self-sacrifice, and suffering endurance define and constitute his "heroic martyrdom."

Milton declares that he is not a poet "to dissect/ With long and tedious havoc fabl'd Knights/ In Battles feign'd (9.29-31). His repudiation of the chivalric romance includes *The Faerie Queene,* therefore, as well as the Renaissance epics of Boiardo, Ariosto, and Tasso. This negative view of Spenserian romance reveals an important change in Milton's thought. As a younger poet he had praised Spenser's "sage and solemn tunes. . . Of Tourneys and Trophies" in whose enchantments "more is meant than meets the ear" ("Il Penseroso," 116-20). Moreover, in his *Apology* Milton had implicitly included Spenser when he expresses his admiration for "those lofty Fables and Romances, which recount in solemne canto's the deeds of Knighthood.'[8] His proposed *Arthuriad* no doubt would have been an extension and development of Spenser's *Faerie Queene*. In the context of *Paradise Lost,* however, Milton undermines the martial deeds of chivalric romance. That these deeds are based on a degenerate concept of heroism is made fully clear in his treatment of war in heaven.

The narration of war, of course, constitutes a principal feature of the traditional heroic poem. Milton complicates this narration, however, by relocating war in Heaven and subverting the ideal of military heroism. The war between the angels has even greater magnitude and significance than the siege of Troy; and in his treatment of military combat Milton illustrates to a greater degree than Virgil the barbarism and destruction of war. Furthermore, he exposes the inadequacy of physical force and material technology in attempting to obstruct providential will. With an aggressive emphasis upon the rebel angels' ignorance of divine power and their perversion of heroic action, the poet invades ancient and modern epics and taking over the machinery of these invaded forms, exposes the baseness to which military heroism can degenerate. At the same time that Raphael's account of the war in Heaven adheres to the conventions of the genre, the poet burlesques the motives and exploits of war in order to degrade it, and through Homeric and chivalric parody he lays open to view Satan's vainglory and self-deceiving pride. The warriors' defiant bragging, their hindering armor, and most particularly the diabolical invention of gunpower and artillery, approach epic farce.[9] By exposing as ridiculous Satan's presumptuous belief that physical might can overthrow the ultimate moral law of God, the poet undermines the old heroic creed. These pretenses of Satan collapse toward the trivial and comic as he fails to perceive the true relationship between the physical and spiritual, the active and contemplative. In attempting to imitate the power of God, he falls into folly and burlesque. He is reduced to a mock-heroic hero, and the war degenerates into

what Arnold Stein calls "epic comedy."[10] Not understanding
that heroism is illusory without moral virtue, Satan's emphasis
on personal glory through war is specious, and despite his guile
and valor, he is doomed:

> For strength from Truth divided and from Just,
> Illaudable, naught merits but dispraise
> And ignominy, yet to glory aspires
> Vain-glorious, and through infamy seeks fame:
> Therefore Eternal silence be their doom.
>
> (6.381-85)

The martial and chivalric similes in Book 1 likewise reveal
the inadequacy of conventional heroism. These similes point
backward and forward in historical time, implicitly relating
the consequences of Satan's rebellion to the condition of man
in the fallen world. The poet compares Satan's warriors to "th'
Heroic Race. . .That fought at *Thebes* and *Ilium*, on each
side/ Mixt with auxiliar Gods" (1.577-79). At first this
reference to the great epic cycles of war seems to raise the
stature of the rebel warriors. Moreover, the comparison of
Satan and his legions with Pharaoh and his army, by transforming the figures into *"Busiris* and his *Memphian* Chivalry" (1.
307) introduces the chivalric ideals of medieval romance in the
identification of Busiris with both Pharaoh and Satan.
Pharaoh's army, however, was defeated, just as were Satan's
legions. This theme of defeat and loss moves as an undercur-
rent throughout the poet's brief survey of heroic legend:

> and what resounds
> In Fable or *Romance* of *Uther's* Son
> Begirt with *British* and *Armoric* Knights;
> And all who since, Baptiz'd or Infidel
> Jousted in *Aspramont* or *Montalban*,
> *Damasco*, or *Marocco*, or *Trebisond*,
> Or whom *Biserta* sent from *Afric* shore
> When *Charlemain* with all his Peerage fell
> By *Fontarabbia*.
>
> (1.578-86)

Milton's reference to Arthur and his knights sets up the
framework of medieval and Renaissance romance that he ex-

plicitly renounces in his invocation in Book 9. The allusion to the battles between Christian and Moslem knights, in addition, captures the chivalric mood of tournament and jousting that were celebrated in French and Italian romances. But the reference to the massacre of Charlemagne's forces by the Saracens, which constitutes the climax of *Chanson de Roland*, creates an elegiac atmosphere suggesting the decline of chivalric heroism. The futility of physical warfare to decide spiritual issues is made clear as Milton describes Christian knights overcome by the victorious infidel. Satan, the archetypal infidel, wins his battles in human history.

The allusion to the *"Romance* of *Uther's* Son" and the image of Saracen knights in battle recall *The Faerie Queene* as well as *Morte D'Arthur* and Continental chivalric epics. In Spenser's romance-epic Arthur plays a central role as knightly champion, and the three Saracen brothers who fight Red Cross represent pagan chivalry. Taking imaginative pleasure in descriptions of "fabl'd Knights/ In Battles feign'd," Spenser used the outer world of physical action and heroic strife as an allegory to define and embody internal, spiritual states of his characters. Their heroic deeds founded in contemplation, Spenser's titular knights are externalizations of inward, spiritual conditions. Spenser's allegorical vehicle of chivalric romance, however, imposed an obstacle for Milton. Denying external action, Milton felt compelled to renounce Spenser's literal level of meaning. For Milton, concepts of Christian virtue had to be treated intrinsically in the poem and on a literal level. If chivalry for Spenser was a suitable vehicle by which moral actions could be understood and evaluated, for Milton chivalry itself was a spiritually inadequate and moribund code. In a radical effort to adapt a traditional genre, Milton liberated himself from the concept of military heroism, achieving an original relation to the epic.

Miltonic Variations on the Pastoral

In the successive stages of the epic, from Virgil and Spenser to Milton, there is a greater criticism of the old heroic creed of *areté* and a correspondingly greater emphasis upon the internalization of action. Evolving through the interaction of each poet's contribution, the heroic poem from the *Aeneid* to *Paradise Lost* concentrates increasingly upon inward experience, contemplation, and the paradise within. Accordingly, there is a persistent shift of center in the genre to the pastoral. As each poet defines true heroic action as being grounded on contemplation, humility, and self-knowledge, his treatment of the pastoral becomes more dominant in the epic.

In *Paradise Lost* the pastoral occupies so central a position that it not only provides the setting of the main action of Temptation and Fall, but operates as the defining value of the whole poem. Mankind's disobedience and "loss of Eden" (the Fall) and the restoration of "the blissful Seat" through "one greater Man" (the Redemption) constitute the theme of the epic. Moreover, the pastoral is the means by which Milton attempts to come to terms with the crucial issue of theodicy, and to "assert Eternal Providence,/ And justify the ways of God to men" (1. 24-25).

Invoking the aid of the Muse, the poet traces the Revelation of God in history by naming the hallowed sources of prophetic inspiration. Milton's biblical imagery is pastoral in his early description of Moses as "That Shepherd, who first taught the chosen Seed" (1. 8). Both literal shepherd watching Jethro's flock on Mount Horeb and moral pastor teaching his flock the Word of God, Moses unites the pastoral and prophetic. The Brook of Siloa which flows by the temple of Jerusalem connects Old and New Testament prophecy: the waters of this Brook, Isaiah says, go softly (Isa. 8), and in them, "Fast by the Oracle of God" (1. 12), Jesus, the Good Shepherd, healed his blind disciple's physical and spiritual vision by sending him to wash there (John 9:7). Comparing Siloa's Brook to the spring of Aganippe on Mount Helicon, "th' *Aonian* Mount," Milton shows that his Muse, who prefers Mount Zion, is not the pagan Muse of classical epic but the "Heav'nly Muse" (1. 6) of God's creative Word. The pastoral and prophetic images of the Bible corroborate the poet's claim that his song "intends to soar/ Above th' Aonian Mount" (1. 14-15), as he insists upon the illuminating experience of withdrawal to pastoral places for manifestations of divine grace and inspiration.

In the invocation to Book 3 Milton develops and extends his treatment of these pastoral places of divine revelation. After lamenting the loss of this external sight, he describes a pastoral landscape, far differernt from the eternal night of Hell and the "darksome Desert" (2. 973) of Chaos. While it, too, represents a condition of consciousness, it is a paradise of the mind. Through spiritual regeneration, fallen man may regain paradise by an inner possession of Eden.

> Yet not the more
> Cease I to wander where the Muses haunt
> Clear Spring, or shady Grove, or Sunny Hill,
> Smit with the love of sacred Song; but chief
> Thee *Sion* and the flow'ry Brooks beneath
> That wash thy hallow'd feet, and warbling flow,
> Nightly I visit.
>
> (3.26-32)

In total physical blindness the poet visits the unlocalized and inward garden of his regenerate imagination. The pastoral images of spring, hill, and brook all look back to the places of God's revelation in the Bible, and are symbols for acts of the creative imagination. Evoking memories of the classical and biblical poetry of blind bards and blind prophets, Milton, the *vates*, describes the clear insight and joy of inner illumination that he has experienced in these places. This *locus amoenus*, moreover, corresponds to and anticipates the physical landscape of Eden, the earthly paradise.[11] While the paradise within lacks the innocence of the external, natural Eden, the *hortus conclusus* of the regenerate mind can be visited in the night of the fallen world.

The poet identifies with the nightingale who "Sings darkling, and in shadiest covert hid/ Tunes her noctural Note" (3. 39-40), and who serves as a symbol of mortal loss and suffering transformed into elegiac song. The symbolic image of the nightingale, deepened and enriched by Ovidian myth and the pastoral tradition, represents the poet's exile from the earthly paradise. Just as Virgil compared Orpheus, mournfully lamenting the loss of his wife, to "philomela sub umbra," so Milton moves from the *"Orphean* Lyre" (3. 17) to the nightingale's song; and like Spenser's Colin, who identifies his melancholy song of loss with that of the nightingale, Milton's epic narrator sees himself as the bird singing of paradise lost in the darkness of the fallen world.

A sightless poet, he mourns his personal deprivation, recalling natural images of the cyclical day and year that are now denied him:

> Thus with the Year
> Seasons return, but not to me returns
> Day, or the sweet approach of Ev'n or Morn,
> Or sight of vernal bloom, or Summer's Rose,
> Or flocks, or herds, or human face divine.
>
> (3.40-44)

He is both exiled from Eden and unable to see the natural beauty of the fallen world. These pastoral images of a paradisal earth recall the Edenic golden age in which all natural things flourished in an eternal spring. They evoke, moreover, a vision of a world whose beauty is made more precious and lovely because it is mortal. Images of passing day and changing seasons illustrate the cycles of nature, which are a result of Man's Fall. Yet the variety and mutability of this familiar, fallen world, despite their meaning for mortal man who must toil by the sweat of his face to assure his own survival are as poignantly beautiful as unfallen Eden.

This elegiac passage in the invocation mounts to a climax with the image of the human face. The face, even divested of its original divine light, is still beautiful to behold. The poet's inability to see the "human face divine" is an even greater deprivation. The human and divine are separate and in tension, but the poet perceives that in the lineaments of the human face there is both a vestige of divinity and the promise and hope restored harmony between man and God.[12]

Although the poet has neither Eden nor the fallen world to see, he does have the insight and spiritual vision to experience another pastoral place, which, unlike Eden, can be visited, and unlike the physical world, is free from fear and care. An attainable ideal in a world of sin, pain, and suffering, the existence of this inner paradise in itself constitues a justification of God's ways to men. The blind, mortal poet consoles himself with an ideal pastoral world of spiritual depth and loveliness. At the same time that he laments his own paradise lost, he shows how a pastoral withdrawal to the inner paradise allows him spiritual *otium* and creative illumination, enabling him to return refreshed and inspired to the experiential world of time, so that he can resume his heroic act of writing his epic poem in physical blindness.

Because of his loss of physical vision, however, he is deprived of the book of nature, and therefore wisdom for him is "at one entrance quite shut out" (3. 50). He prays for "Celestial Light" to "Shine inward," so that he "may see and tell/ Of things invisible to mortal sight" (3. 52-55). The blind poet's prayer for spiritual light merges almost imperceptibly with the visionary description of omniscient God bending down His own eye to see "Our two first Parents"

> . . . in the happy Garden plac't,
> Reaping immortal fruits of joy and love,
> Uninterrupted joy, unrivall'd love
> In blissful solitude.
>
> (3. 66-69)

This description of Eden from the divine perspective, unlike the full and sensuous description of Book 4, is characterized by brevity, generality, and moral emphasis. It is both brief and general because from God's comprehensive view Eden is a pastoral enclave in vast cosmic space, and He is not concerned mainly with external, sensuous particularities. The fruits of the Garden, for example, are not physical, but fruits of joy and love. For God, joy and love define and constitute the life of prelapsarian mankind in Eden.

Milton introduces the celestial paradise as well as the inner paradise in Book 3 before he fully describes the natural external Garden, in order to show how God will compensate for the loss of Eden. In the celestial council God the Father tells His Son that though Satan will be successful in seducing mankind, He will offer grace to fallen man. God declares, however, that without "The rigid satisfaction" of divine justice, "death for death" (3. 211), grace cannot be extended toward him. Freely offering himself as ransom, Messiah, the exemplary hero, volunteers to descend, join human nature, and die for man. Whereas Satan had offered to "undertake/ The perilous attempt" (2. 419) and "seek/ Deliverance" (2. 464-65) for the rebel angels by perverting innocent mankind, the Son will deliver sinful man by undergoing his punishment. A worldly hero, Satan seeks to win glory and satisfy his lust for revenge; the supernatural Christ, in contrast, is heroically obedient and freely renounces glory for shame. "Account me man," he tells the Father,

> . . . I for his sake will leave
> Thy bosom, and this glory next to thee
> Freely put off, and for him lastly die
> Well pleas'd, on me let Death wreck all his rage.
>
> (3.238-41)

The Almighty accepts the Son's offer to be subject to death, and ordains his incarnation: "And be thyself Man among men on Earth" (3. 283). Foreshadowing the poet's pastoral description of Heaven, God foretells the Messiah's life and purpose on earth, using horticultural symbols: He will be "of Virgin seed" (3. 284); He will restore many men "As from a second root" (3. 288); His righteousness will be "transplanted" (3. 293) in man and through faith. Recognizing that His Son's offer to atone for mankind is an act of heavenly compassion, the Father praises Him:

> . . . because in thee
> Love hath abounded more than Glory abounds,
> Therefore thy Humiliation shall exalt
> With thee thy Manhood also to this Throne.
>
> (3.311-14)

The Son has shown virtues diametrically opposed to Satan's activism and blind faith in his own strength. "To be weak is miserable," Satan declares to Beelzebub, "Doing or Suffering" (1. 157-58). The Son's obedience, humility, and assumption of human weakness constitute aspects of His contemplative nature. Satan's heroic ambition for glory is implicitly contrasted with the Son's pastoral humility. Accordingly, the pastoral becomes for Milton the suitable vehicle through which to describe the lowliness of humility of the Son.

With its thrones, harps, jasper and crowns of gold, Milton's description of Heaven resembles the Book of Revelation; furthermore, it foreshadows the "New heav'n and earth" (3. 355) that will spring from the ashes of the world following the future resurrection of the dead.[13] Heaven in *Paradise Lost*, however, is more pastoral than the New Jerusalem of St. John the Divine, and has much in common with Virgil's Elysian Fields. *"Elysian* Flow'rs" (3. 359) grow beside the amber stream of "the river of Bliss" (3. 358), and the "Immortal Amarant" (3. 353), transplanted to grow in Eden, links the heavenly and earthly paradises. Like haemony, which in Milton's masque bears a bright flower in another country, the amaranth unites the spiritual and natural, the mystical and pastoral. The amaranth grew in Eden by the Tree of life, but because of mankind's Fall, was removed to heaven "where it first grew" (3. 356), and blooms by the Fount of Life. Pastoral images symbolizing life and order recur throughout Milton's description of the celestial landscape. The "Trees/ Of life" bear "ambrosial fruitage" and "vines/ Yield nectar" (5. 426-28). Heaven is adorned "With Plant, Fruit, Flow'r Ambrosial" (6. 475) as well as gems and gold. The angels weave the unfading amaranth blossoms and wreathe garlands, binding them into "thir resplendent locks" (3. 361). They sit "In fellowships of Joy" in "blissful Bow'rs/ Of *Amarantin* Shade" and "By the water of Life" (11. 76-80).

Praising the Son, the angels spontaneously play their harps of gold, and this recreation, like that of the exalted spirits of Elysium, represents pastoral *otium* in Heaven. Moreover, like Virgil's chorus chanting by the rolling Eridanus in the Elysian Fields, the singing of the angels by the river of bliss suggests an otherworldly harmony. The disorder and discord of Hell are replaced by the order and concord of Heaven. Instead of the rebel angels' ambition and nervous restlessness, there is tranquil *otium*. The angels' celestial harmony is the "unexpressive nuptial Song" in the apotheosis of *Lycidas*. This blissful *otium*, however, does not constitute the only state of being for the angels. They also wait to serve God, standing like the "Bright-harness'd Angels" of the Nativity Ode in readiness for action. These angels, as John R. Knott Jr. points out, reconcile pastoral *otium* and epic heroism.[14] They are images of the two manifestations of Divinity named in Spenser's "Mutabilitie Cantos," the heavenly Sabbath of God, which is contemplative, and "that great Sabbaoth God," who is powerful and active. The Son, like the angels, reconciles contemplation and action, pastoral and epic. Whereas the aspiring Renaissance poet hoped to ascend generically from pastoral to epic, Messiah descends from contemplation in pastoral Heaven to heroic action in the world of history.

In contrast to both internal and celestial paradises is the pastoral, in which the poet compares the situation in Hell to the fallen world of nature and history. Through similes and allusions he brings the freshness, natural light, and color of the countryside to the oppressively dark, urban setting of Hell, but he also shows the relation between the condition of rebel angels and fallen man. At the same time that these pastoral images take us outside Hell into the recognizable world, they ironically pull us deeper into the consciousness of Hell.

Four descriptive passages in Book 1 illustrate this ironic treatment of the pastoral. First, the famous simile (1. 300-303) in which the numberless angels are compared to the "Autumnal Leaves that strow the Brooks/ In *Vallambrosa*" provides a momentary relief, because of its naturalness, coolness, and particularity, after the "utter darkness' (1. 72) and "burning Marl" (1. 296) of Hell. The simile evokes the diversity, movement, and vivid colors of newly fallen leaves. Newly fallen from Heaven, these angel forms still have a residue of their original beauty. This same image, however, reduces the significance and titanic size of Satan's legions. Like the fallen leaves of autumn, they are innumerable, disparate, and confused, severed from the tree of life. Spiritually unfruitful, they rapidly wither. And mortal man's confusion and loss are as inevitable as autumn and death in winter, because human life after the Fall is ruled by nature's cycles. Echoes of Homer, Virgil, and Dante in this enduring simile reinforce the idea of recurrent fall, both seasonal and spiritual. The seasonal reference,

moreover, foreshadows the appearance of "inclement Seasons"
(10. 1063) following the Fall in the Garden. Adam refers to the

> . . . Rain, Ice, Hail and Snow,
> Which now the Sky with various Face begins
> To show us in this Mountain, while the Winds
> Blow moist and keen, shattering the graceful locks
> Of these fair spreading Trees.
>
> (10.1063-67)

After his disobedience, Adam becomes tragically aware that
the change from perpetual spring to the inclement seasons is a
sign of mankind's alienation from heaven and nature.

The poet's description of the fall of Mulciber from Olympus
likewise refers to time — the season of the year and divisions of
day:

> Nor was his name unheard or unador'd
> In ancient *Greece*; and in *Ausonian* land
> Men call'd him *Mulciber*; and how he fell
> From Heav'n, they fabl'd, thrown by angry *Jove*
> Sheer o'er the Crystal Battlements; from Morn
> To Noon he fell, from Noon to dewy Eve,
> A Summer's day; and with the setting Sun
> Dropt from the Zenith like a falling Star,
> On *Lemnos* th' *Aegean* Isle.
>
> (1. 738-46)

Instead of the Italian world of Virgil's and Dante's tormented
shades, Milton re-creates the idealized world of Homeric
Greece. The image of this almost leisurely fall through the
vastness of space and the whole of a summer's day evokes an un-
troubled calmness very different from his previous description
of Lucifer "Hurl'd headlong flaming from th' Ethereal Sky" (1.
45). In that passage he describes a heart-stopping plummet
through space, corroborating it with a style of breathless
aspirates and kinetically taut sound values. In the passage
describing Mulciber's gradual descent from the crystal bat-
tlements, on the other hand, the poet produces an atmosphere
that is pleasantly remote, easy, and serene. Mulciber drops out
of the blue Mediterranean sky like a falling star, and the
peaceful pastoral image of summer's day and setting sun are

beheld from an Aegean Isle. The casual but abrupt intrusion of "thus they relate,/ Erring" (1. 746-47), however, breaks the lyrical spell the poet has cast. Dismissing the pagan myth, he returns to the narrative of Satan in Hell. He deflates and constricts the spaciousness of his free-floating image to that of Satan's self-bondage, showing the ironic discrepancy between fable and the real fall.

Third, the bee simile (1. 767-74), well established in the epic tradition, compares the multitude of fallen angels to bees in springtime. Emphasizing their density, social organization, and industrious activity, the simile also reduces their stature, divests them of individuality, and likens them to a domestic swarm mindlessly adoring and protecting the ruler bee with stinging barbs. Similarly, the image of the "straw-built Citadel" (1. 773) diminishes Pandemonium to a tiny beehive, suggesting, moreover, that their monument to self-idolatry is insubstantial and ephemeral. However, the simile is proleptic as well as deflationary. The facts that the dome of St. Peter's at Rome is shaped like a hive and that the insignia of the Barberini Pope was a bee suggest both Satanic power in the world of men and the pretenses of Satan's Pandemonium. Milton's allusive bee simile, moreover, recalls two passages in Virgil's poems, his mock-epic treatment of the beehive in Book 4 of *Georgics* and a simile in Book 6 of the *Aeneid*. In this simile Virgil compares the voices of the damned hovering about Lethe's stream of forgetfulness to the murmuring of the bees in cloudless summertime. Simile and allusion, then, help interpret both the folly of the fallen angels' activities and their desperate need as damned souls to seek oblivion in Hell.

Finally, in the concluding simile of Book 1, the poet compares the fallen angels to fairy elves

> Whose midnight Revels, by a Forest side
> Or Fountain some belated Peasant sees,
> Or dreams he sees, while over-head the Moon
> Sits Arbitress, and nearer to the Earth
> Wheels her pale course; they on thir mirth and dance
> Intent, with jocund Music charm his ear.

(1.782-87)

Milton has moved from the military pomp of Pandemonium into a moonlit pastoral world of fairy elves and innocent rustics. Evoking the mood of the English countryside of *A Midsummer Night's Dream*, in which the moon-goddess as queen of faery reigns, and Bottom sees elves revel at night, he deceptively relieves the mounting tension created by the fallen angels clashing "on their sounding shields the din of war" (1. 668). Although the poet seems to be contrasting pastoral innocence and epic ambition, this scene is not so innocent as it first appears. These fairy elves, small and trivial looking to the superstitious peasant, are demonic powers like the "pert Fairies and the dapper Elves" of Comus, and their reveling in the dark woods may be the "Nocturnal sport" of those who worship "Dark veil'd *Cotytto*." Illusory as the light of the mutable moon in which they dance, they are sinister forces in the fallen, natural world. The atmosphere of the moonlit forest, moreover, recalls a scene in Virgil's epic in which the poet describes Aeneas's ambiguous encounter with Dido in the Mourning Fields. He sees or thinks he sees her, and Virgil compares the hero's doubt to one who "sees or fancies he has seen the moon rise amid the clouds" (6. 453-59). By his ironic counterpoint of the pastoral with the epic and nether world, Milton shows their interaction, and the consequence is an ambiguous treatment of the pastoral.

Another example of the illusory nature of the pastoral world in the epic context is the episode in which the poet narrates Satan's cosmic voyage toward earth in Book 3. Inviting the reader to view the vastness of space through Satan's eyes, the poet reveals his character's state of consciousness. Struck with wonder, Satan surveys round as he stands "So high above the circling canopy/ Of Night's extended shade" (3. 55-56) He feels envy, however, recognizing the tremendous breadth and beauty of his adversary's domain, the created universe. He considers the possibility, as he makes his way to the world to seduce its "puny habitants" (2. 366), of other worlds in other stars'

> . . . nigh hand seem'd other Worlds,
> Or other Worlds they seem'd, or happy isles,

Like those *Hesperian* Gardens fam'd of old,
Fortunate Fields, and Groves and flow'ry Vales.

(3.566-69)

This may be an illusion of Satan's, but he "stay'd not to en-
quire" (3. 571), for if he did discover that other paradises exist,
he would have consciously to acknowledge the futility of his attempt, by either force or guile, to vanquish the omnipresent
Creator. In order for Satan to adhere to his existential lie of
self-sufficiency he cannot afford to know the unlimited
resources of God's power.

The poet imaginatively plays with the awesome possibility of
life on other worlds, but emphasizes its illusory nature through
the repetition of "seemed." He does make the reader think,
however, that among those "thousand thousand Stars" (7. 383)
in boundless space, there may be a plurality of Arcadias or
Edens. The whole universe is filled and sanctified by God's
presence, which is an inexhaustible source of cosmic creativity.
The angel Michael later tells Adam that God is not confined
within "narrow bounds" of the Garden but is everywhere:

Adam, thou know'st Heav'n his, and all the Earth,
Not this Rock only; his Omnipresence fills
Land, Sea, and Air. . .

(11.355-37)

That God's created universe may be filled with isles and
enclaves of "Groves and flow'ry Vales" suggests that the
plenum of cosmic space is essentially pastoral, animate, vernal,
and idyllic. In contemplative and recreative *otium*, God has
freely created a paradisal universe, which, because of His omnipresence, is itself the *locus ille locorum*.

In Book 4 the poet follows Satan to the earthly paradise: "So
on he fares, and to the border comes/ Of Eden . . ." (4.
131-32). For Satan, exiled from Heaven, Eden is the place to
revenge himself on God through guile. Bounding over the walls
of the *hortus conclusus*, Satan shows contempt for God's pro-
hibitions. In an extended simile Satan is compared to a wolf:

. . . As when a prowling Wolf,
Whom hunger drives to seek new haunt for prey,

Watching where Shepherds pen thir Flocks at eve
In hurdl'd Cotes amid the field secure,
Leaps o'er the fence with ease into the Fold.

(4.183-87)

The symbolic image of the wolf invading the sheepfold derives, of course, from both classical and biblical pastoral. Like the wolf that in Virgil's third and seventh *Eclogues* represents a hostile, destructive force assaulting the vulnerable Arcadian world of innocence and harmony, Satan, driven by his hunger for revenge, intrudes upon Eden, the sheepfold, to prey upon God's innocent lambs, Adam and Eve. In addition, Satan resembles Turnus in the *Aeneid*, with whom Virgil compares a wolf lying in wait about a sheepfold, roaring beside the pens while bleating lambs are safe beneath their mothers (11. 59-64). Milton's pastoral simile, moreover, recalls the admonition in St. Matthew concerning ravening wolves in sheep's clothing, the warnings of Piers and Diggon in Spenser's moral eclogues, and Saint Peter's invective in *Lycidas*.

Satan is like a dangerous and cunning wolf, but he is also like the thief in Saint John (10.1) who climbs into the sheepfold: "So clomb this first grand Thief into God's Fold:/ So since into his Church lewd Hirelings climb" (4. 193-94). In this multiple simile Milton reveals more about Satan and his vulnerable victims, as he looks at the unfallen Garden from the point of view of the fallen world in which wolves prey on sheep, thieves force their way into defenseless people's homes, and corrupt pastors deceive and exploit their flocks. With the permutations of the vehicle, the unknown primal Garden becomes a fold, house, and church, in a recognizable fallen world. This, and other similes in the poem, make the reader more aware of the narrator, who knows that pastoral innocence will be destroyed.

Milton's Garden of Eden and Its Sources

Milton's Garden is an image of an archetype. Arnold Stein has described the Garden as a representation of "an archetypal state that can be known only through the metaphysical creation of an image."[15] To create this image, the poet draws upon the biblical *Gan Eden*, and the whole pastoral tradition of mythical earthly paradises, the classical Golden Age, and Arcadias. By combining and converting these traditional elements he gains great imaginative power, for this kind of encyclopedic inclusion and synthesis creates a sense of the archetypal and universal. He uses the *loci amoeni* of the epic, moreover, to rival his predecessors in order to surpass them and discredit their imperfect ideal of paradise. Milton's Garden represents both unfallen nature and the perfection of mankind, which reflect the heavenly order.

Milton's description of the "blissful Bower" (4. 690) of Adam and Eve recalls Spenser's Bower of Bliss, which, like the other enchanted gardens of allegorical romance-epic, represents the false paradise in which a temptress lures the hero through its false-seeming beauty and enthralls him with sensual vice. Distinct similarities may be found in the techniques with which the poets describe the false and true paradise. For example, they compare their respective gardens with other traditional earthly paradises in order to depreciate and dismiss them. Acrasia's Bower is "more sweet and holesome" than either Rhodope, Tempe, Ida, Parnassus, "or Eden selfe" (2.12.52). Similarly, the Garden of Eden surpasses that fair field of Enna, the grove of Daphne, the Niserian Isle, and Mount Amara (4. 269-81). The poets, moreover, use similar conventional motifs representing their pastoral landscapes. For example, there are parallel passages describing birds melodiously singing in harmony with winds and murmuring waters.

Milton's use of terms from art seems to correspond to Spenser's emphasis upon artifice in the Bower of Bliss. The nuptial bower in the Edenic Garden has a roof of "inwoven shade," shrubs that "Fenc'd" up its verdant wall, and flowers in "wrought/ Mosaic," making a "rich inlay" that "Broider'd" the ground (4. 690-703). But the art of this bower, unlike that of Acrasia's Bower, is the work of *deus artifex* and not of fallen man. The bower of Adam and Eve was "Chos'n by the sovran Planter," and "he fram'd/ All things to man's delightful use"

(4. 691-92). Roof, fence, and floor are all products of God's art in nature. The beauty of flowers in the Edenic Garden, unlike those which "nice Art" cunningly arranges in "Beds and curious Knots," is not an artificial one, but that which "Nature boon/ Pour'd forth profuse" (4. 240-43). The image of the "curious Knots," moreover, prefigures the "Serpent sly/ Insinuating" who weaves "with Gordian twine/ His braided train" (4. 346-48), and later, in Book 9, Satan's artfully deceptive appearance as a serpent, whom the poet describes as "erect/ Amidst his circling Spires" (9. 501-2). In contrast to Acrasia's Bower, in which art and nature compete, the Garden is a sacred place where this dualism is both reconciled and transcended by the sacramental order of grace. Whereas the art of Acrasia's Bower has sinister designs on fallen man, art in Eden is created for the obedience to God of unfallen Adam and Eve and for their love of one another. The Bower of Bliss is characterized by excess, sophisticated artificiality, and sterility; the Edenic bower, by ordered profusion, innocent nature, fruition, and growth.

Milton's sensuous image of Eve is superficially similar to Spenser's description of the two wanton maidens in the Bower. They, too, are naked, beautiful, and have loose-flowing tresses. Eve is modest, however, and her hair is like a veil; her "swelling Breast" is hidden "under the flowing Gold/ Of her loose tresses" (4. 494-97). The two "naked damzelles" immodestly expose their breasts and bodies to entice and arouse their viewer. In contrast to Eve's unself-conscious innocence is the craft of the temptresses, who act very deliberately and artfully in creating a desired effect. Whereas the damzelles self-consciously display their sexual charms in order to tempt Guyon, Eve is innocently unaware that she is the object of the Tempter's lust and voyeuristic glances. As Adam and Eve embrace and kiss in the Garden,

> . . . aside the Devil turn'd
> For envy, yet with jealous leer malign
> Ey'd them askance.

> (4.502-4)

The damzelles arouse lust but do not gratify; Eve and Adam
sexually fulfill their pure and innocent love in the nuptial
bower.

Finally, the relation between Eve and Adam differs greatly
from that of Acrasia and Verdant. Acrasia dominates,
possesses, and enervates her lover; Eve, on the other hand,
yields to Adam "with coy submission, modest pride,/ And
sweet reluctant amorous delay" ("4. 310-11). Understanding
their proper relationship in the natural hierarchy, Adam and
Eve express their love to each other with "endearing smiles"
and "youthful dalliance" (4. 337-38). There is no melancholy
song of *carpe diem* to tell them of the withering virgin rose or
the desperate need to snatch passing joys. Eve's own love song
to Adam does not resist passing time but integrates the passage
of the day, lyrically reenacting the diurnal cycle. In contrast to
Verdant, whose languorous passivity is a perversion of *otium*,
Adam and Eve actively accept their "daily work of body or
mind" (4. 618). Going hand in hand to their inmost bower,
they also look forward to the first light of morning when they
will rise, and at their "pleasant labor" (4. 625) reform the exuberantly growing garden around them.

Of all the earthly paradises that influenced Milton's treatment of Eden, Spenser's Garden of Adonis is the most important. But despite the borrowing of his predecessor's thematic
imagery, he says of Eden that it is a "Spot more delicious than
those Gardens feign'd/ Or of reviv'd *Adonis*" (9. 439-40). It is
more delicious, doubtless, because his Garden of Eden is not
"feign'd" but a biblical truth and authentic. However, there
are significant analogies between the two earthly paradises. In
addition to their use of commonplace motifs in describing the
hortus conclusus, perpetual spring, and *locus uberimmus*,
both poets insist upon the harmony between the physical and
erotic and the spiritual. They both compare the topography of
their delicious paradises to the organic imagery of the human
body. The "hairy sides" of the "rural mound" (4. 135), the
"shaggy hill" (4. 224), the "veins/ Of porous Earth" (4.
227-28), and "the flow'ry lap" (4. 225) of the Garden, like the
myrtle-covered Mount in Spenser's Garden, reflect the close
relation between nature and mankind,[16] in regard especially to

their physical love, fertility, and procreation. When Eve gives an account of her own creation, the images of birth, "waters issu'd from a Cave" (4. 454), suggest the delivery of Mother Nature. A place of healthy sensuality and natural generation, Milton's Garden recalls the Garden of Adonis, which is "the first seminary/ Of all things." Just as the "Almighty Lord . . . bad them to increase and multiply" in the Garden of Adonis, so God ordains a purposeful sexual life in Eden. Milton's "genial Angel" (4. 712) assumes the role of Spenser's "Old Genius," who presides over generation. The innocent sexuality and fruitfulness of the Garden reflect the love Adam and Eve feel for one another. Their sexual fulfillment suggests, as does that of Spenser's Venus and Adonis, a union between themselves and God. Like Venus and Adonis, they are Universal Parents of their idyllic Garden.

When Milton hails wedded love, he celebrates their sexual communion with a pastoral epithalamium like Spenser's for the "steadfast love and happy state" of Cupid and Psyche, and his own in the epilogue to his *Mask*. All three epithalamia praise the union of heavenly and physical *eros*. The marriage hymn for Adam and Eve contrasts the moral purity and simplicity of their physical union with both joyless lust and the "starv'd Lover" (4. 769) of courtly love tradition, corruptions of sexuality in the fallen world. Whereas Cupid and Psyche in marriage conceive Pleasure, Adam and Eve are progenitors of "a Race/ To fill the Earth" (4. 732-33), the "thousand thousand naked babes" of the Garden of Adonis.

In the lyrical close of this epithalamium, the poet as "the wakeful nightingale" sings to the blissful lovers:

> . . . Sleep on,
> Blest pair; and O yet happiest if ye seek
> No happier state, and know to know no more.
>
> (4.773-75)

Epithalamium turns to elegy here, evoking a sense of foreboding and impending doom. Just as "wicked Tyme" in the Garden of Adonis mows the "flowring herbes and goodly things," so the Fall, intimated in the passage, will usher in devouring time, death, and the ruin of this fragile pastoral world.

The Garden of Eden, Milton's vision of the ideal pastoral life too fragile to last, resembles Colin Clout's vision on Mount Acidale. Milton's description of "All Trees of noblest kind" (4. 217) around the Garden recalls Spenser's hill bordered by "all trees of honour" that bud in winter as in summer. Colin's pastoral song of love piped against a background of the *locus amoenus* is like Eve's love lyric and the grateful couple's hymn of love for God. Their spontaneous, inspired poetry, like Colin's, expresses a contemplative reflection of cosmic order and love, and reveals in their poetry-making how grace takes over from nature. Adam and Eve are graceful in both their physical beauty and spiritual virtue. Reminiscent of Spenser's dancing Graces on Mount Acidale is Milton's description of music and dance in the Garden of Eden:

> . . . while universal *Pan*
> Knit with the *Graces* and the *Hours* in dance
> Led on th' Eternal Spring.
>
> (4.266-68)

Just as Colin Clout's vision of the Graces dissolves at the intrusion of Calidore, Milton's vision of prelapsarian grace fades away as he remembers the imminent assault of Satan and mankind's subsequent Fall. In a mid-line intrusion, Milton alludes to the ominous myth of Proserpine, which proleptically suggests Satan's seduction in the Garden and the Fall of Eve, creating a poignant atmosphere of precariousness and loss:

> . . . Not that fair field
> Of *Enna*, where *Proserpin* gath'ring flow'rs
> Herself a fairer Flow'r by gloomy *Dis*
> Was gather'd, which cost *Ceres* all that pain
> To seek her through the world.
>
> (4.268-72)

This elegiac suggestion of *et in Arcadia Ego* intrudes into the music of Pan and the dancing Graces, and dissolves the pastoral *otium*. Moreover, the poet's identification of Eve with Proserpine, a symbol of transient spring, suggests that Eve is the cause of this dissolution. "Herself a fairer Flow'r," Eve brings about the fading of all flowers.[17] Proserpine becomes Queen of Hades, and in Spenser's account, sits under a tree of golden apples in her black garden of cypress, poppy, and gall. The fact that Eden, like the vision on Mount Acidale, is doomed makes its beauty far greater for fallen man because it intensifies his longing for lost innocence and grace.

Milton's representations of both the celestial and earthly paradises show his indebtedness to Virgil's Elysian Fields. Since he emphasizes the typological relationship between heaven and earth, the Garden of Eden resembles Virgil's heavenly Arcadia. Like the "full flood of Eridanus," which "rolls" amid the forest, the Edenic rivers are described as "Rolling on Orient Pearl and sands of Gold" (4. 238). Moreover, the contemplative and otherworldly aspects of Elysium enrich the spiritual meaning of the numinous Garden. Just as *pater Anchises* contemplates among the exalted spirits, father Adam contemplates the presence of "Millions of spiritual Creatures" walking "the Earth/ Unseen" (4. 677-78), who praise their Creator with sacred songs. This supernatural dimension of the Garden suggests that physical nature is consecrated by a spiritual reality, and Adam and Eve are mystically initiated into solemn responsibilities. They are devoted, like the angels, to a divine purpose and manifest it by their obedience to and worship of God.

Perspectives and Pastoral Modes

After depicting the many delights of Eden with some sensuous particularity, the narrator surveys the whole idealized scene in a sweeping, generalized phrase that anticipates Augustan topographical poetry: "Thus was this place,/ A happy rural seat of various view" (4. 246-47). Suggesting the spatial depth and order of his *locus amoenus*, he also gives his reader an extensive view of many prospects, groves, level downs, hillocks, valleys, caves, and waters. The "various view" denotes many topographical prospects, but it connotes multiple moral perspectives. This topographical comprehensiveness suggests the omniscient view of God. It is not only God's prospect, however, that characterizes the poet's representation of Eden, but the perspectives of Satan, Adam and Eve, and the narrator as well. Each one of these moral perspectives interprets the Garden differently. For Satan, the Garden, which arouses his ambivalent feelings of envy and hatred, is the place where the prospect is the ruin of mankind. The promising outlook of innocent Adam and Eve, on the other hand, is the place in which to live happily, love, and praise God for their "choice/ Unlimited of manifold delights" (4. 434-35). The narrator sees the Garden as a sacred place that is doomed to fall, and from which he as postlapsarian man is exiled.

The continual interaction between the perspectives of the narrator and unfallen Adam and Eve informs the poet's representation of Eden. Although the reader is invited to share imaginatively unfallen mankind's perception of Eden, the narrator's experiential knowledge provides a resisting element that complicates and deepens the emotional significance of the Garden. Where, for example, the reader is introduced to the Garden, the narrator makes him aware, as Adam and Eve are not, of Satan's presence there, perched "like a Cormorant" (4. 196) on the Tree of Life. In this representation of mankind's original joy and love, the Garden is ironically overshadowed by the intrusion of evil and imminent woe.

An integral part of Milton's exploitation of the pastoral in the poem, then, is the disparity between innocence and experience, a tension that causes both suspense and inevitability. This disparity, moreover, defines and controls Milton's use of the pastoral in recreative, plaintive, and moral modes. By contrasting the moral mode of the narrator and the implicit modes of Adam and Eve, first recreative and then plaintive, the poet both expresses and enacts the contrast between the prelapsarian and postlapsarian conditions of mankind, resulting in an enrichment of the theme of the poem. The poet, furthermore, traces a progression through these three modes by dramatizing the characterizational development of Adam and Eve from prelapsarian innocence (recreative) to postlapsarian experience (plaintive), and finally to a regenerate, enlightened innocence (moral) that corresponds to that of the narrator of the poem.

In the four invocations, Milton uses the narrator to represent the condition of fallen but regenerate man. Exiled from Eden, he laments the loss of past perfection. He reveals, moreover, the defects of his mortal nature, acknowledging that his condition is both dark and low. Meditating on those personal circumstances which cause him to suffer, most particularly his physical handicap, he describes his corporeal eyes, which "roll in vain" to find the "piercing ray" (3. 23-24) of light. He is cut off from the light of Eden and now without physical sight, cut off also from "the cheerful ways of men" (3. 46) and the book of Nature's works. Furthermore, the political situation in England intensifies his feelings of loneliness, alienation, and personal danger. He is

> . . . fall'n on evil days
> On evil days fall'n, and evil tongues;
> In darkness, and with dangers compast round,
> And solitude.
>
> (7.25-28)

He identifies himself with Orpheus, the archetype of inspired poet who with his lyre descended into Hell, and was later attacked by the hostile Bacchantes. Like Orpheus, he hears the "barbarous dissonance" (7. 32) of enemies who would take his life, and knows that the Muse of epic poetry, who is no more than 'an empty dream" (7. 39), could not defend her own son. Living in a violent, corrupt, and sinful nation, he is a solitary outcast fearing that he might fail in his heroic venture in "an age too late, or cold/ Climate. or Years" (9. 44-45). He suspects that the senescence of the world, the northern cold, and his own years, all having their origin in the Fall, may "damp" his "intended wing/ Deprest" (9. 45-46). The poet uses the narrator, therefore, to make personal "all our woe,/ With loss of *Eden*" (1. 3-4). As that voice of human woe, he constitutes an important aspect of the thematic pattern of the poem.

But the theme of his poem includes the restoration of paradise. Accordingly, the mood of these invocations, while at first clearly elegiac or plaintive, is modulated by the narrative voice, to moral earnestness expressing regenerate hope and Christian faith. He humbly invokes the living Spirit to illumine, raise, and support him. Because wisdom is "at one entrance quite shut out" (3. 50), he prays that "Celestial Light" may "Shine inward" (3. 51-52), and that he can therefore have the insight and spiritual vision to justify God's ways to men. He cannot see nature's beauty, yet he is free to wander without fear in an internal garden of the regenerate spirit "where the Muses haunt" (3. 27). Although he recognizes that he has "fall'n on evil days" and knows the fate of Orpheus, whose secular Muse could not save him, he calls upon Urania, the "Heav'nly born" (7. 7) Christian Muse who, despite his country's hostility to poets and prophets, will govern his song and find "fit audience. . . though few" (7. 31). Conceding his advancing age, bad climate, and a "world of woe," he prays to his celestial patroness to bring the inspired Word nightly to his ear. And like the Holy Spirit, the narrator himself seems to sit "brooding on the vast Abyss" (1. 21) of his mind and heart, making it pregnant with the Word that resounds through the words of the poem. The narrator moves, after all, from the plaintive to moral mode; his voice is that of fallen humanity which, having lost primal innocence, can regain through suffering, self-knowledge, and grace, the promise of redemption and the paradise within.

Both the plaintive and moral modes of the narrator color the reader's response to the pastoral in the poem, not only in the invocations but in the narration itself. The narrator's description of the Garden and Adam and Eve exemplifies these modes, because through retrospective elegy and proleptic irony the reader is made to anticipate the Fall even in passages that depict the harmony of nature and human perfection. Overtones of the Fall pervade every description. While describing the prelapsarian Garden, which reflects the order, variety, and generosity of the Creation, the narrator's images obliquely and ironically foreshadow the Fall and the fallen world of nature to which Adam and Eve must descend after their expulsion. The rivers of Paradise, which "united fell/ Down the steep glade, and met the nether Flood" (4. 230-31), and the rich trees, which "wept" (4. 249), anticipate the elegiac atmosphere[18] of their loneliness, sorrow, and fear, upon hearing Michael's command to leave their Garden. As has been noted, the ominous analogue to Proserpine brings a sense of doom to the Garden in its foreshadowing of Eve's fate. The Garden, then, reflects mankind's potentiality for sin and sorrow as well as innocence and joy.

Describing Adam and Eve, who together in their original purity embody the wholeness of human nature, the narrator emphasizes the ideal of their virtuous nakedness. They are "with native Honor clad/ In naked majesty" (4. 288-89). In their "Simplicity and spotless innocence" (4. 318) they do not conceal "those mysterious parts" (4. 312), the narrator comments, but then adds darkly:

> Then was not guilty shame: dishonest shame
> Of Nature's works, honor dishonorable,
> Sin-bred, how have ye troubl'd all mankind
> With shows instead, mere shows of seeming pure,
> And banisht from man's life his happiest life.
>
> (4.313-17)

Even in the idyllic scene in which Adam and Eve are surrounded by playful animals, the serpent "of his fatal guile/ Gave proof unheeded" (4. 349-50). From the point of view of Adam and Eve, this scene is wholly recreative, taking place in their perpetual sunshine holiday or holy day. An aspect of this golden age is harmony among animals, as in both Isaiah's version of a pastoral millennium and Virgil's Fourth *Eclogue*. The mirthful sport of the prelapsarian animals refreshes them as they rest "Under a tuft of shade" after "thir sweet Gard'ning labor" (4. 325-29). Enjoying their pastoral *otium*, they recline on the soft bank, feast on the fruits of the Garden, and for diversion watch the animals sport, ramp, and gambol. Milton's Garden is far more rich and diverse than the usual Arcadian landscape; it has lions and kids, "Bears, Tigers, Ounces, Pards" (4. 344), elephants, and snakes. These humble and affectionate creatures, the narrator reminds us, are "since wild" (4. 341), and many are hostile predators of the wilderness. But for the time being they give cheer to the happy couple in the Garden. "Th' unwieldy Elephant" participates in the little pastoral zoo "To make them mirth," and with ponderous jocularity wreathes "His lithe proboscis" (4. 345-47). The narrator's reminders, however, momentarily change his amused tone as he intimates that this innocent *otium* is precarious.

The gardening of Adam and Eve is in the recreative mode, for it is an easy and light activity, unlike work as fallen man knows it. This "pleasant labor" provides them with physical exercise and satisfaction.[19] Their gardening is only strenuous enough "to recommend cool *Zephyr*" and make "ease/ More easy, wholesome thirst and appetite/ More grateful" (4. 329-31). Moreover, as Adam tells Eve after she describes her bad dream, gardening is a "fresh imployment" that will divert and console her "Among the Groves, the Fountains, and the Flow'rs (5. 125). Gardening is contemplative as well as recreative; by tilling and keeping the sacred Garden, Adam and Eve can better know both the Creator, by joining in His will for order, and the interdependence of man and nature. For mankind, too, would increase, multiply, and replenish the earth. In describing their "morning's rural work" (5. 211), the poet suggests an analogue between the trees and vines in the Garden and the moral and psychological relationship between Adam and Eve in their domestic bliss. They hasten to

> . . . where any row
> Of Fruit-tree overwoody reach'd too far
> Thir pamper'd boughs, and needed hands to check
> Fruitless imbraces: or they led the vine
> To wed her Elm; she spous'd about him twines
> Her marriageable arms, and with her brings
> Her dow'r th' adopted Clusters, to adorn
> His barren leaves.
>
> (5.212-19)

Gardening likewise teaches them to see more fully their proper place in Paradise, "Lords of all" (4. 290). Finally, by assisting in natural generation and renewal, Adam and Eve participate in the divine process of regeneration.

God gave them Paradise "To Till and keep, and of the Fruit to eat" (7. 320), and He gave them rest as well as labor. Adam tells Eve that whereas "other Creatures all day long/ Rove idle unimploy'd . . .Man hath his daily work of body or mind/ Appointed, which declares his Dignity" (4. 616-19). Fallen man toils by the sweat of his face as he brings forth bread from a cursed ground strewn with thorns and thistles; the husbandry of Adam and Eve is easy, cheerful, and serene. Unfallen man's georgics exemplify a golden age when "*Spring* and *Autumn*. . .Danc'd hand in hand" (5. 394-95), and a *locus amoenus* in which the thornless rose and "Flow'rs of all hue" flourish (4. 256).

The recreative mode of the traditional pastoral reveals the shepherd's unawareness, even if momentarily, of the inimical forces threatening his fragile peace and freedom. Similarly, Adam and Eve enjoy a privileged position in their Garden, an idyllic enclosure surrounded by cosmic strife and sorrow. Unaware of how brief an interlude their idyll is, their pastoral life is far more precious and fragile than they can know. Their innocence, unlike that or Arcadian shepherds, is not achieved or feigned, but actual. Whereas the shepherds play, dance, or make songs in epicurean *otium*, seeming to ignore or even repress the problems of the real world outside their *locus amoenus*, Adam and Eve are wholly innocent of evil. Consequently, their recreation, whether gardening or song, is free of the ambiguity that colors that of the shepherd.

The characteristic recreative activity of the pastoral is the creation of poetry. The pastoral song, piped or sung by the Arcadian shepherd, represents the spontaneous and free response to the idyllic world of nature. Whether in love song or singing match, the shepherd enjoys his *otium* in a spirit of pure play. Adam and Eve likewise enjoy the making of pastoral song in their Garden. Their spontaneous poetry expresses their love, gratitude, and *otium*.

As Satan had jealously perceived, Adam and Eve are "Imparadis't in one another's arms" (4. 506). Their love and communion with each other is Eden for Eve. Her pastoral lyric takes as its theme this Eden of love that she feels for Adam. It is a love song based on a circular pattern in which the phrases in the first half (4. 641-49) are repeated, nearly word for word, in the second (4. 650-56). This circularity expresses the sense of simultaneous recurrence and constancy:[20] "All seasons and thir change, all please alike" (4. 640). In each half Eve lyrically re-creates the progress of a day, as in "L-Allegro" and "Il

Penseroso," from morning through the night, first in Paradise with Adam, and then without him:

> Sweet is the breath or morn, her rising sweet,
> With charm of earliest Birds; pleasant the Sun
> When first on this delightful Land he spreads
> His orient Beams, on herb, tree, fruit, and flow'r,
> Glist'ring with dew; fragrant the fertile earth
> After soft showers; and sweet the coming on
> Of grateful Ev'ning mild, then silent Night
> With this her solemn Bird and this fair Moon,
> And these the Gems of Heav'n, her starry train.
>
> (4.641-49)

The song in this half shows how her feeling of love is in harmony with the idyllic setting and how the passage of the Edenic day seems timeless to her when she is with Adam, as she participates in the fullness of existence. Nature is beautiful for her, invested with spiritual and human meaning. Her personification of the moon and stars has the effect of animating and harmonizing the whole universe with sweetness, sympathy, and love. She believes in a universe that is personal and cares about her. In the second half she describes how she thinks it would be without Adam. Nature is divested of its human sympathy, and her own language accordingly lacks the earlier rhapsodic amplitude:

> But neither breath of Morn when she ascends
> With charm of earliest Birds, nor rising Sun
> On this delightful land, nor herb, fruit, flow'r,
> Glist'ring with dew, nor fragrance after showers,
> Nor grateful Ev'ning mild, nor silent Night
> With this her solemn Bird, nor walk by Moon
> Or glittering Star-light without thee is sweet.
>
> (4.650-56)

Without Adam, she feels that everything in Eden would be altered. The negations do not cancel out the physical beauty of the pastoral day, but nature is no longer in harmony with her emotional needs. Hastening time rather than timelessness predominates. The moon is no longer fair nor does it have a "starry train." Instead, it is merely an inhuman celestial sphere, and the "glittering Star-light" seems distant, remote, and coldly indifferent to her lonely yearning for Adam.

Adam is the archetypal poet, forerunner of the psalmist David and Milton himself.[21] At Creation, God endowed Adam with intellect, innate knowledge, language, and intuitive perceptions. When he waked to find himself in the Garden, he discovered "all real, as the dream/ Had lively shadow'd" (8. 310-11). With the wholeness of man's nature before the Fall, Adam experiences a vision of the ideal that is actualized in the Garden Paradise. He is able to know, moreover, the essential nature of the prelapsarian animals, and as lord and poet of the Garden he names each one. Perceiving the right relationship between word and thing, Adam names them, and in so doing, humanizes the world of animals. He is a maker of poems, psalmlike hymns that resemble the "Celestial voices to the midnight air" and that "lift our thoughts to Heaven" (4.682-88).

Two hymns sung by Adam and Eve, during their first night together and the next morning, exemplify the innocent poet's pastoral song. Unlike the conventional love-complaints and singing matches of Arcadian shepherds, Adam's recreative poetry gives fresh life to the singer's faith and gratitude.

The evening hymn praises the "Maker Omnipotent" (4. 725) who created the heavens under which Adam and Eve stand at their "shady Lodge" (4. 720) before consummating their love. This spontaneous hymn expresses their humble thanks for their happiness and love for one another, "the Crown of all our bliss/ Ordain'd by thee" (4. 728-29). Just before they taste of the "Perpetual Fountain of Domestic sweets" (4. 760), they reveal their desire for children:

> . . . and this delicious place
> For us too large, where thy abundance wants
> Partakers, and uncropt falls to the ground.
> But thou hast promis'd from us two a Race
> To fill the Earth, who shall with us extol
> Thy goodness infinite.
>
> (4.729-34)

This hymn, finally, praises God for the "gift of sleep" (4. 735).

After the night in which Satan had disturbed Eve's rest with her dream, Adam and Eve sing a sunrise hymn. The narrator describes it as "unmeditated" (5. 149) and "In various style" (5. 146), emphasizing both inspired spontaneity and freedom from set form. In a world of *otium* there is no need for any intermediary to constrain Adam's making of poetic prayer. Their "holy rapture" (5. 147) is sufficient, and the style of the hymn demonstrates Adam's understanding of both God's hierarchical order and intrinsic poetic form. Liturgical in tone, the hymn joyfully praises god with images of motion and light. He calls successively upon heavenly bodies to join them in praising God. The image of divine *stasis* ("Almighty. . .who sit'st above these Heavens") is contrasted with the dynamic movement of the sun climbing and setting, the mists rising and falling, angels circling God's throne, and the planets circling in "mystic Dance" (5. 153-91). Adam's song corresponds thematically to Eve's in that he also praises the "ceaseless change" of the universe: "Let your ceaseless change/ Vary to our great Maker still new praise" (5. 183-84). Glorifying the variety of the created universe, Adam's own "various style" is expressively appropriate. His description of the early morning sky, "Till the Sun paint your fleecy skirts with Gold" (5. 187), and his exhortation to the pines to wave their tops, give the hymn a sense of immediacy in the Garden. The song moves downward from God and heaven, to tall trees, birds, and thence to the creatures of the earth, those who "stately tread, or lowly creep" (5. 201). All of nature, winds, trees, plants, birds, and creatures of the earth, seem to be restored after sleep and at sunrise join in praise.

The aubade that first morning, sung after Adam and Eve have slept in their marriage bed, echoes the pastoral epithalmium, *Song of Songs*:

> . . . Awake
> My fairest, my espous'd, my latest found,
> Heav'n's last best gift, my ever new delight,
> Awake, the morning shines, and the fresh field
> Calls us.

(5.17-21)

Like the voice of the beloved bidding his fair one to rise up and come away, Adam, on "his side/ Leaning half-rais'd" (5. 11-12), wakens Eve after their night of love with a delicate description of the dawn light in the Garden.

Eve has had a disturbing dream, however, which has caused an "unquiet rest" (5. 11) for her. This disturbance to her well-being is revealed in the prophetic dream itself. Inspired by Satan, it recalls Red Cross Knight's dream of a false Una at Archimago's hermitage. Both dreams have the semblance of pastoral loveliness, emphasize the appearance of things, and are erotic in mood. Eve, who has been beguiled by her own reflected image in the pool, is easily deceived by shadows and illusions, and Satan plays on her vulnerability in the dream. The setting of the dreams is pastoral and the atmosphere, romantically nocturnal.

The false poetry of Satan in the dream exploits conventional pastoral attitudes and motifs. Assuming the rhetoric of courtly lover, he lyrically catalogues the sensuous delights of nature to Eve, the rural maiden, "Nature's desire" (5. 46), and invites her to enjoy the pleasures of a romantic night with him. In the darkness Eve mistakes the "gentle voice" (5. 37) for Adam's. "Why sleep'st thou Eve?" (5. 38) the voice asks, parodically imitating Adam's aubade. Just as Satan falsely assumes Adam's role as lover, so "the night-warbling Bird" that "Tunes sweetest his love-labor'd song" (5. 40-41) is a demonic parody of the poet's own nightingale, who "Tunes her nocturnal Note" (3. 40) and sings to the "Blest pair" to "Sleep on" (4. 773-74) in their loving embrace. Satan's amorous serenade describes the moonlight in the darkened garden, and this "more pleasing light/ Shadowy sets off the face of things" (5. 42-43). With "ravishment" (5. 46) in mind, his words are flattering and his tone incantatory; and all this, in the nocturnal landscape, has the effect of a charm.

The Eden of her dream becomes an enchanted garden, a false paradise of ambiguities, deceptions, and illusions. Eve succumbs to Satan's seduction by eating the forbidden fruit, and with her tempter flies "up to the Clouds" (5. 86). Her flight, a "high exaltation" (5. 89), is thrilling for her as she has a godlike prospect from above. But the very means of her physical elevation and flight, denied to mankind, suggests that it is evil.[22] The dream of sin becomes a nightmare as Eve is abruptly abandoned by her guide in the midst of her excitement, and she feels great relief on awakening: "but O how glad I wak'd/ To find this but a dream!" (5. 92-93).

Thus the Garden of Eden, "A happy rural seat of various view," is now seen from the perspective of Eve's demonic dream. The nocturnal Garden, with its illusory images, resembles Spenser's Bower of Bliss. The recreative mode of the pastoral that had characterized the lives of unfallen Adam and Eve degenerates into a Satanic perversion of it: *otium* becomes reason alseep; pastoral song, a vehicle for temptation; *eros*, Satan's cynical means of revenging himself upon God.

Creation as Pastoral

Because omniscient God knows that Satan has entered Paradise and effectively agitated Eve's mind, even causing her tears, He sends Raphael to instruct Adam and "advise him of his happy state" (5. 234) and the conditions necessary to maintain that happiness. Although Raphael's primary task is to remind Adam of his duty to obey, God tells the "sociable Spirit" (5. 221) that he should visit the Garden, and "as friend with friend/ Converse with *Adam*" (5. 229-30). God wants Adam's experience with Raphael to be recreative, "To respite his daylabor with repast/ Or with repose" (5. 231-32). This recreative and contemplative respite with a friend is intended to cheer Adam by giving him encouragement.

The narrator contrasts Adam's modest and naturally courteous meeting with his "god-like Guest" with the "tedious pomp" of the worldly court:

> Meanwhile our Primitive great Sire, to meet
> His god-like Guest, walks forth, without more train
> Accompanied than with his own complete

Perfections; in himself was all his state,
More solemn than the tedious pomp that waits
On Princes, when thir rich Retinue long
Of Horses led, and Grooms besmear'd with Gold
Dazzles the crowd, and sets them all agape.

(5.350-57)

This meeting confirms that the relationship between God and man, spirit and nature, is harmonious. The heroic angel, who knows of "th' invisible exploits/ Of warring Spirits" (5. 565) is greeted by pastoral man.

The narrator describes the pastoral atmosphere of the sociable Spirit's call and mankind's entertainment with what David Daiches calls a "domestic simplicty of language."[23] The little scenes in which Adam sits in the door of his cool bower away from the midday sun, or Eve prepares a salad of fruits and nuts for their luncheon guest, and the open-air meal itself, served on a table "Rais'd of grassy turf" with "mossy seats" (5. 391-92) about it, all suggest that mankind's entertainment of the angel is natural, simple, and humble. The domestic good humor of the phrase, "No fear lest Dinner cool" (5. 396), is not bathetic but consistent with the pastoral naturalism of the scene.

This scene resembles both the bucolic banquet of Aeneas and Evander and the simple rural repast of Calidore and Melibee. In Virgil's Arcadian kingdom, as in Spenser's, the hero is taught moral lessons regarding pastoral ideals. From Evander, Aeneas learns the values of humility and peace; from Melibee, Calidore learns that the pastoral is a state of mind free from ambition and envy. These rustic teachers provide the epic heroes with a contemplative education in the need for internalizing the pastoral. Their meals represent not only pastoral courtesy but pastoral communion. Thus the simple and pleasant picnic that Adam and Eve share with Raphael is in effect a sacramental communion, symbolizing the infusion and rarefaction of nature by spirit. Everything physical and creaturely, even hunger and sexual drive, is material for sanctification.

Raphael's lesson, moreover, is like that of Evander and Melibee in that it explains the moral values of mankind's innocence, obedience, humility, and love. His explanation of the physical and moral hierarchy is based on an organic and pastoral analogy in order to aid Adam's understanding. Within man, as among the elements and other living creatures, there are degrees of excellence. Comparing man to a flowering plant, Raphael describes the evolutionary purification that his nature can undergo:

> . . . So from the root
> Springs lighter the green stalk, from thence the leaves
> More aery, last the bright consummate flow'r
> Spirits odorous breathes.
>
> (5. 479-82)

According to Raphael, matter is essentially good and aspires upward through progressive sublimation, to become more excellent.[24] From the root down in the earth grows the upward green stalk, and from this "lighter" stalk "More aery" leaves bud, and then finally "the bright consummate flow'r," facing heavenward, breathes an incorruptible perfume. The spiritual processes in man follow the same ascent from earth to heaven. The "gradual scale" (5. 484) that Raphael describes is "the scale of Nature . . .whereon/ In contemplation of created things/ By steps we may ascend to God" (5. 509-12).

Raphael tries to satisfy Adam's natural "desire/ of knowledge within bounds" (7. 119-20) by giving accounts of the war in Heaven "By terrible Example the reward/ of disobedience" (6. 910-11), and of the Creation of the World as a glorious example of God's wisdom, which "ordain'd/ Good out of evil to create" (7. 187). At the very structural center of the poem, in Books 6 and 7, the poet juxtaposes the anarchic destruction of Satan's evil with the orderly re-creation of God's good.

The poet implicitly contrasts the debased currency of old epic heroism with the pervasive pastoral imagery of the Creation. On the second day of the battle in Heaven, the rebel angels disrupt and violate the "Celestial soil" (6. 510) by mining it for gunpowder. Later the loyal angels, defending themselves against Satan's artillery, pluck up "the seated Hills with all thir load,/ Rocks, Waters, Woods" (6. 644-45), and uplifting the shaggy tops, hurl them at their foes. Only when the Son commands the "uprooted Hills" to retire "Each to his place" (6. 781-82) is the pastoral landscape of Heaven restored. On the final day, the rebel angels are routed by the Son. They lose all resistance and courage, dropping "down thir idle weapons" (6. 839). In the climactic simile, the poet compares the rebel warriors to a "Herd/ Of Goats or timorous flock" (6. 856-57), echoing the separation of redeemed sheep from reprobate goats at the Last Judgment in Saint Matthew (25: 37). Reducing the heroic stature of the rebel warriors in this pastoral simile, the poet also exposes their lost freedom of wills as they blindly follow their leader off the "Crystal wall of Heav'n. . . Into the wasteful Deep" (6. 860-62).

Raphael's re-creation of the Creation emphasizes the theme of God's power to restore and create anew. The account of the Creation both temporally and logically follows that of the war, because God's Creation is His answer to Satan's revolt.[25] God can "repair/ that detriment" of Satan's destruction, "and in a moment will create/ Another World" and moreover, "out of one man a Race/ Of men innumerable, there to dwell" (7. 152-56). The description of this Creation enacts the Creator's divine power, intelligent energy, and love for man. These divine attributes are expressed most particularly in pastoral settings, motifs, and images.

On the third day, the Word, God's "begotten Son" (7. 163), creates the green world of plants and trees. Beginning with a nearly word-for-word quotation from Genesis,

> . . . Let th' Earth
> Put forth the verdant Grass, Herb yielding Seed,
> And Fruit Tree yielding Fruit after her kind
> Whose Seed is in herself upon the Earth,
>
> (7.309-12)

the poet amplifies, develops, and enriches the biblical account through vivid, recurring pastoral images:

> He scarce had said, when the bare Earth, till then
> Desert and bare, unsightly, unadorn'd,
> Brought forth the tender Grass, whose verdure clad

> Her Universal Face with pleasant green,
> Then Herbs of every leaf, that sudden flow'r'd
> Op'ning thir various colors, and made gay
> Her bosom smelling sweet: and these scarce blown,
> Forth flourish'd thick the clust'ring Vine, forth crept
> The smelling Gourd, up stood the corny Reed
> Embattl'd in her field: and th' humble Shrub,
> And Bush with frizzl'd hair implicit: last
> Rose as in Dance the stately Trees, and spread
> Thir branches hung with copious Fruit: or gemm'd
> Thir Blossoms.
>
> (7.313-26)

He progresses from the "Desert and bare" earth to simple rudimentary plant life, "tender Grass" and "Then Herbs of every leaf." Ascending the scale of nature to larger, more complex forms, he describes flowering plants, vines, gourds, then the "humble Shrub,/ And Bush," and finally "the stately Trees" that bear blossoms or fruit. In ascending the chain of being he establishes God's hierarchical principle of order and degree. Second, the poet emphasizes the dynamic processes of growth. The Creation takes place, and is taking place, continually. The plants "that sudden flow'r'd/ Op'ning thir various colors," the gourd creeping forth, and the trees rising, all suggest, in Milton's time-lapse imagery, the animate process of fruition, growth, and budding. Third, the correspondence with human images confirms the idea that the natural world was created for man, and that man and nature live in harmony. "Her Universal Face" and "Her bosom" personify earth as a fruitful and benevolent mother, and the "frizzl'd hair" of the bush suggests its human characteristics. That the gourd crept forth, the corny reed stood up, and the trees rose as in dance, recapitulates the stages of human development from infancy to maturity. Finally, the stately trees, as they participate in the cosmic dance, symbolize the joyful celebration of nature. The plentitude, diversity, order, and harmony, the divine beauty of the Creation itself, are expressed and embodied in the lyrical justification of God's ways to men. The "Earth," Raphael says, "now/ Seem'd like to Heav'n" (7. 327-28).

In his description of the fourth day, when God created the celestial bodies of the "Firmament of Heav'n" (7. 344), the

Creator is represented as a husbandman who "sow'd with Stars the Heav'n thick as a field" (7. 358). This georgic figure of the husbandman scattering seed-stars both manifests the generosity of the Creator and suggests the life and inherent fertility of the whole physical universe that guarantee its continual regeneration and plenitude.

The passage describing the sea creatures likewise uses pastoral images to show the plenitude, peace, and contentment with which God has endowed the natural world. The "Shoals/ Of fish" swarm "With Fry innumerable" as they "Glide under the green Wave" (7. 400-402). In a variant on the pastoral, they are seen to "Graze the Seaweed thir pasture, and through Groves/ Of Coral stray" (7. 405-6). Their vivid colors, "wav'd coats dropt with Gold" (7. 406) are illuminated as they dart through a watery Eden. Enjoying a life of aquatic *otium*, the sea creatures take their recreation, free from danger and care. No carnivore threatens their idyllic existence. Shell creatures are "at ease" (7. 407), innocent fish "sport" (7. 404), and "bended Dolphins play" (7. 410).

Raphael's account, describing the creation of land animals that are born "perfect forms,/ Limb'd and full grown" (7. 455-56), represents the tremendous vitality and kinetic energy of God and His created life. The wild beast rises up from the ground:

> The grassy Clods now Calv'd, now half appear'd
> The Tawny Lion, pawing to get free
> His hinder parts, then springs as broke from Bonds,
> And Rampant shakes his Brinded Mane; the Ounce,
> The Libbard, and the Tiger, as the Mole
> Rising, the crumbl'd Earth above them threw
> In Hillocks; the swift Stag from under ground
> Bore up his branching head.
>
> (7.463-70)

The earth quakes in its delivery of life, and the beasts in their birthing embody all the majesty, power, and energy of their maturity. The cattle pasture at once, and the fleeced flocks, like plants, rise up, bleating. Each creature, from "*Behemoth* biggest born of Earth" (7. 481) to the "Minims of Nature" (7. 482), to which Adam was to give a name, including "The Serpent subtl'st Beast of all the field" (7. 495), is the magnanimous creation of God, and lives, humble and obedient, in peaceful harmony.

The Creator's "Master work, the end/Of all yet done" (7. 505-6), which is Man, constitutes the climax of order in the Creation. Man shares with the animals their creatureliness; unlike them, however, he is made in the image of God. Accordingly, he is a creature "not prone/And Brute" (7. 506-7) as they,

> . . . but endued
> With Sanctity of Reason . . .erect
> His Stature, and upright with Front serene.
>
> (7. 507-9)

Man is "self-knowing, and from thence/ Magnanimous" and "grateful to acknowledge whence his good/ Descends" (7. 510-13). Blessed by the Creator to "Be fruitful, multiply, and fill the Earth" (7. 531), Man is given dominion over it. God then brings Man "into this delicious Grove" (7. 537), the Garden of Eden, and in this sacred pastoral place he is given "all th' Earth yields" (7. 541) and God provides. In the golden world of Eden, Adam lives a blissful life, secure and free from care and coercion. The Creator has given him free will so that he can obey Him or not; He has given him the Tree of Knowledge of good and evil, which stands in his paradise Garden not as a symbol of compulsion but as God's pledge that He will not take away man's freedom. The Tree is a real, concrete means by which Man is able to disobey if he freely chooses.

When the six days of the Creation are completed, the angels sing a hymn of gratitude. This song on the Sabbath day of rest reasserts the theme of Books 6 and 7, which is that God can both expel the destructive forces from Heaven and create out of "the vast immeasureable Abyss" (7. 211) of formless matter a universe of order, love, and joy. The angels conclude their hymn in a celebration of mankind's idyllic condition: "thrice happy if they knew/ Their happiness" (7. 631-32), lines that recall Virgil's in *Georgics* on the happiness of simple Italian husbandmen: "too happy, should they come to know their blessings!" (O fortunatos nimium, sua si bona norint . . .) (2. 459)

Raphael's poetry of heaven extends and illuminates the relationship between the pastoral and heroic even as it asserts the central theme of theodicy in the poem: God can create good out of evil. Although Satan attempts to destroy the pastoral goodness of Heaven, God's armed angels engage in warfare to prevent that attempt, and the Son as epic hero defeats him and his rebellious forces. Moreover, seeing that Satan's war had "dispeopl'd Heav'n" (7. 151), God repairs "That detriment" (7. 153) by creating "Another World," an earthly paradise, for another race, mankind. The apparent opposition between pastoral and heroic, then, is understood as a divine dialectic moving from pastoral to heroic to new pastoral, a dialectic that will be repeated after mankind succumbs to Satan in the Garden of Eden.

Paradise Lost (II)

Subversion of Pastoral Eden

At Adam's own request Raphael, the "Divine Historian" (8. 6-7), has told him who his enemy is, given a narrative of the revolt in Heaven, and the consequences of disobedience. He has taught Adam, further, to understand that God uses evil to create more good. He has described the Creation of the natural world and explained to him Man's place in the hierarchical moral order, emphasizing obedience and temperance. Yet, for all this, Adam exceeds the boundary of knowledge by questioning God's wisdom rather than expressing humble and joyful wonder. Adam's speculative questions regarding what he vainly presumes is wasteful disproportion in the Creation in effect judges `the divine order and finds it wanting. In so doing, Adam reveals a potential intellectual pride that will lead to mankind's Fall and destroy the idyllic happiness of which the angels had sung. His inquiry is, as he says a little later, a "fond impertinence" (8. 195). Even though this discussion with Raphael regarding celestial motions seems both contemplative and recreative, Adam's excessive curiosity and implicit moral indictment are contrary to the pastoral ideal of humility and contentment.

In contrast to Adam's abstruse thoughts on "things remote/ From use obscure and subtle" (8. 191-92), Eve perceives that the natural world she cares for, "Her Nursery" (8. 46) of budding and blossoming flowers, needs her attention and she departs. Although "such discourse" (8. 48) delights her, she is "lowly wise" (8. 173) and thinks primarily of what concerns them, that which lies before them in daily life. Eve's thought, unlike Adam's, is still very much in the pastoral mode. Her "Lowliness Majestic" (8. 42) and grace characterize her present state.

Adam's emotional speech to Raphael on his love for Eve likewise reveals his vulnerability and potential weakness. He describes the passion he feels for her as a "Commotion strange" (8. 531) and confesses that he becomes "Here only weak/ Against the charm of Beauty's powerful glance" (8. 532-33). Moreover, he excitedly tells Raphael that when he approaches her loveliness,

> . . . so absolute she seems
> And in herself complete, so well to know
> Her own, that what she wills to do or say,
> Seems wisest, virtuousest, discreetest, best;
> All higher knowledge in her presence falls
> Degraded, Wisdom in discourse with her
> Loses discount'nanc't, and like folly shows;
> Authority and Reason on her wait.
>
> (8.546-54)

Here Adam is betraying his disposition to let human love become idolatry. Adam recalls Spenser's Colin as his irrational passion for Eve threatens to disturb their pastoral *otium*. By permitting Eve's power over him to be nearly godlike and in substituting God's creature for the Creator, he reveals that he is likely to fall. Chiding Adam, Raphael in a pastoral debate attempts to rectify Adam's dangerous tendencies — to intellectual pride, sexual passion, and idolatory. Although he does temporarily restrain these tendencies, the "half abasht" (8. 595) Adam responds by acting with a kind of aggressive impertinence as he asks Raphael a personal question regarding the physical union of heavenly spirits. The affable angel's celestial blush expresses more than his words. With the parting sun Raphael must leave, and he both blesses Adam and summarizes his warning implications with an explicit admonition:

Be strong, live happy, and love, but first of all
Him whom to love is to obey, and keep
His great command; take heed lest Passion sway
Thy Judgment to do aught, which else free will
Would not admit.

(8.633-37)

In the invocation to Book 9 the narrator explicitly changes
the pastoral mood of contemplation and recreation to that of
tragic action:

No more of talk where God or Angel Guest
With Man, as with his Friend, familiar us'd
To sit indulgent, and with him partake
Rural repast, permitting him the while
Venial discourse unblam'd: I now must change
Those Notes to Tragic.

(9.1-6)

Whereas his earlier representation of Paradise was pastoral, he
will remove his reader, with Adam and Eve, from the golden
age into "a world of woe" (9. 11). Necessity demands that his
vision be tragic, including mutability, human suffering, and
history. His reference to paradise early in the book, "There was
a place,/ Now not, though Sin, not Time, first wrought the
change" (9. 69-70), ominously foreshadows its imminent ruin
as Satan enters the Garden.

Satan's embittered and plaintive soliloquy is a eulogy to the
pastoral world in which he identifies the relationship of Adam
and Eve with the landscape, the "sweet interchange/ Of Hill,
and Valley, Rivers, Woods and Plains" (9. 115-16). But Eden
cannot be an enclave of peace for him, nor can it be a refuge.
Tormented by "the hateful siege/ Of contraries" (9. 121-22),
Satan's own state of consciousness is a hell from which he cannot escape. His own ambivalence toward mankind and Eden,
and his "relentless thoughts" (9. 130), give him no peace; only
through destruction does he think he can "find ease" (9. 129).
Both "Ambition and Revenge" (9. 168), two characteristics of
the classic hero, cause him to aspire, and ironically, to "Descend" (9. 169). In his 'foul descent" (9. 163), Satan, who

aspired to the "highth of Deity" (9. 167), enters the mouth of a snake and demonically incarnates himself.

The interchange between Adam and Eve on the morning of the fatal day does not have, in spite of its courteous address, the sweetness of their earlier conversations. Eve's apparently impulsive proposal to separate so that they can garden without interruption reveals her discontent with both the Garden and her relationship with Adam. Rather than perceiving the natural luxuriance of the Garden as a cause for grateful wonder, she complains that its "wanton growth" (9. 211) tends to wildness. This wanton growth and potential wildness, however, are reflections of Eve's state of mind. Moreover, she sees gardening not as a recreative and contemplative employment to enhance their *otium*, but as work too great for them to do unless they efficiently divide their labors. Further, she argues in her extreme conscientiousness that interruptions by affectionate looks, smiles, and casual discourse prevent them from doing sufficient work.

Her proposal to separate, however, is motivated by complex, unexpressed feelings. She may be unaware herself of what unconscious, ambivalent urges compel her. Whether testing Adam's love, or willfully desiring an opportunity to prove her independence and intellectual equality, or indeed eager to relive that "high exaltation" (5. 89) in her dream of sin, Eve's proposal hastens the dramatic process already begun, of the Fall.

Adam has learned Raphael's moral lesson that the will is free only when it obeys reason,[1] and although his reply to Eve's proposal is painstaking in its rationality, it is too pedagogic and impersonal. He is not firm enough, finally, to withstand her persistent self-assertiveness. She pretends to have her feelings hurt and petulantly remarks:

> But that thou shouldst my firmness therefore doubt
> To God or thee, because we have a foe
> May tempt it, I expected not to hear,
>
> (9.337-41)

and she expresses her resentment:

> Let us not then suspect our happy State
> Left so imperfect by the Maker wise,
> As not secure to single or combin'd.
> Frail is our happiness, if this be so,
> And *Eden* were no Eden thus expos'd.
>
> (9.337-41)

Her phrase *frail is our happiness* ironically defines the intrinsic precariousness and vulnerablity of the pastoral condition. Not being able to persuade Eve's will, Adam reluctantly gives her permission to part: "Go; for thy stay, not free, absents thee more" (9. 372).

The movement in Book 9 from apparently secure bliss into a drama of ambiguous expectations and relationships, of temptation and sin, is bridged by a number of pastoral and mythological similes that enrich and intensify the critical moment of separation. Just as Eve softly withdraws her hand out of her husband's, she is compared to

> . . . a Wood-Nymph light,
> *Oread* or *Dryad*, or of *Delia's* Train,
> Betook her to the Groves, but *Delia's* self
> In gait surpass'd and Goddess-like deport.
>
> (9.386-89)

Although Eve's innocent beauty is evoked in the simile, the narrator suggests her giddiness in the ambiguous word *light*. There is something ominous, moreover, in the epithet *goddess-like* implying the pagan and idolatrous.[2] Unlike the immortal Diana, however, Eve is not armed "with Bow and Quiver" (9. 390), and only with her rude "Gard'ning Tools" (9. 391) she cannot withstand the assault of her enemy. By comparing Eve with Pomona and Ceres, the poet identifies her with both a georgic landscape during its autumnal harvest and myths about seduction and the loss of virginity:[3]

> . . . or *Pomona*, thus adorn'd
> Likest she seem'd, *Pomona* when she fled
> *Vertumnus*, or to *Ceres* in her Prime,
> Yet Virgin of *Proserpina* from *Jove*.
>
> (9.393-96)

Adam views Eve's fateful departure with an aching loss never before felt in Eden. She has never seemed lovelier or more precious to him than when she leaves his sight: "Her long and ardent look his Eye purse'd/ Delighted, but desiring more her stay" (9. 397-98).

Evil in the form of the serpent intensifies her isolation. Narrowly watched by Satan, Eve begins her gardening alone. The poet returns both to his earlier Proserpine analogy, in which he implicitly compared Eve to "a fairer Flow'r by gloomy*Dis*/. . . gather'd" (4. 270-71), and to his identification of her with the goddess of flowers, "as when *Zephyrus* on *Flora* breathes" (5. 16). Varying and elaborating the flower figure, he describes Eve

> . . . oft stooping to support
> Each Flow'r of slender stalk, whose head though gay
> Carnation, Purple, Azure, or speckt with Gold,
> Hung drooping unsustain'd, them she upstays
> Gently with Myrtle band, mindless the while,
> Herself, though fairest unsupported Flow'r,
> From her best prop so far, and storm so nigh.
>
> (9.427-33)

For the last time we see an innocent Eve in pastoral recreation, and the narrator's ironic moral insight complicates this image of her unfallen simplicity and beauty. The ironic interaction between Eve's separateness and her idyllic loveliness as she gardens among the drooping flowers emphasizes her own frailty and vulnerability. She is like the flower because she is gay now that she has gained independence from her husband, yet like the flower she props she is fragile and not self-sufficient needing Adam, "her best prop," to support her because without him she will droop, unsustained.

The image of the menacing snake in the Garden recalls Virgil's recreative third *Eclogue*, in which the shepherd Damotas warns his friends: "Qui legites flores ete humi nascentia fragra,/ frigidus, o pueri, fugite hinc, latet anguis in herba" (3. 92-93) (Ye who cull flowers and low-growing strawberries, away from here, lads; a chill snake lurks in the grass). Just as the snake endangers Virgil's classical Arcadia, so the Serpent amidst Eve's fragrant flowers, "his Head/ Crested aloft" (9. 499-500), insinuates his destructive evil in the Garden of Eden.

In his description of Satan in the Garden, the poet uses a simile comparing him to a city-dweller in a pastoral landscape who enjoys its idyllic charms:

> As one who long in populous City pent,
> Where Houses thick and Sewers annoy the Air,
> Forth issuing on a Summer's Morn to breath
> Among the pleasant Village and Farms
> Adjoin'd, from each thing met conceives delight,
> The smell of Grain, or tedded Grass, or Kine,
> Or Dairy, each rural sight, each rural sound.
>
> (9.445-51)

Whereas Paradise is like the country, Hell is like a subterranean city. The excessive artifice and luxury of Satan's "high Capital" (1. 756), Pandemonium, with its grim technology, rows of "Starry Lamps and blazing Cressets fed/ With *Naphtha* and *Asphaltus*" (1. 728-29), represents the inorganic, the unnatural, the urban. Moreover, Satan himself is sophisticated in his experience, and urbane in his flattering manipulation of the "fair Virgin" (9.452), Eve, a naive young woman, with whom the narrator associates the smells, sights, and sounds of the country. When the Serpent lies to Eve about how he by happenstance came upon the "goodly Tree" (9. 576), he compares the "savory odor" (9. 579) of its fruit to humble and homely rural smells. It pleased his sense more, he says,

> Than smell of sweetest Fennel, or the Teats
> Of Ewe or Goat dropping Milk at Ev'n,
> Unsuckt of Lamb or Kid, that tend thir play.
>
> (9.581-83)

The last phrase ironically suggest that Eve, a pastoral lamb herself, is untended in her innocent play.

Satan's amorous flattery of Eve, while calculating in its intent, is not wholly hypocritical. Indeed, Satan is Adam's sexual rival. Seeing her, the Tempter himself is tempted by her grace, beauty, and innocence:

> . . . her Heav'nly form
> Angelic, but more soft, and Feminine,
> Her graceful Innocence, her every Air
> Of gesture of least action overaw'd
> His Malice, and with rapine sweet bereav'd
> His fierceness of the fierce intent it brought.
>
> (9.457-62)

The oxymoron *rapine sweet* ironically reveals Satan's state of consciousness; he who would rape and plunder is himself seized Momentarily conquered,

> That space the Evil one abstracted stood
> From his own evil, and for the time remain'd
> Stupidly good.
>
> (9.463-65)

The second oxymoron, *stupidly good*, suggests not Satan's "hateful siege/ Of contraries" (9. 121-22), but his momentary transcendence of all contradictions. In a kind of ecstasy, beyond reason and self-control, Satan is "disarm'd" (9. 465) of guile, hate, envy, and revenge. He is transported, as Comus was upon hearing the Lady's song, by an epiphany of human grace. But the "hot Hell" of his destructive pride "that always in him burns" (9. 467) jolts him from what Comus had called the "sober certainty of waking bliss." Instead, Satan's internal hell "tortures him now more" (9. 469) and alienated from God and man, he soon recollects his purpose. With self-loathing he disparages that "sweet Compulsion" which momentarily "transported" (9. 473-74) him so that he forgot his obsessive hatred. He ruefully recognizes, however, that his only pleasure and joy is "to destroy." "Other joy," he laments, "To me is lost" (9. 477-79).

Eve's encounter with the Tempter in the Garden catches her off guard, because she has never seen a speaking snake, and unnerves her, because the whole ambience of the situation is so much like her dream that she has an uncanny sense that all this has happened before.

In his strategy to seduce Eve, Satan continually attempts to undermine pastoral values. For example, he praises her "Celestial beauty" and tells her that she should be "universally admir'd,"

> . . . but here
> In this enclosure wild, these Beasts among,
> Beholders rude, and shallow to discern
> Half what in thee is fair, one man except,
> Who sees thee? (and what is one?) who shouldst be seen
> A Goddess among Gods, ador'd and serv'd
> By Angels numberless, thy daily Train.
>
> (9.540-48)

Referring with contempt to the sacred *locus amoenus* as "this enclosure wild," Satan means to debase it as a primitive place unworthy of her beauty. Although he hastily excepts man from the animals, he underplays her husband's importance, trying to blur the distinction between Adam and the beasts who are "Beholders rude." By offering "numberless" admirers as preferable to Adam's single love, he appeals to Eve's vanity. Satan vulgarizes both divine beauty and Heaven, moreover, by suggesting that the angels have a more expert eye for physical pulchritude. He extols her as "A Goddess," thereby slyly urging her to be dissatisfied with her human limitations and to be resentful of her role as Adam's helpmeet, studying "household good,/ And good works in her Husband to promote" (9. 233-234). After degrading the Garden, slighting Adam, and raising Eve above her proper place in the hierarchy, Satan tries to discredit God as a "Threat'ner" (9. 687) who wants to keep her "low and ignorant" (9. 704) so that she will continue to worship Him.

Satan says that God would be a mean-spirited, envious tyrant if He should be angry "For such a petty Trespass" (9. 693) as her eating the fruit. Instead, He should praise her for her "dauntless virtue" (9. 694). Implicitly disparaging both obedience and humility, Satan advocates courageous pride and the ambition to be "as Gods" (9. 790). Further, Satan's pretended ignorance of the nature of death, "whatever thing Death be" (9. 695), and his trivialization of God's penalty, "So ye shall die perhaps" (9. 713), are evasive, and calculated to minimize their significance.

Once Satan has excited her with the prospect of being "Sovran of Creatures, universal Dame" (9. 612), Eve, "yet sinless" (9. 659), is dominated by her cavalier, and, her curiosity aroused, is ready to be led to the Tree itself. Satan histrionically addresses it, using an incantatory tone in a hostile parody of religious worship:

> —O Sacred, Wise, and Wisdom-giving Plant,
> Mother of Science, Now I feel thy Power
> Within me clear, not only to discern
> Things in thir Causes, but to trace the ways
> Of highest Agents, deem'd however wise.
>
> (9.679-83)

This act of idolatry is meant to appeal to whatever is left of Eve's sense of spirituality, but the worship cunningly replaces the Creator with an inanimate tree. Satan has promised her that once she has tasted its fruit, she will, as he claims he has already done, turn her thoughts to "Speculations high or deep" and with capacious mind consider "all things visible in Heav'n/ Or Earth" (9. 602-4). This newly gained intellectual ability will be used in just the kind of forbidden knowledge that Raphael had rejected.

Satan tempts Eve with a world beyond the Garden and pastoral *otium*. Ignoring God's injunction and her own human limitations, Eve rejects the pastoral ideals of contentment, humility, and love. In her discontent, aspiration, and self-love, she has succumbed to Satan's temptation, for "his words replete with guile/ Into her heart too easy entrance won" (9. 733-34). Satan emboldens her with his command, "Reach then, and freely taste" (9. 732), and his reference to freedom here has a rich duplicity: he gives her license to taste and enjoy her emancipation with full swing, yet we are reminded of her natural freedom of moral choice: "Freely they stood who stood, and fell who fell" (3. 102). As she reaches, then, she falls.

Eve greedily devours the forbidden fruit "without restraint" (9. 791), and initiates the process of her moral degeneration. Feeling intoxicated and gay after her transgression, she exhibits self-deceiving perceptions. Eve impersonates Satan in her pagan idolatry of the tree, and her caricature of God as "Our great Forbidder, safe with all his Spies/ About him" (9. 815-16) is like Satan's public view. Moreover, she is selfish in her attitude toward Adam. Although she is jealous, she wants to dominate her husband and she considers what strategy to use when dealing with him. Returning to Adam finally, she is ready to lie to him.

While Eve degerates into the unloving nymph of pastoral tradition, Adam begins to resemble the disconsolate lover-shepherd. After their disagreement over Eve's proposal to separate, Adam, waiting eagerly for her return, has woven a chaplet of flowers for her as a peace offering. This garland is "to adorn/ Her tresses, and her rural labors crown,/ As Reapers oft are wont thir Harvest Queen" (9. 841-43). The simile returns to earlier comparisons of Eve with pastoral figures, and it recalls, moreover, Pastorella's "flowry garland" in Arcadia. Holding his simple gift, Adam, in noble innocence, is still part of the pastoral world. Eve has aspired, on the other hand, to universal admiration and godhead, has been seduced and is intoxicated, and the humble reaper's garland can no longer please her.[4] Eve's harvest of time and death is a "bough of fairest fruit" (9. 852) newly gathered. As a consequence of her sin and his passion for her, Adam will reap only sorrow.

As Eve, with "bland words" (9. 855), tells her story, she still seems feverish with exhilaration, and "in her Cheek distemper flushing glow'd" (9. 887). Her "Count'nance blithe" (9. 886) is contrasted with Adam's amazement and chilled horror. The poet symbolizes the loss of Paradise in Adam's unconscious gesture: "From his slack hand the Garland wreath'd for Eve/ Down dropp'd, and all the faded Roses shed" (9. 893-94). In this compressed image the poet dramatizes Adam's horror, and the faded roses sugggest the mutability of love and death's incursion into the garden of innocence. Although Adam loses his grip on happiness, he tries to control his reply to Eve. He does not blame her for what has happened, for his love is too great. Moved by his romantic passion, Adam is willing to sacrifice everything, even his own life, for her. Whereas Adam expresses his selfless love, Eve exhibits only self-love as she encourages him in his willingness to die for her: "O glorious trial of exceeding love" (9. 961). Motivated by self-interest, she offers him the fruit she thinks may kill him. When Adam, faithless to God, decides to eat of the fatal tree, he is determined, deliberate, and undeceived:

> . . . he scrupl'd not to eat
> Against his better knowledge, not deceiv'd,
> But fondly overcome with Female charm.
>
> (9.997-99)

Eating the forbidden fruit, Adam's change is as instantaneous as was Eve's. In mortal sin, both Adam and Eve "swim in mirth" (9.1009), and he teasingly praises her "elegant" (9. 1018) taste. Not facing his guilt, Adam recklessly and rebelliously extols the tree as the source of his newly experienced pleasure:

> Much pleasure we have lost, while we abstain'd
> From this delightful Fruit, nor known till now
> True relish, tasting; if such pleasure be
> In things to us forbidden, it might be wish'd
> For this one Tree had been forbidden ten.
>
> (9.1022-26)

Moreover, their innocent love is degraded into lust. As if the fruit had been an aphrodisiac, it "inflames" their "Carnal desire" (9. 1013) and they want to gratify themselves sexually. The poet's language recreates Adam's callous levity and sexual excitement. He begins to "cast lascivious Eyes" (9. 1014) at Eve and moves her "to dalliance" (9. 1016). Adam's own words reflect his coarsened attitude toward Eve, whom he depersonalizes as a willing object of his erotic pleasure. His invitation, "now let us play" (9. 1027), and his phrase "to enjoy thee" (1032) both reveal Adam's sensual crudeness. Seizing Eve's hand that had clasped his in innocent love and faith, and that she had withdrawn from his when she left him, Adam leads her to a shady bank on which to copulate:

> Her hand he seiz'd, and to a shady bank,
> Thick overhead with verdant roof imbowr'd
> He led her nothing loath; Flow'rs were the Couch,
> Pansies, and Violets, and Asphodel,
> And Hyacinth, Earth's freshest softest lap.
>
> (9.1037-41)

The Garden itself is still naturally beautiful and unspoiled, but for Adam and Eve it has become merely a convenient and comfortable place for self-gratification. Not having deteriorated so quickly as Adam and Eve, it has maintained its pastoral loveliness. The moral climate created by their lust, however, profanes its sacredness, and as they are no longer a part of it, its beauty is now withdrawn.

Their once innocent sexuality degenerates by an act that "seals" (9. 1043) their lust, humiliation, and guilt. Indulgently, they take "thir fill of Love" (9. 1042), but this "solace of thir sin" (9. 1044) is an illusory escape from self-knowledge to a temporary refuge of erotic gratification. "Sunk in carnal pleasure" (8. 593), as Raphael warned, their sexual passion, unlike their love in the nuptial bower, is only of the flesh. This "seal" is not of "mutual help" and "mutual love" (4. 727-28), but "mutual guilt" (9. 1048). The ironic consequence of their sexual seal is mutual alienation, resentment, and hostility.

Neither their sexual consummation nor their "grosser sleep" (9. 1049) has restored them. After being "Encumber'd" with "conscious dreams" (9. 1050-51), they are aware of their newly acquired "knowledge" and instinctively react to their guilt by wanting to hide and cover their nakedness. What they know, as Adam acknowledges, is "Both Good and Evil, Good lost, and Evil got" (9. 1072). Having lost their innocence, they feel the need to hide from each other as well as from "God or Angel" (9. 1081). Adam's plaintive wish that he might "In solitude live savage" (9. 1085) expresses his desire to hide from light itself. He would be "obscur'd" in "some glade" of "highest Woods impenetrable" (9. 1085-86). These images of wilderness ironically look back to innocent Adam's passionately loving and loyal declaration to fallen Eve:

How can I live without thee, how forgo
Thy sweet Converse and Love so dearly join'd,
To live again in these wild Woods Forlorn?

(9.908-10)

He feels that without Eve the Garden would be a wilderness.
Further, Adm's wish for a wilderness to conceal him was
ironically foreshadowed by both Eve's fear of wanton growth
and Satan's derogatory description of the Garden as an
"enclosure wild." Now, with Eve, Adam hopes to hide in that
wilderness, which the light of star and sun cannot reach.
Adam's guilty need to withdraw into solitude exemplifies a corrupted use of the pastoral. His unnatural retirement is for
escape and not for spiritual restoration and return.

They choose the figtree for its large leaves which they gather
and sew together to conceal "The Parts of each from other,
that seem most/ To shame obnoxious" (9. 1092-93):

 . . . there soon they chose
The Figtree, not that kind for Fruit renown'd,
But such as at this day to *Indians* known
In *Malabar* or *Decan* spreads her Arms
Branching so broad and long, that in the ground
The bended Twigs take root, and Daughters grow
About the Mother Tree, a Pillar'd shade
High overarch't, and echoing Walks between.

(9.1100-7)

The simile of the figtree operates in several ways. By implication, the Garden is becoming a wilderness; the golden age
degerates into primitivism. Moreover, the banyan provides
them with a cool, dark shelter, but this enclosed bower is like
Spenser's labyrinthine wood of Error, which heaven's light cannot penetrate.[5] This figtree is "not that kind for Fruit
renown'd"; it is fruitless and therefore in effect sterile and unnatural, unlike the fruitful trees of the prelapsarian garden. Its
fruitlessness suggests the couple's fallen condition and their
futile attempt to hide moral guilt by covering their genitals.
The "Mother Tree" suggests Mother Eve, and the many tendrils

of the figtree, the savage offspring of fallen mankind multiply-
ing sin and error. The poet identifies Adam and Eve with "Indians" and "Americans," savage children of nature living in
primitive conditions:[6]

> There oft the *Indian* Herdsman shunning heat
> Shelters in cool, and tends his pasturing Herds
> At Loopholes cut through thickest shade: Those Leaves
> They gather'd, broad as *Amazonian* Targe,
> And with what skill they had, together sew'd.
> To gird thir waste, vain Covering if to hide
> Thir guilt and dreaded shame; O how unlike
> To that first naked Glory. Such of late
> Columbus found th' American so girt
> With feather'd Cincture, naked else and wild
> Among the Trees on Isles and woody Shores.
>
> (9.1108-18)

Adam and Eve, like the Indian, are now pagans. The "*Amazo-
nian* Targe," or shield, moreover, suggests that fallen man is
now in a warlike state. Through the pastoral simile in which
Adam and Eve are implicitly compared to an "*Indian* Herdsman" tending "his pasturing Herds/ At Loopholes out through
thickest shade," the original moral stature of unfallen man is
degraded. The Indian herdsman is not an Arcadian shepherd
or Edenic gardener, but a primitive peasant who toils in a
jungle of necessity and care. Finally, the poet creates a special
atmosphere in this simile, a hushed mood of remoteness,
loneliness, and melancholy. Of this atmosphere Donald R.
Pearce writes:

> When Milton describes how Eden's fig tree is formed
>
> . . . a pillared shade
> High overarched and echoing walks between
>
> it is pictured stillness in the lines, not any verbal resonance that
> strikes us. The image is that of pastoral arcades gulfed in some
> large, dreamlike silence, punctuated by intermittent footsteps.[7]

The primitivism and savagery of postlapsarian man are

reflected in the world of nature. When Eve bit into the forbidden fruit,

> Earth felt the wound, and Nature from her seat
> Sighing through all her Works gave signs of woe,
> That all was lost.
>
> (9.782-84)

Earth trembled and nature groaned a second time when Adam succumbed to his passion for Eve and transgressed God's law:

> Sky low'r'd, and muttering Thunder, some sad drops
> Wept at completing of the mortal Sin
> Original.
>
> (9.1002-4)

In Book 10 the poet develops the theme of the destruction by Original Sin of the harmony in nature, and between man and nature, as between Adam and Eve. With the Fall, the "Angels turn askance/ The Poles of Earth" (10. 668-69), tilting its axis, or shifting the orbit of the sun. Consequently, extremes of cold and heat afflict the earth, and Eden no longer enjoys perpetual spring. Accompanying this new "Discord," Death introduced a "fierce antipathy" (10. 707-9) among the animals. Many of them began to war and, becoming predatory carnivores, "Devour'd each other" (10. 712). They fled man in fear or developed a hostility toward him, and "with count'nance grim/ Glar'd on him passing" (10. 713-14).

All these terrible changes in nature, however, are external manifestations of what mankind has internally undergone. The guilty pair has lost pastoral *otium* with their inocence; they are "not at rest or ease of Mind" (11. 1120). Corresponding to the disturbances in nature, their human nature is characterized by rain, high winds, and stormy turbulence:

> They sat them down to weep, nor only Tears
> Rain'd at thir Eyes, but high Winds worse within
> Began to rise, high Passions, Anger, Hate,
> Mistrust, Suspicion, Discord, and sook sore
> Thir inward State of Mind, calm Region once
> And full of Peace, now toss't and turbulent.
>
> (11.1121-26)

The inner paradise has been swept away by the tempest of high passions. Victims of those passions and "sensual Appetite" (11. 1129), the human psyche, once whole and harmonious, has become corrupted and is at war with itself. The emotional chaos that overwhelms them marks the guilty couple's miserable fate.

Judgment and the Georgic

The poet describes God's two judgments, the pain of childbirth and the burden of work, which are the immediate punishment of Adam and Eve. Hearing "the voice of God" (10. 97) in the Garden, they try to hide themselves from His presence. The Son tells them that He "will greatly multiply" (10. 193) Eve's sorrow by her conception: "Children thou shalt bring/ In sorrow forth" (10. 194-95). What had been God's blessing now becomes His curse. As Adam later laments in his soliloquy:

> . . . O voice once heard
> Delightfully, *Increase and multiply*,
> Now death to hear!
>
> (10. 729-31)

In their innocence, "our first parents" wanted to have children who would be "partakers" of God's abundance, and "a Race/ To fill the Earth" who would "extol" God's "goodness infinite" (4. 730-34) with them. Now the prospect for their progeny is terrible. Adam's "Fair Patrimony" is a curse: "So disinherited how would ye bless/ Me now your Curse!" (10. 821-22). Sin and Death, and not the "genial angel," will preside over their marriage bed: the sorrowful song of violated Philomel will replace the "spousal" sung by the amorous nightingale.

God's curse of labor for livelihood, like the curse of labor in childbirth, is a physical consequence of the Fall. The blessed ground of the earth is cursed, and the estrangement between fallen man and nature results in his work upon cursed ground:

Because thou hast hearken'd to the voice of thy Wife,
And eaten of the Tree concerning which
I charg'd thee, saying: Thou shalt not eat thereof,
Curs'd is the ground for thy sake, thou in sorrow
Shalt eat therof all the days of thy Life;
Thorns also and Thistles it shall bring thee forth
Unbid, and thou shalt eat th' Herb of the Field,
In the sweat of thy Face shalt thou eat Bread,
Till thou return unto the ground.

(10.198-206)

Having surrendered *otium*, man can no longer dress flowers in a bountiful paradisal garden but will toil strenuously in a cursed ground of thorns and thistles, and in the sweat of his face eat his hard-earned bread.

Both of these curses, however, involve a paradox that will allow mankind, through God's redemptive grace, to regenerate. Although the curse of work exemplifies a fallen world of necessity and constraint, this georgic labor offers a promise of meaning and satisfaction for man. Just as Jove in Virgil's *Georgics* imposed continual labor upon man, God's curse of work will teach man to use his moral strength in adversity. Man cannot return to the idyllic world of recreative *otium*, but he can still enjoy the goodness of country life, and by working in harmony with the cycle of seedtime and harvest, know God. The georgic rather than pastoral ideal is the hope of fallen man. Adam will recognize, after his soliloquy and forgiveness of Eve, that work is now better than idleness, and that there is no harm in laboring to earn bread, for it will sustain him and give him purpose.

Similarly, the curse of childbirth, painful though it will be, is the means of promise and hope. When Adam later rejects Eve's proposal to deceive Death by remaining childless, he tells her that this resolution, although it expresses her willingness for self-sacrifice, cannot be good because "wilful barrenness" is an act of human pride that cuts them "off from hope" (10. 1042-43). Eve's "Seed shall bruise/ The Serpent's head" (10. 1031-32), and

Pains only in Child-bearing were foretold,

And bringing forth, soon recompens't with joy,
Fruit of thy Womb.

(10.1051-53)

The Son comes to the Garden, however, not only as a judge
of transgressors but as Savior. He has told the Father that
"Whoever judg'd, the worst of mee must light" (10. 73). In his
divine compassion, he tempers "Justice with Mercy" (10. 78).
Pitying Adam and Eve as they stand "Before him naked to the
air" (10. 212), receiving God's judgment, the Son

> . . . disdain'd not to begin
> Thenceforth the form of servant to assume,
> As when he wash'd his servants' feet, so now
> As Father of his Family he clad
> Thir nakedness with Skins of Beasts, or slain,
> Or as the Snake with youthful Coat repaid;
> And thought not much to clothe his Enemies.

(10.213-19)

He accepts fallen man as he is. Serving both man and snake in
fatherly sympathy, humility, and love, the Son clothes their
physical nakedness. He clothes man, moreover, with "his Robe
of righteousness" to cover "inward nakedness, much more/Op-
probrious" (10. 221-22). The Son serves in Eden as a pastor,
providing mankind with protection and physical care.

In contrast to the Son as pastor and servant, Satan in his apparently triumphant return to Hell, is the old epic hero. The
Son is meek, humble, and loving; Satan is vengeful, proud,
and self-loving. Preparing the reader for the epic mood of
Satan's return to Pandemonium, the narrator describes the full
assembly of fallen angels

> . . . now expecting
> Each hour their great adventurer from the search
> Of Foreign Worlds.

(10.439-41)

Satan's self-aggrandizing rhetoric in proclaiming victory over
God plays up his epic heroism. He has returned, he announces
to his followers, from his "adventure hard/ With peril great
achiev'd" (10. 468-69). But his oratory, like his theatrical en-

trance and physical presence, is "false glitter" (10. 452). After having avoided Adam because of his intellect, courage, and heroic physique, Satan recognized that he was a "foe not informidable" (9. 486) and seduced the weaker Eve. In Hell the cowardly Satan publicizes the enormous risks he took in his perilous heroic quest. His speech is a perversion of truth and true heroism, and the metamorphosis of his followers and then of himself is an external manifestation of that perversion. Whereas the Son of God freely assumes the form of servant, Satan is changed into the form of the snake he had permitted himself to be.

The scene in the infernal grove, moreover, is a perversion of the Garden. Just when Satan and his followers have degenerated into hissing serpents, they see "A Grove hard by, sprung up with this thir change" (10. 548). The trees here seem to be "laden with fair Fruit like that/ Which grew in Paradise" (10. 550-51). Imagining "For one forbidden Tree a multitude/Now Ris'n (10. 554-55), they roll their serpents' bodies and climb up the trees in order to slake their "scalding thirst" and feed "hunger fierce" (10. 556). Like intemperate Tantalus in Spenser's punitive Garden of Proserpine, they cannot appease their appetites. Not being able to abstain, like Eve, they seize the delusive fruit, "fondly thinking to allay/ Thir appetite with gust" (10. 564-65). The fruit, however, is Dead Sea fruit of "bitter ashes" (10. 566). These apples of Sodom resemble Mammon's apples in Proserpine's garden. Enacting God's curse that he shall grovel upon his belly and eat dust, Satan and his followers "writh'd thir jaws/ With soot and cinders fill'd" (10. 568-69). And like Tantalus, "oft they fell/ Into the same illusion" (10. 570-71), tormented by their hunger and thirst, and continually being punished for their self-deception. The grove in Hell, then, is an infernal parody of the Garden of Eden. It is a false paradise of illusions, and like the Garden of Proserpine an ironic anti-pastoral of temptation, tormented discontent, sterility, and death.

In contrast to Satan's return and punitive metamorphosis, Adam's soliloquy and the reconciliation of Adam and Eve dramatize their gradual process of recovery. Satan's epic return to Hell and his public address first appear to prove the victory of evil; Adam's lonely soliloquy appears to be an expression of human defeat. Satan's triumph, however, becomes a defeat, and Adam's apparent defeat, while beginning in despair and grief, reveals the initial stage of his restoration. His humble acceptance of responsibility, and his struggle with conscience, in contrast to Satan's willful self-deception, demonstrate fallen man's search for self-knowledge. While Satan attempts to justify his own actions with public rationalizations, Adam introspectively works his way to a justification of God's ways to men as his trust in divine mercy grows.

Adam's lament in many ways is like the evolving meditation of the Arcadian shepherd in *Lycidas*. Both the shepherd-poet and Adam begin in despair and resentment, and then, because they cannot come to terms with death, turn to false consolations. Adam's notion of death as being merely physical, "how glad would lay me down/ As in my Mother's lap!" (10. 777-78) and a means of escaping God's "dreadful voice" (10. 779), corresponds to the shepherd's fiction of nature's sympathy; both allow their "frail thoughts" to "dally with false surmise." Both Adam and the shepherd must, however, reject these "evasions vain" (10. 829), no matter how comforting they might be. Finally, both elegiac soliloquies, starting in grief and doubt, develop ultimately into faith in God's justice and mercy.

Although Eve has no such ratiocinative soliloquy, she has become a vessel of God's redemptive grace. Unlike Adam who, still unregenerate, is incapable of forgiving her, Eve has experienced a spiritual and psychological change. In humility, meekness, and grace, she asks Adam for his pardon, thereby restoring their original and proper hierarchical relationship. "Both have sinn'd," Eve says, "but thou/ Against God only, I against God and thee" (10.930-31). Accordingly, she importunes Heaven:

> . . . that all
> The sentence from thy head remov'd light
> On me, sole cause to thee of all this woe,
> Mee mee only just object of his ire.
>
> (10.933-36)

Willing to bear the punishment for both, and offering her life for Adam, Eve humbly on her knees reenacts the Son's offer to undergo punishment for mankind. "His heart relented" (10. 940), Adam raises her from the ground in a symbolic act of human love. Eve, who had initiated sin, initiates a new stage toward regeneration.

After their personal reconciliation, Adam and Eve confess their sin, begging God for His pardon. The narrator in this description ritually echoes the language of their contrition as if he were participating in the liturgy himself:

> . . . they forthwith to the place
> Repairing where he judg'd them prostrate fell
> Before him reverent, and both confess'd
> Humbly thir faults, and pardon begg'd, with tears
> Watering the ground, and with thir signs the Air
> Frequenting, sent from hearts contrite, in sign
> Of sorrow unfeign'd, and humiliation meek.
>
> (10.1098-114)

In contrast to the self-raising of pride and its inevitable fall, Adam and Eve, who fell from grace, fall prostrate in their sin and humility, to be raised by God's love and mercy.

History and the Return of the Epic

The narrator describes "Prevenient Grace descending," which "had remov'd/ The stony from thir hearts, and made new flesh/ Regenerate grow instead" (11. 3-5), fulfilling the Father's merciful promise to offer fallen man grace:

> . . . for I will clear thir senses dark,
> What may suffice, and soft'n stony hearts
> To pray, repent, and bring obedience due.
>
> (3.188-90)

Moreover, prevenient grace, which is that divine grace operating on the human will preparatory to action, underscores fallen man's total depravity, the sovereignty of God, and justification by faith alone. Through self-examination and acknowledgment of sin, Adam and Eve have come to a recognition as crucial as Adam's tragically ironic "We know/ Both Good and Evil, Good lost, and Evil got" (9. 1071-72).

Through contemplation, then, Adam and Eve recognize that they are dependent on God and turn to Him. Descending upon them in their contemplation, prevenient grace aids their repentance. The poet returns to the horticultural symbols God used when the Son offered to die for man. In so doing, he unites the themes of piety, humility, and grace with the pastoral mode. The traditional epic celebrates heroic deeds that exemplify the ideal of rational self-sufficiency, which is analogous to a salvation dependent on human achievement; the pastoral, with its reference continually inward, is Milton's poetic vehicle for justification by faith. The Son's figure describing the "first fruits on Earth" (11. 22), which spring from God's "implanted Grace in Man" (11. 23), is elaborately developed in a horticultural conceit:

> Fruits of more pleasing savor from thy seed
> Sown with contrition in his heart, than those
> Which his own hand manuring all the Trees
> Of Paradise could have produc't, ere fallen
> From innocence.
>
> (11.26-30)

Introducing the paradox of *felix culpa*, the Son contrasts fallen man's internal, spiritual gardening with unfallen man's external, physical gardening. However, the "more pleasing savor" of sacramental fruit is far better. The fragrance resembles Raphael's description of the "bright consummate flow'r" that "Spirits odorous breathes" (5. 481-82). The images of sowing and manuring, moreover, suggest that prayerful repentance is an active husbandry, but it is an activity cooperating with divine love and grace that makes regeneration possible.

God sends Michael, however, to "drive out the sinful Pair" (11. 105) from the Paradise they have lost. In His instructions to the Angel, God tempers His justice with mercy. The sentence of "Perpetual banishment" (11. 108) must be executed, but God tells him to "send them forth, though sorrowing, yet in peace" (11. 117). The heavenly messenger is told to "reveal/ To *Adam* what shall come in future days" (11. 114), and this prophetic vision will show him how "supernal Grace" will contend "With sinfulness of Men" (11. 359-60). Further, Michael will enlighten Adam as to how Satan will be punished by woman's seed.

Whereas Raphael, "the sociable Spirit," had engaged in leisurely pastoral recreation with innocent mankind, Michael, the angelic warrior who drove the rebel angels out of Heaven, must "Without remorse" (11. 104) expel fallen mankind from Paradise. Dressed with "lucid Arms" and "military Vest" (11. 240-41), Michael brings sorrowful man a tragic epic vision of history, warfare, and suffering.

The poet's description of the vigilant, all-seeing cherubim ironically returns to a mythlogical, pastoral simile only in order to surpass and negate it:

> . . . all thir shape
> Spangl'd with eyes more numerous than those
> Of *Argus*, and more wakeful than to drowse,
> Charm'd with *Arcadian* Pipe, the Pastoral Reed
> Of *Hermes*, or his opiate Rod.
>
> (11.129-33)

The "*Arcadian* Pipe" was a soporific for many-eyed Argus, who failed at his task; the flaming warriors, on the other hand, are alert, at military attention, prepared for heroic action. The Son signaled for the "Trumpet" (11. 74) and the "Angelic blast" (11. 76), not the pastoral reed, to summon Michael's forces to receive their divine commission.

Michael's arrival comes at an ironic moment, for Adam and Eve have just "found/ Strength" and "new hope" (11. 138-38). They think that they can look forward to life together, "though in fall'n state, content" (11. 180) in their beloved home. Eve perceives, however, that the changes in Eden will necessitate a life very different from their earlier *otium*:

> . . . But the Field
> To labor calls us now with sweat impos'd,
> Though after sleepless Night; for see the Morn,

All unconcern'd with our unrest, begins
Her rosy progress smiling.

(11. 171-75)

Eve in her love lyric had envisioned nature uncaring without
Adam; now she sees that it is that way even with him. Although
she personifies nature, the dawn is indifferent to them, "All
unconcern'd" with their physically deprived condition. Know-
ing that she must stay with her husband, however, Eve promises him "never from thy side henceforth to stray,/ Where'er
our day's work lies" (11. 176-77). At the same time Adam, seeing "mute signs in Nature" (11. 194), has a presentiment of
greater change. The signs showing nature's cruelty are omens
foreshadowing their expulsion: the air is "suddenly eclips'd,"
"The Bird of Jove" drives out "Two Birds of gayest plume,"
and "the Beast that reigns in Woods" pursues a hart and hind
(11. 183-89), which like the two birds correspond to Adam and
Eve.

As executor of God's judgment, Michael, "solemn and
sublime" (11. 235), announces the divine sentence:

But longer in this Paradise to dwell
Permits not; to remove thee I am come,
And send thee from the Garden forth to till
The ground whence thou wast tak'n, fitter Soil.

(11.260-63)

The plaintive mode now pervades Milton's pastoral world. The
traditional plaintive mode in Virgil and Spenser consisted of
love-complaint, funeral elegy, or lament upon having to leave
Arcadia, but Eve's moving lament combines all three:

O unexpected stroke, worse than Death!
Must I thus leave thee Paradise? thus leave
Thee Native Soil, these happy Walks and Shades,
Fit haunt of Gods? where I had hope to spend,
Quiet though sad, the respite of that day
That must be mortal to us both.

(11.268-73)

The poet's larger achievement in this lament lies in raising
emotions of man's dashed hopes, his homesickness and

nostalgia for lost innocence. As Eve undergoes these experiences, the immediacy and intensity of her passionate lament voice a kind of universal eegy.

Eve grieves, moreover, as a mother for her children. Her instinctively maternal love of the flowers that she has bred, named
and nurtured, is reflected in her sorrow for their loss:

> . . . O flow'rs
> That never will in other Climate grow,
> My early visitation, and my last
> At Ev'n, which I bred up with tender hand
> From the first op'ning bud, and gave ye Names,
> Who now shall rear ye to the Sun, or rank
> Your Tribes, and water from th' ambrosial Fount?
>
> (11.273-79)

Finally, Eve has identified her love with the "nuptial Bower"
that she had adorned with those flowers:

> Thee lastly nuptial Bower, by mee adorn'd
> With what to sight or smell was sweet; from thee
> How shall I part.
>
> (11.280-82)

To comfort her, Michael gently explains that her "native soil"
is not a localized, physical place, but that her real home is in
abiding with Adam. Whereas Eve's pastoral condition is clearly
in the plaintive mode, Michael's is in the moral:

> Whom thus the Angel interrupted mild.
> Lament not *Eve*, but patiently resign
> What justly thou hast lost; nor set thy heart,
> Thus over-fond, on that which is not thine;
> Thy going is not lonely, with thee goes
> Thy Husband, him to follow thou art bound;
> Where he abides, think there thy native soil.
>
> (11.286-92)

Michael also assuages Adam's horror at the thought of expulsion from Paradise. Although Adam's regret is more
spiritual than Eve's sorrow for domestic life, he also emphasizes
the specialness of place. He fears that being removed from his
birthplace is the same as being taken away from communion
with God:

> This most afflicts me, that departing hence,
> As from his face I shall be hid, depriv'd
> His blessed count'nance.

(11.315-17)

He had hoped for a future as a patriarch who would show his sons those holy places which God had consecrated by His appearance:

> On this Mount he appear'd, under this Tree
> Stood visible, among these Pines his voice
> I heard, here with him at this Fountain talk'd.

(11.320-22)

Adam would mark these places of theophany with altars of turf and stone

> . . . in memory,
> Or monument to Ages, and thereon
> Offer sweet smelling Gums and Fruits and Flow'rs.

(11.325-27)

The altars are the sacred counterpart of Eve's nuptial bower. His pious insistence on building altars and raising monuments to commemorate a sacred time reveals that he understands devotion as merely the preservation of the past. Michael corrects his limited and potentially superstitious belief; God is confined neither to a particular time nor to a circumscribed place. The Angel reassures Adam with the knowledge of God's omnipresence, telling him that God is not confined to 'this Rock only" (11. 336). By calling Paradise a rock, Michael anticipates the time when the *locus amoenus* will become no more than "an Island salt and bare" (11. 834). God had given him, Michael continues, "All th' Earth. . . to possess and rule,/ No despicable gift" (11. 339-40). God is not only in the past but in the present and future. Accordingly, Michael will reveal to the progenitor of the human race what will befall his descendants in that future. Leading him to the highest hill of Paradise, the heavenly messenger grants Adam a revelation of human history. The great vision, in its spatial and temporal sweep, shows him the relative unimportance of his isolated pastoral enclave.

This revelation of the future, an epic convention, corresponds to the visions of Aeneas and Red Cross Knight. All three epic heroes are fallible human beings who have a divine mission to fulfill. As a consequence of irresponsible individualism and pride, however, each has been deflected from that mission and has undergone a period of suffering. Aeneas's descent into hell, Red Cross's ordeal in the Cave of Despair, and Adam's soul-searching soliloquy are crucial episodes that dramatize their struggle with conscience and their need for spiritual guidance. They must gain self-knowledge from spiritual instructors, and learn patience and humility. Moreover, they must learn to surrender their individual pride and selflessly submit to providential will.

Both Michael and Anchises, as spokesmen for that will, instruct their students in the necessity for righteous deeds. That Adam and Aeneas learn their lesson in pastoral places emphasizes the inward, contemplative nature of true heroism. In these pastoral places they contemplate a vision of providential will manifesting itself in redemptive history, thus uniting the pastoral and epic.

Adam, like Aeneas, learns from the vision his future role in history. Aeneas will be father of the Roman Empire; Adam's vision foretells the future of the human race, from the Fall to the end of time. Adam's vision shows the consequences of his sin on mankind in history and man's continual falling away from God. At the same time it reveals the encounter of God and man in which the love of God contends with sinful man, and His Word manifests itself dynamically in biblical events through the righteous deeds of just men and the "Chosen Seed." Finally, in the redemptive process of history, "one greater Man" comes to save fallen man and regains the Paradise that the first man had lost.

Adam's process of regeneration parallels that of Red Cross Knight. His conscience-stricken soliloquy in Book 10 resembles the spiritual crisis of Red Cross in his confrontation with the Giant Despair. In these scenes Adam and Red Cross reveal their suffering and guilt as they hope for death. They are rescued from their despair, however, by Eve and Una. Adam, like Red Cross, humbly acknowledges his sinfulness. The Knight is healed and instructed in the House of Holiness, and Adam spiritually recovers through Michael's teaching. The aged holy man, Contemplation, like Michael, grants the hero a prophetic vision. Although the vision is mystical in Spenser's work and primarily historical in Milton's, both are prophetic revelations that provide the epic hero with his identity and vocation defined by divine purpose. Red Cross discovers that he is a warrior-saint who will slay the Dragon and liberate Una's parents from bondage; Adam discovers that he and Eve will beget the human race, from which "one greater Man" will be born to deliver mankind from sin and restore Paradise. Finally, Michael's mystical vision, like that of Contemplation, reveals Christ's incarnation and sacrifice as the means by which the faithful will be received into heavenly bliss. Neither hero is ready, however, to "enter into glory" (12. 456); each must first fulfill his role in human history.

Milton's purpose in dividing Adam's vision, which in Book 11 extends from the story of Cain and Abel to Noah and the Flood, into scenes is to dramatize and define the operation of sin in human history. For Adam this journey into time and space is also a journey of self-discovery. The external actions he sees are manifestations of what has happened to him internally. These human events are historical moments that crystallize the results of man's ambition, greed, and violence.

In this series of miniature dramas, Michael reveals the destruction of pastoral innocence and the growth of corrupt and violent civilizations. The first scene, for example, shows Cain's murder of Abel, establishing the themes of sin and death in the fallen world and the violent disruption of pastoral peace. The biblical pastoral setting, with its new-reaped sheaves, sheep-walks, and folds, evokes a sense of the goodness and peace of country life, of harvest and pastoral care. The image of the altar, a symbol of the Covenant, suggests man's piety and devotion.

The entrance of "A sweaty Reaper" (11. 433) on this peaceful georgic scene, however, recalls God's curse of work. Cain has brought first fruits for sacrifice, but the green ear and yellow sheaf are "Uncull'd, as came to hand" (11. 436). Abel

the shepherd brings the "Choicest and best" (11. 438) of is
flock to the altar as an offering to God, and because he exemplifies pastoral meekness and obedience, God shows His acceptance of the sacrifice with a sign from Heaven. God is
displeased, however, with Cain's offering, "for his was not
sincere" (11. 443). God will not accept a ritual sacrifice if it is
not offered with purity of heart. The reaper rages inwardly,
feeling jealousy and malice toward the good shepherd, recalling Satan's envy of the Son. In blind hatred Cain smites Abel
"into the Midriff with a stone/ That beat out life" (11. 445-46).
The poet's simple monosysllabic words capture the elemental
and primitive violence of Cain's deed. Abel falls, "and deadly
pale," he groans "out his Soul with gushing blood effus'd" (11.
446-47). The shepherd's corpse at the altar is a human
sacrifice. This is the "fruit" of man's disobedience, which
"Brought Death into the World, and all our woe" (1. 3).

Adam beholds the first death, which is a result of human
sin: "But have I now seen Death? Is this the way/ I must return
to native dust?" (11. 462-63). He does not understand why the
"meek man, who well had sacrific'd" (11. 451) was punished:
"Is Piety thus and pure Devotion paid?" (11. 452), he cries in
terror, questioning God's justice. Michael, "also mov'd" (11.
453), tells Adam that the murderer and victim are to be his
sons. He tells him also that "th' unjust the just hath slain" (11.
455),

> . . . but the bloody Fact
> Will be aveng'd, and th' other's Faith approv'd
> Lose no reward, though here thou see him die,
> Rolling in dust and gore.
>
> (11.457-60)

Adam must learn that there is an immutable justice, a system
of reward and punishment that transcends the temporal, fallen
world.

In a later scene Adam sees the sons of Lamech on a
"spacious Plain" (11. 556) busily engaged in many kinds of
secular and civilized activities. The lives of these people are far
more sophisticated than those of the shepherd and reaper. "A
Bevy of fair Women, richly gay/ In Gems and wanton dress"

(11. 582-83) dance to the music of a harp and sing "Soft amorous Ditties" (11. 583). The "Nuptial Torch" (11. 590) is lit, and "marriage Rites invok't (11. 591) to the pagan god Hymen. Adam, having witnessed the earlier scenes of "hate and death, or pain much worse" (11. 601), thinks that this vision seems much better. Michael explains to him, however, that these men are descendants of Cain, and although they appear "studious. . ./ Of Arts that polish Life" (11. 609-10), they are "Unmindful of thir Maker" (11. 611). The women "that seem'd/ Of Goddesses" (11. 614-15) are bred only to tempt men into sin.

Adam's first vision reveals through the single characters of Cain and Abel the incursion of violence into the pastoral world; another scene shows Cain's descendants beginning a nonpastoral culture; the next exhibits the growth of towns and "Cities of Men with lofty Gates and Tow'r" (11. 640). This vision resembles Virgil's description of the shield Mulciber made, which was given to Aeneas in Arcadia. Just a Aeneas's shield portrays the triumph of personified Discord in the slaughter of warfare, Michael's vision reveals the devastation of the whole pastoral way of life by "Giants of mighty Bone, and bold emprise" (11. 642). These lawless warriors, like Satan's rebel angels, are in constant battle, and their warfare destroys a once lovely and innocent world. A band of marauders drive "A herd of Beeves, fair Oxen and fair Kine/ From a fat Meadow ground" (11. 647-48). They attack shepherds and seize for booty "Ewes and thir bleating Lambs" (11. 649). What had been an enclave of bucolic tranquillity becomes a bloody battleground in which peaceful nature has been plundered and violated:

> Where Cattle pastur'd late, now scatter'd lies
> With Carcasses and Arms th' ensanguin'd Field
> Deserted.
>
> (11.653-56)

The warring biblical giants who violate the harmony of nature, murder men, and destroy the landscape live in a "heroic age." They embody the ideals of martial heroism and, like Satan, exalt physical might as heroic virtue, and war as a glorious enterprise, aspiring to gain fame and "renown on Earth" (11. 698):

> Such were those Giants, men of high renown;
> For in those days Might only shall be admir'd
> And Valor and Heroic Virtue call'd;
> To overcome in Battle, and subdue
> Nations, and bring home spoils with infinite
> Man-slaughter, shall be held the highest pitch
> Of human Glory, and for Glory done
> Of triumph, to be styl'd great Conquerors.
>
> (11.689-96)

Enoch, the first "just man," condemns their "Sword Law" (11. 672) and brutal deeds, understanding that true justice is founded on moral and religious ideals. Alone, Enoch dares "to be just,/ And utter odious Truth" (11. 703)4). Like the angel Abdiel, this just man in righteous zeal condemns the sinfulness and violence of "Death's Ministers" (11. 676). Although Enoch cannot turn them to God, he is saved by God from their "violent hands" (11. 669) and lifted up to Heaven.

In the continuous encounter between God and man in history there emerge men who, like Enoch, exemplify the true heroism of righteous deeds. Noah is another such just man. The next scene in Adam's vision is not of "heroic" war, but of a degenerate age:

> All now was turn'd to jollity and game,
> To luxury and riot, feast and dance,
> Marrying or prostituting, as befell,
> Rape or Adultery, where passing fair
> Allur'd them; thence from Cups to civil Broils.
>
> (11.715-19)

Noah, like Enoch before him, "testifi'd against thir ways" (11. 720) and "to them preach'd/ Conversion and Repentance" (11. 723-24). He is a moral pastor who admonishes 'thir wicked ways" and sets before them "The paths of righteousness" (11. 812-14), but it is all in vain. Being warned by God, he builds an ark and stores provisions. God judges and sentences sinful humanity once more, and the Flood constitutes a second Fall.

Noah is a man of peace and humility, and like a shepherd he provides shelter from the Flood for the animals as well as his family. The ark, "one small bottom" (11. 753), is what is left of the pastoral enclave, but despite its diminutive size it holds "every Beast, and Bird, and Insect small" (11. 734). This "floating Vessel," which rides "tilting o'er the Waves" (11. 747), is surrounded and threatened by a hostile environment, a "Sea without shore" (11. 750), a kind of return to Chaos after man's repeated rebellion against God.

The Garden of Eden itself is dislodged, swept away, and transformed in the great deluge:

> . . . then shall this Mount
> Of Paradise by might of Waves be mov'd
> Out of his place, push'd by the horned flood,
> With all his verdure spoil'd, and Trees adrift
> Down the great River to the op'ning Gulf,
> And there take root an Island salt and bare,
> The haunt of Seals and Orcs, and Sea-mews' clang.
>
> (11. 829-35)

What had originally been an earthly Paradise of perpetual spring and an idyllic garden of human love and natural fruition, becomes a bleak, remote island of dead stone. Instead of a *locus amoenus*, where man lived in happiness, it is a *locus odiosus*, distant from all men, and the sounds there are not the "amorous descant" of the "wakeful Nightingale" (4. 602-3), but the dissonant, reverberating cries of the sea-mew.

The description of this displaced, barren island recalls Spenser's "Rock of vile Reproach" in his Bower of Bliss canto:

> A daungerous and detestable place
> To which nor fish nor fowle did once approach,
> But yelling meawes, with seagulls hoars and bace,
> And cormoyraunts, with birds of ravenous race,
> Which still sat wayting on that wastfull clift,
> For spoile of wretches.
>
> (2.12.8)

The Garden of Eden has been transformed into a Rock of vile Reproach, and like Spenser's Rock is a symbol of "shame and sad reproach" for those "miserable wights" who have "spent their looser daies in leud delights" (2. 12. 9).

More important, however, the carrying away of the Garden of Eden in the Flood shows that "God attributes to place/ No sanctity" (11. 836-37). Adam and Eve had lamented their expulsion from the Garden; now there is no more Paradise anywhere on earth. Paradise cannot be located in outward physical space.

Just as God repaired "That detriment" of destruction in the rebellion in Heaven by creating "Another World" (7. 152-56), He again creates more good out of evil by raising yet "another World" (11. 877) after the Deluge. Noah, a just man and type of Christ, is saved in order to found a new world. When the Flood recedes and the dove returns with its olive leaf, Noah descends from the ark and sees a rainbow "Betok'ning peace from God, and Cov'nant new" (11. 867). Adam's question regarding the meaning of the rainbow implicitly identifies its symbolic nature with the fresh pastoral beauty of a second Creation:

> But say, what mean those color'd streaks in Heav'n,
> Distended as the Brow of God appeas'd,
> Or serve they as a flow'ry verge to bind
> The fluid skirts of that same wat'ry Cloud,
> Lest it again dissolve and show'r the Earth?
>
> (11.879-83)

Moreover, the poet's description of the rainbow and the chastened, restored earth, never to be destroyed again by flood, emphasizes its pastoral beauty:

> . . . but when he brings
> Over the Earth a Cloud, will therein set
> His triple-color'd Bow, whereon to look
> And call to mind his Cov'nant: Day and Night
> Seed-time and Harvest, Heat and hoary Frost
> Shall hold thir course.
>
> (11.895-900)

Michael's georgic images of the natural order, of the recurring cycle of seasons and man doing his daily work in "Seed-time and Harvest," console Adam. He has a more spiritual consolation, however, in Michael's prophecy at the very conclusion of the book: ". . .till fire purge all things new,/ Both Heav'n and Earth, wherein the just shall dwell" (11. 900-901). This vision of the Last Day expresses the eschatological hope for final purgation and immutable bliss.

The Shepherd-Hero

In the final book of the poem, Milton extends and develops the major thematic patterns of Michael's vision. God manifests His redemptive purpose in just men who, loving God, fulfill His will in human history, and in man's internalization of paradise. Through man's faith and righteous deeds, God will continue to create a greater good out of destructive evil. These themes point forward to, and converge in, Milton's portrayal of Christ the Hero-Redeemer. Whereas the deeds of just men, from Enoch through Moses, are the epic embodiment of heroic virtue, the internalization of paradise in regenerative man constitutes Milton's pastoral theme. The Messiah, as "one greater Man" who delivers sinful humanity and regains "the blissful seat," Eden, unites the heroic with the pastoral.

In the narration of Book 12 Michael returns, "with transition sweet" to a "world restored" (12. 3-5). He first describes the descendants of Noah, "This second source of Men" (12. 13). These God-fearing men "dwell/ Long time in peace by Families and Tribes/ Under paternal rule" (12. 23-34). Their pastoral lives are pious, peaceful, and plentiful:

> Laboring the soil, and reaping plenteous crop,
> Corn, wine and oil; and from the herd or flock,
> Oft sacrificing Bullock, Lamb, or Kid,
> With large Wine-offerings pour'd, and sacred Feast,
> Shall spend thir days in joy unblam'd.
>
> (12.18-22)

However, like the shepherd Abel, and the shepherds who lived in the days of the giants, their peace and plenty are threatened by hostile forces. The archetypal tyrant, Nimrod, "Of proud ambitious heart," like Satan and Cain, is "not content/ With fair equality, fraternal state," and claims "Dominion undeserv'd/ Over his brethren" (12. 25-28). The pastoral community gives way to "A City and Tow'r" (12. 44), peaceful patriarchal rule, to dominion and empire. Nimrod is an ambitious rebel as well as despot. Having usurped human authority, he aspires to godhead. Like the fallen angels, the tyrannical Nimrod founds another empire. The Tower in his city "intends/ Siege and defiance" (12. 73-74) to God. However, God in judgment and derision sets

> Upon thir Tongues a various spirit to rase
> Quite out thir Native Language, and instead
> To sow a jangling noise of words unknown.
>
> (12.52-55)

The Tower is named "Confusion" (12. 62), another Pandemonium. The "hubbub strange" (12. 60) of profane unintelligible tongues recreates the dreadful din of the fallen angels' forked tongues as they are degraded into snakes. As Man had lost the Garden of Eden, his original home, he now loses his original sacred language, in which God and Adam spoke together and in which Adam named God's creatures in the Garden.

In his narration of the reign of patriarch Abraham, the exodus of Moses and the Chosen People, the conquest of Canaan, and biblical history up to the Nativity, Michael emphasizes both the operation of a providential plan of salvation and the typological meaning of historical characters and events. Having introduced various types of Christ through Old Testament history, Michael reaches the climax of his revelation of God's redemptive purpose in the incarnation and sacrifice of Messiah. With this prophecy, Milton makes a full circle back to the early poems of his career, the Nativity Ode and "The Passion." As in the Nativity Ode, Michael's description of the Messiah's birth expresses and enacts the solemnity of the scene in Bethlehem. In contrast to the ornate imagery and spacious treatment of the Ode, however, the plain style of the narration is consistent with Michael's disciplined, austere character. The "simple Shepherds, keeping watch by night" (12. 365) is a description returning to the biblical pastoral mode, but the poet eschews both his earlier classical pastoral images and apocalyptic tone. Whereas the Ode, whose theme is the Incarnation, is in the spirit of the Gospel according to John, this unadorned narration of the Nativity, with its emphasis upon historical event, resembles the synoptic gospels:

> . . . yet at his Birth a Star
> Unseen before in Heav'n proclaims him come,
> And guides the Eastern Sages, who enquire
> His place, to offer Incense, Myrrh, and Gold;
> His place of birth a Solemn Angel tells
> To simple Shepherds, keeping watch by night;
> They gladly hither haste, and by a Choir
> Of squadron'd Angels hear his Carol sung,
> A Virgin is his Mother, but his Sire
> The Power of the most High.
>
> (12.360-69)

The Messiah's pastoral origins have a particular thematic significance because as contemplative hero He embodies the virtues of lowliness, humility, and mercy; He is the Good Shepherd who will restore Eden.

Adam misunderstands, however, the nature of the Redeemer's heroism and the promise of the Kingdom. He thinks that Christ is an active epic hero, and expects Him to defeat the Serpent in physical combat in order to win an earthly kingdom. Michael corrects Adam's response by teaching him that the warfare is spiritual and that the battleground is within the heart of man:[8]

> . . . Dream not of thir fight,
> As of a Duel, or the local wounds
> Of head or heel: not therefore joins the Son
> Manhood to Godhead, with more strength to foil
> Thy enemy; nor so is overcome
> *Satan*, whose fall from Heav'n, a deadlier bruise,
> Disabl'd not to give thee thy death's wound:
> Which hee, who comes thy Saviour, shall recure,
> Not by destroying *Satan*, but his works
> In thee and in thy Seed.
>
> (12.386-95)

The Son will restore Paradise not by the epic warrior's active physical combat but by fulfilling the law of God "Both by obe-

dience and by love" (12. 403). In Michael's narration of
Christ's sacrifice, Milton finally concludes his uncompleted
poem, "The Passion." In contrast to the early poem, which
celebrates the sacrifice of the Son with lofty rhetorical
language and allusions to classical heroes like Hercules,
Michael's economic narration of the crucifixion is stripped and
severe, aptly expressing its stark tragedy. For example, Michael
describes Christ being

> Seiz'd on by force, judg'd, and to death condemn'd
> A shameful and accurst, nail'd to the Cross
> By his own Nation, slain for bringing Life.
>
> (12.412-14)

Further, Michael applies the meaning of the Son's humiliation
and death to Adam and all humanity:

> But to the Cross he nails thy Enemies,
> The Law that is against thee, and the sins
> Of all mankind, with him there crucifi'd,
> Never to hurt them more who rightly trust
> In this his satisfaction.
>
> (12.415-19)

The Redeemer corresponds to the Just Man in history, who
fulfills God's will by suffering for Him, but He is also God,
Who suffers for fallen man. Although through his sin Adam
had lost his primal innocence and a future in the Garden for
himself and for his descendants, God's love and His redemptive
grace have given man another chance. God does not want to
withdraw His love. The Son's martyrdom, His suffering as man
for Man, is the "God-like act" that "annuls" man's doom, "the
death," Michael tells Adam, "Thou shouldst have di'd/ In sin
for ever lost from life atonement (12. 427-29). The vicarious
atonement of Christ frees sinful man to hope for salvation
through faith and the power of grace.

Christ's Resurrection and the promise of the Last Judgment
are the final events of Michael's prophecy of redemptive
history. In the Millennium, "When this world's dissolution
shall be ripe," God will "reward/ His faithful, and receive
them into bliss" (12. 459-62). Both Heaven and earth shall be

Paradise, Michael promises, a "far happier place/ Than this of *Eden*, and far happier days" (12. 464-65).

Upon completion of Michael's revelation, Adam expresses his new understanding of the virtues of humility, obedience, and fortitude, which form the basis for heroic knowledge and righteous deeds. True heroic virtue is founded on service and love of God. Whereas Satan believes that heroic action springs from personal strength and pride, Adam has learned through the example of the Servant of God that weakness, suffering, and regenerate goodness overcome evil

> . . . by things deem'd weak
> Subverting worldly strong, and worldly wise
> By simply meek; that suffering for Truth's sake
> Is fortitude to highest victory,
> And to the faithful Death the Gate of Life;
> Taught this by his example whom I now
> Acknowledge my Redeemer ever blest.
>
> (12.567-73)

Just after Adam accepts Christ, and just before his expulsion from the earthly Garden, Michael promises him[9]: "A paradise within thee, happier far" (12. 587). The original Garden will be swept away in the Flood, and now it must be transformed from an external, localized place to an inner condition. The pastoral enclave of Eden will become the enclave of the human heart. Even in "the world's wilderness' (12. 313), regenerate man can find ease and solace with God in that pastoral sanctuary. This "paradise within," however, must be recovered by works of faith, virtue, patience, temperance, and love. The paradise within is far more profound and rich than that of man's original innocence; it is "far happier," since it is an authentically human condition that encompasses man's experience and forgiveness, and his unconditional trust in God's judgment and grace.

The Transformation of the Pastoral

In the concluding scene Milton recapitulates the dialectical progression of the poem from the pastoral to the georgic and the heroic, and implies, finally, a spiritual contemplation of a pastoral Heaven beyond the reach of all three.

Michael tells Adam to awaken Eve, who has been calmed "with gentle Dreams" (12. 595) revealing "The great deliverance by her Seed to come" (12. 600). That Eve's mood, as well as Adam's, has changed profoundly, is shown by her words to her husband:

> . . . but now lead on;
> In mee is no delay; with thee to go,
> Is to stay here; without thee here to stay,
> Is to go hence unwilling; thou to mee
> Art all things under Heav'n, all places thou,
> Who for my wilful crime art banisht hence.
>
> (12.614-19)

Her gentle expression of faithfulness, loyalty, and love echoes Ruth's words to Naomi in the biblical pastoral idyll. Moreover, Eve echoes both her own innocent song of love and Michael's exhortation to cherish wherever Adam abides as her native soil. Consoled by her dream, she has recovered the "paradise within," and with Adam continues in her spiritual regeneration.

In contrast to the "paradise within," the external, physical pastoral place is transitory and fragile. It was the *locus amoenus* of mankind's innocence, and now both Adam and Eve know that they must leave their childlike innocence and the Garden behind them,

> . . . for now too nigh
> Th' Arch-Angel stood, and from the other Hill
> To thir fixt station, all in bright array
> The Cherubim descended.
>
> (12.625-28)

The atmosphere in the Garden itself has changed from peaceful resignation to imminent catastrophe. God's angelic warriors, symbolic of His Judgment, descend to guard the gates of Paradise. Just as the Roman soldiers in Virgil's first *Eclogue* seized Meliboeus's Arcadian home, God's soldiers take over

Eden. Yet their awesome physical presence is momentarily dispelled. They appear,

> . . . on the ground
> Gliding meteorous, as Ev'ning Mist
> Ris'n from a River o'er the marish glides.
>
> (12.628-30)

Although the image of the meteor intensifies the heavenly fire of the guardian cherubim as they land on earth, they seem to vaporize into an intangible, luminous mist. Eden's landscape is permeated with heavenly spirits, and there is something mysterious and foreboding about this Miltonic transformation of Virgilian twilight as the mist "gathers round fast." (12. 631).

The sword of justice blocks the way back to the unapproachable Garden, barring Adam and Eve from their home of pastoral innocence and primal unity. The cherubim lift up their flaming swords

> . . . which with torrid heat,
> And vapor as the *Libyan* Air adust
> Began to parch that temperate Clime.
>
> (12.634-36)

Scorched with waves of heat, the *locus amoenus* is changed into a frightening wasteland. In spite of the terrible changes that the Garden is undergoing, Adam and Eve are reluctant to leave; they feel a sorrowful nostalgia for their native home. With memories of lost happiness, they look back for the last time at "all th' Eastern side. . .of Paradise, so late thir happy seat" (12. 641-42). This last phrase elegiacally recalls "A happy rural seat of various view" (4. 247). Adam and Eve no longer have a bright future as their prospect. The Garden, guarded now by cherubim with flaming swords, seems remote, cloistered, and even unreal.

More real is the everyday image of "the Laborer's heel/Homeward returning" (12. 631-32). With this image the poet moves away from pastoral ease toward the georgic world. God's judgment has sentenced fallen man to a lifetime of hard labor. But the georgic world in which he will labor, with its recurring cycle of seed-time and harvest, offers him promise and satisfaction. Just as the pastoral is internal as well as physical, his georgic condition in the experiential world has also an internal, spiritual meaning. Adam must labor in the sweat of his face, but mankind will also sow God's seed with righteous deeds and grow the spiritual fruits of prayer; although Eve must labor to bring children forth, mankind will grow "the Promis'd Seed" (12. 623) that will restore all. "The Laborer's heel," then, recalls God's prophecy that although the Serpent will bruise man's head, the heel of woman's seed will bruise his head.

As Adam and Eve leave the Garden, they move from recreative and contemplative *otium* into a life of hardship demanding active labor, steadfastness, and faith. Moreover, regenerate man must go into the mutable world of history and suffering, which demands his heroic deeds in spiritual warfare. Armed "With spiritual Armor," he must be "able to resist/ *Satan's* assaults" (12. 491-92). Like Aeneas and Calidore after their experience in the pastoral enclave, Adam has gained greater self-knowledge as he prepares to enter the fallen world. Adam, like Aeneas, has come through a period of spiritual crisis, to a greater contemplative understanding of his divine purpose and duty in the world and, like Calidore, he has learned the true meaning of the pastoral, in spite or because of his "lucklesse breach." Both Adam and Calidore have learned, moreover, about the heavenly gift of grace, and although Arcadia and the Garden of Eden have been physically destroyed, these regenerate men have recovered peace through the paradise within them. Consequently, they better understand the nature of their heroic duty in a violent and corrupt world.

Adam's spiritual regeneration is itself a heroic action that is indirectly responsible for the liberation of all mankind, for the redemption of Christ is possible through Adam. For Adam, Christ embodies both the true heroism he can emulate, and the pastoral enclave within his soul where he can find spiritual ease and fellowship with God.

Before Adam and Eve is an unfamiliar, perilous world of pain, labor, and death, but they are reassured in their knowledge that they can have Providence for their guide, and they can wipe their tears: "The World was all before them, where to choose/This place of rest, and Providence thir guide" (12. 646-47). Although "Homeward" seems at first to refer to the Garden that was man's first home, or the temporary home of the exiled laborer, it points toward the certain grave, and man's final "place of rest," which is his spiritual home with God. Then regenerate man will "enter into glory, and resume/His Seat at God's right hand" (12. 456-57). This is the celestial paradise where "Elysian Flow'rs" grow beside "the river of Bliss' (3. 358-59) and the angels sit "In fellowships of joy" in "blissful Bow'rs/ Of *Amarantin* Shade" (11. 76-80).

What appears to be Michael's unresponsive impatience as he physically urges Adam and Eve on is an act of watchful compassion. Catching either hand of "Our ling'ring Parents" (12. 638), who now seem so much like children, he is solicitous, demonstrating God's nearness and fatherly care. Even in His Judgment God does not want to withdraw His love.

Bewildered, afraid, and sad, "Some natural tears they dropp'd, but wip'd them soon" (12. 645). God had told Michael to "send them forth, though sorrowing, yet in peace" (11. 117), and now as Adam and Eve wander through Paradise, they are able to conquer their despair with peace of heart. Cast out of Paradise, they bring the burden of humanity to the heroic world of moral choice, certain only that they will be challenged by trials of faith in which they must prove true before God.

Michael no longer leads them by the hands, but in a pledge of communion and love the banished couple hold hands as they did in their innocence. The love of God for mankind is still revealed through the depths of love that Adam and Eve feel for one another.

As they leave Paradise, their steps are "wand'ring" and "slow" (12. 648). They are "solitary" (12. 649) because they have discovered human sorrow, yet they have discovered, in their spiritual maturity, a greater love, faith, and hope. Adam and Eve have fallen from recreative bliss to plaintive loss, but finally they have progressed to moral awareness, prepared to do righteous deeds in the georgic and heroic worlds, trusting that they will finally participate in a transcendent pastoral Paradise.

Notes

Chapter 1. Virgil

1. Hallett Smith, *Elizabethan Poetry: A Study in Conventions, Meaning, and Expression* (Cambridge, Mass: Harvard University Press, 1952) p. 2.

2. *Pastoral* (London: Methuen & Co., 1971), pp. 32-33.

3. My thinking on Virgil's *Eclogues* is much indebted to Michael C. J. Putnam, *Virgil's Pastoral Art: Studies in the Eclogues* (Princeton, N.J.: Princeton University Press, 1970).

4. I have followed the Loeb Classical Library translation of Virgil's poetry.

5. Thomas J. Rosenmeyer, *The Green Cabinet: Theocritus and the European Pastoral Lyric* (Berkeley and Los Angeles: University of California Press, 1969)), p. 98.

6. "*Et in Arcadia Ego*: Poussin and the Elegiac Tradition," in *Meaning in the Visual Arts* (New York: Doubleday & Co., 1955), pp. 295-320.

7. Putnam, *Virgil's Pastoral Art*, p. 229.

8. Rosenmeyer, *The Green Cabinet*, p. 158.

9. Putnam, *Virgil's Pastoral Art*, p. 253.

10. Rosenmeyer, *The Green Cabinet*, p. 157.

11. *Self-Consuming Artifacts: The Experience of Seventeenth-Century Literature* (Berkeley and Los Angeles: University of California Press, 1972), p. 10.

12. Rosenmeyer, *The Green Cabinet*, p. 229.

13. Alexander G. McKay, *Vergil's Italy* (Greenwich, Conn: New York Graphic Society, 1970), p. 29.

14. Jacques Perret, "The *Georgics*" (1957); reprinted in *Virgil: A Collection of Critical Essays*, ed. Steele Commager (Englewood Cliffs, N.J.: Prentice-Hall, Inc., 1966), pp. 29-30.

15. *The Country and the City* (London: Chatto & Windus, 1973), p. 14.

16. Quoted in Eugene M. Waith, *The Herculean Hero in Marlowe, Chapman, Shakespeare, and Dryden* (New York: Columbia University Press, 1962), p. 16.

17. A. S. P. Woodhouse, *The Heavenly Muse: A Preface to Milton*, ed. Hugh MacCallum (Toronto: University of Toronto Press, (1972), p. 187.

18. Davis P. Harding, *The Club of Hercules: Studies in the Classical Background of Paradise Lost* (Urbana: The Univerrsity of Illinois Press, 1962), p. 33.

19. Brooks Otis, "The Originality of the Aeneid," in *Virgil*, ed. D. R. Dudley (London: Routledge & Kegan Paul, 1969), p. 41.

20. Ernst R. Curtius suggests that the term *locus amoenus*, pleasance, is derived from Virgil's description of the Elysian Fields. *European Literature and the Latin Middle Ages*, trans. Willard R. Trask (London: Routledge & Kegan Paul, 1953), p. 192.

21. Michael C. J. Putnam, *The Poetry of the Aeneid: Four Studies in Imaginative Unity and Design* (Cambridge, Mass.: Harvard University Press, 1965), p. 134.

22. McKay, *Vergil's Italy*, pp. 76-77.

23. Smith, *Elizabethan Poetry*, p. 323.

Chapter 2: Spenser

1. In *English Literary Criticism: The Renaissance*, ed. O. B. Hardison, Jr. (New York: Appleton-Century-Crofts, Goldentree Books, 1963), p. 167.

2. Citations from Spenser and E. K. in my text are to *The Complete Poetical Works of Spenser*, ed. R. E. Neil Dodge (Boston: Houghton Mifflin Co., Cambridge Edition, 1936).

3. William Nelson, *The Poetry of Edmund Spenser* (New York: Columbia University Press, 1963), pp. 30-31.

4. For discussion of *The Shepheardes Calender* along these lines see Patrick Cullen, *Spenser, Marvell, and Renaissance Pastoral* (Cambridge, Mass: Harvard University Press, 1970). Cullen's book was especially helpful in the present study.

5. A. C. Hamilton, "The Argument of Spenser's *Shepheardes Calender*" (1956); reprinted in *Spenser: A Collection of Critical Essays*, ed. Harry Berger (Englewood Cliffs, N.J.: Prentice-Hall, Inc., 1968), p. 34.

6. *Myths, Dreams, and Mysteries*, trans. Philip Mairet (New York: Harper & Row, 1960), pp. 35-36, 52.

7. Alice S. Miskimin, *The Renaissance Chaucer* (New Haven, Conn.: Yale University Press, 1975), p. 264.

8. *The Burden of the Past and the English Poet* (Cambridge, Mass.: Harvard University Press, 1970), p. 43.

9. Patrick Cullen, "Initiation and Metamorphoses: The Golden-Age Eclogue in Spenser, Milton, and Marvell," *PMLA* 84 (1969): 1565.

10. *Homo Ludens: A Study of the Play-Element in Culture* (London: Routledge & Kegan Paul, 1949), pp. 180-81.

11. Hardison, ed., *English Literary Criticism*, p. 104.

12. Cullen, *Spenser, Marvell, and Renaissance Pastoral*, p. 105.

13. Columbia edition of *The Works of John Milton*, ed. Frank Allen Patterson (New York: Columbia University Press, 1931-42), 3. 1: 165-66.

14. Cullen, *Spenser, Marvell, and Renaissance Pastoral*, pp. 64-65.

15. Ibid., p. 69.

16. Ibid., p. 70.

17. Peter Bayley, *Edmund Spenser: Prince of Poets* (London: Hutchinson University Library, 1971), p. 35.

18. Hamilton, "The Argument of Spenser's *Shepheardes Calender*," pp. 35.

19. Smith, *Elizabethan Poetry*, p. 37.

20. Cullen, *Spenser, Marvell, and Renaissance Pastoral*, p. 85.

21. Ibid., pp. 91, 111.

22. Smith, *Elizabethan Poetry*, p. 39.

23. Kathleen Williams, *Spenser's World of Glass: A Reading of The Faerie Queene*

(Berkeley and Los Angeles: University of California Press, 1966), p. 203.

24. Isabel G. MacCaffrey, "Allegory and Pastoral in *The Shepheardes Calender*," *English Literary History*, 36 (1969): 99.

25. Smith, *Elizabethan Poetry*, pp. 40-41.

26. I adopt the term *regulative fiction* from Frank Kermode, *The Sense of an Ending: Studies in the Theory of Fiction* (New York: Oxford University Press, 1966).

27. Cullen, *Spenser, Marvell, and Renaissance Pastoral*, p. 122.

28. S. K. Heninger, Jr., "Sidney and Milton: The Poet as Maker," in *Milton and the Line of Vision*, ed. Joseph A. Wittreich, Jr. (Madison: University of Wisconsin Press, 1975), p. 70.

Chapter 3: *The Faerie Queene*

1. Cullen, *Spenser, Marvell, and Renaissance Pastoral*, p. 10.

2. Nelson, *The Poetry of Edmund Spenser*, pp. 121-22.

3. "An Apologie for Poetrie," *English Literary Criticism*, pp. 123-24.

4. Merritt Y. Hughes, *Virgil and Spenser* (Berkeley and Los Angeles: University of California Publications in English, vol. 2, no. 3, 1929), p. 405.

5. "An Apologie for Poetrie," p. 105.'

6. Ibid., p. 112.

7. Ibid., pp. 123-24.

8. Smith, *Elizabethan Poetry*, p. 327.

9. A. C. Hamilton, "Spenser's Pastoral," *ELH* 33 (1966): 518-31.

10. A. C. Hamilton, *The Structure of Allegory in The Faerie Queene* (Oxford: At the Clarendon Press, 1961), p. 39.

11. Nelson, *The Poetry of Edmund Spenser*, pp. 169-70.

12. Northrop Frye, *Fables of Identity: Studies in Poetic Mythology* (New York: Harcourt Brace, 1963), p. 78.

13. Williams, *Spenser's World of Glass*, p. 31.

14. Nelson, *The Poetry of Edmund Spenser*, pp. 176-77.

15. Frye, *Fables of Identity*, p. 80.

16. Kathleen Williams, "Milton, Greatest Spenserian," in *Milton and the Line of Vision*, ed. Joseph A. Wittreich, Jr. (Madison: University of Wisconsin Press, 1975), p. 50.

17. Joseph E. Duncan, *Milton's Earthly Paradise: A Historical Study of Eden* (Minneapolis: University of Minnesota Press, 1972), pp. 26-28.

18. Williams, *Spenser's World of Glass*, p. 72.

19. Nelson, *The Poetry of Edmund Spenser*, p. 186.

20. I am indebted for the reading of this episode to C. S. Lewis, *The Allegory of Love: A Study in Medieval Tradition* (London: Oxford University Press, 1938), pp. 325-26.

21. Williams, *Spenser's World of Glass*, pp. 76-77.

22. Maurice Evans, *Spenser's Anatomy of Heroism* (Cambridge: Cambridge University Press, 1970), p. 152.

23. Thomas P. Roche, Jr., *The Kindly Flame: A Study of the Third and Fourth Books of Spenser's Faerie Queene* (Princeton, N.J.: Princeton University Press, 1965), p. 102.

24. Williams, *Spenser's World of Glass*, p. 103.

25. Nelson, *The Poetry of Edmund Spenser*, p. 222.

26. Graham Hough, *A Preface to The Faerie Queene* (London: Gerald Duckworth & Co., 1962), p. 178.

27. A. Kent Hieatt, *Chaucer, Spenser, Milton: Mythopeic Continuities and Transformations* (Montreal: McGill-Queen's University Press, 1975), p. 97.

28. Roche, *The Kindly Flame*, pp. 130-31.

29. Ibid., pp. 167-68.

30. Ibid., p. 183.

31. Lewis, *The Allegory of Love*, p. 351.

32. Nelson, *The Poetry of Edmund Spenser*, p. 287.

33. Arnold Williams, *Flower on a Lowly Stalk: The Sixth Book of The Faerie Queene* (East Lansing: Michigan State University, 1967), p. 58.

34. Williams, *Spenser's World of Glass*, p. 212.

35. Marinelli, *Pastoral*, pp. 69-70.

36. *Spenser's Image of Nature: Wild Man and Shepherd in "The Faerie Queene"* (New Haven, Conn.: Yale University Press, 1966), p. 2.

37. Williams, *Flower on a Lowly Stalk*, pp. 56-57.

38. Ibid., p. 83.

39. Williams, "Milton, Greatest Spenserian," p. 42.

40. Frye, *Fables of Identity*, p. 80.

41. Nelson, *The Poetry of Edmund Spenser*, p. 300.

42. Bayley, *Edmund Spenser: Prince of Poets*, p. 98.

Chapter 4: Milton

1. Quoted in Hughes, *Virgil and Spenser*, p. 319.

2. *The Works of John Milton*, 3. 1: 237.

3. Citations from Milton's poetry in my text are to *Complete Poems and Major Prose*, ed. Merritt Y. Hughes (New York: The Odyssey Press, 1957).

4. Winifred Maynard, ed. "The Nativity Ode," in *John Milton: Odes, Pastorals, Masques*, ed. John Broadbent (Cambridge: University Press, 1975), p. 9.

5. Renato Poggioli, *The Oaten Flute: Essays on Pastoral Poetry and the Pastoral Ideal* (Cambridge, Mass.: Harvard University, 1975), p. 129.

6. Ibid., p. 127.

7. A. C. Hamilton alludes to this work in "The Argument of Spenser's *Shepheardes Calender*," pp. 31-32. *The Works of Michael Drayton*, ed. J. William Hebel (Oxford: University Press, 1932), 2: 517.

8. Cullen, "Initiation and Metamorphoses," *PMLA* 84: 1567.

9. Maynard, "The Nativity Ode," pp. 11-12.

10. Cullen, "Initiation and Metamorphoses," *PMLA* 84: 1566.

11. *The Works of John Milton*, 12: 247-49.

12. Ibid.

13. Lorna Sage, ed. "L'Allegro and Il Penseroso," in *John Milton: Odes, Pastorals, Masques*, ed. John Broadbent (Cambridge: University Press, 1965), p. 65.

14. S. K. Heninger, Jr., "Sidney and Milton: The Poet as Maker," in *Milton and the*

Line of Vision, ed. Joseph A. Wittreich, Jr. (Madison: University of Wisconsin Press, 1975),p. 80.

15. Rosemond Tuve, "Structural Figures of *L'Allegro* and *Il Penseroso*" (1957); reprinted in *Milton: Modern Essays in Criticism*, ed. Arthur E. Barker (New York: Oxford University Press, A Galaxy Book, 1965), p. 64.

16. Don Cameron Allen, *The Harmonious Vision: Studies in Milton's Poetry* (Baltimore, Md.: The Johns Hopkins Press, 1954), p. 8.

17. Bridget Gellert Lyons, *Voices of Melancholy: Studies in Literary Treatments of Melancholy in Renaissance England* (London: Routledge & Kegan Paul, 1971), p. 152.

18. Allen, *The Harmonious Vision*, p. 10.

19. Harold E. Toliver, *Pastoral Forms and Attitudes* (Berkeley and Los Angeles: University of California Press, 1971), p. 156.

20. Lyons, *Voices of Melancholy*, p. 153.

21. Allen, *The Harmonious Vision*, p. 19.

22. Sage, "L'Allegro and Il Penseroso," p. 69.

23. John M. Wallace, "Milton's *Arcades*" (1959); reprinted in *Milton: Modern Essays in Criticism*, ed. Arthur E. Barker (New York: Oxford University Press, A Galaxy Book, 1965, p. 81.

24. *Lives of the English Poets* (New York: E. P. Dutton & Co., Everyman's Library, 1950), 1: 99.

25. Smith, *Elizabethan Poetry*, p. 292.

26. *The Works of John Milton*, 4: 310.

27. Peter Mendes, ed. "Arcades and Comus," in *John Milton: Odes, Pastorals, Masques*, ed. John Broadbent (Cambridge: University Press, 1965), p. 102.

28. Ibid., p. 106.

29. John Hollander, "Milton's Renewed Song"(1961); reprinted in *Milton: Modern Essays in Criticism*, ed. Arthur E. Barker (New York: Oxford University Press, A Galaxy Book, 1965), p. 46.

30. Ibid., p. 48.

31. For a fuller discussion of the brothers, see Gale H. Carrithers, "Milton's Ludlow Mask: From Chaos to Community" (1966); reprinted in *Critical Essays on Milton from ELH* (Baltimore, Md.: The Johns Hopkins Press, 1969), esp. pp. 105-11.

32. Roger B. Wilkenfeld, "The Seat at the Center: An Interpretation of *Comus*" (1966); reprinted in *Critical Essays on Milton from ELH* (Baltimore, Md.: The Johns Hopkins Press, 1969), p. 136.

33. The Lady's condition recalls Romans 7:23: "But I see another law in my members, warring against the law of my mind, and bringing me into captivity to the law of sin which is in my members."

34. Edgar Wind, *Pagan Mysteries in the Renaissance* (New York: W. W. Norton & Co., 1958), p. 73.

35. Ibid., p. 69.

36. *The Works of John Milton*, 12: 29.

37. Harold Bloom, *The Anxiety of Influence: A Theory of Poetry* (New York: Oxford University Press, 1973), p. 15.

38. "'Eager Thought': Dialectic in *Lycidas*" (1962); reprinted in *Milton: Modern*

Essays in Criticism, ed. Arthur E. Barker (New York: Oxford University Press, a Galaxy Book, 1965), p. 113.

39. According to Arthur E. Barker's structural analysis of the poem, *Lycidas* consists of an introduction and conclusion, and three parallel movements in which Lycidas is lamented as poet-shepherd, priest-shepherd, and poet-priest-shepherd. See "The Pattern of Milton's 'Nativity Ode'" (1940); reprinted in *Milton: Modern Judgements,* ed. Alan Rudrum (London: Macmillan, 1968), p. 48.

40. Poggioli, *The Oaten Flute,* p. 89.

41. Josephine Miles, "The Primary Language of *Lycidas*" (1948); reprinted in *Milton's Lycidas: The Tradition and the Poem,* ed. C. A. Patrides (New York: Holt, Rinehart and Winston, 1961), p. 98.

42. Putnam, *Virgil's Pastoral Art,* p. 23.

43. Allen, *The Harmonious Vision,* p. 61.

44. Cleanth Brooks and John E. Hardy, "Essays in Analysis: *Lycidas*" (1951); reprinted in *Milton's Lycidas: The Tradition and The Poem,* ed. C. A. Patrides (New York: Holt, Rinehart and Winston, 1961), p. 151.

Chapter 5: *Paradise Lost* (I)

1. Woodhouse, *The Heavenly Muse,* p. 96.

2. "An Apologie for Poetrie," p. 123.

3. *The Works of John Milton,* 3. 1: 237.

4. John M. Steadman, *Milton and the Renaissance Hero* (Oxford: Clarendon Press, 1967), p.xvi.

5. *The Works of John Milton,* 3. 1: 239.

6. Harding, *The Club of Hercules,* p. 51.

7. Bloom, *The Anxiety of Influence,* p. 30.

8. *The Works of John Milton,* 3. 1: 304.

9. Arnold Stein, *Answerable Style: Essays on "Paradise Lost"* (Seattle: University of Washington Press, 1953), pp. 17-37.

10. Ibid., p. 23.

11. Duncan, *Milton's Earthly Paradise,* p. 266.

12. David Daiches, *Milton* (London: Hutchinson University Library, 1957), p. 180.

13. Duncan, *Milton's Earthly Paradise,* p. 253.

14. *Milton's Pastoral Vision: An Approach to Paradise Lost* (Chicago: University of Chicago Press, 1971), p. 83.

15. Stein, *Answerable Style,* p. 62.

16. C. S. Lewis, *A Preface to Paradise Lost* (London: Oxford University Press, 1942), pp. 47, 49.

17. Knott, *Milton's Pastoral Vision,* p. 120.

18. William G. Madsen, "Earth the Shadow of Heaven: Typological Symbolism in *Paradise Lost*" (1960); reprinted in *Milton: Modern Essays in Criticism,* ed. Arthur E. Barker (New York: Oxford University Press, A Galaxy Book, 1965), pp. 255-56.

19. Duncan, *Milton's Earthly Paradise,* pp. 152-53.

20. Isabel G. MacCaffrey, *"Paradise Lost" as "Myth"* (Cambridge, Mass.: Harvard University Press, 1959), p. 77.

21. William G. Riggs, *The Christian Poet in "Paradise Lost"* (Berkeley and Los Angeles: University of California Press, 1972), p. 73.

22. John Carey and Alastair Fowler, eds., *The Poems of John Milton* (London: Longman Annotated English Poets Series, 1968), p. 679n.

23. Daiches, *Milton*, p. 197.

24. Lawrence Babb, *The Moral Cosmos of "Paradise Lost"* (East Lansing: Michigan State University, 1970), p. 40.

25. George Williamson, "The Education of Adam" (1963); reprinted in *Milton: Modern Essays in Criticism*, ed. Arthur E. Barker (New York: Oxford University Press, A Galaxy Book, 1965), p. 291.

Chapter 6: *Paradise Lost* (II)

1. Williamson, "The Education of Adam," p. 298.

2. Woodhouse, *The Heavenly Muse*, p. 265.

3. Carey and Fowler, eds. *The Poems of John Milton*, p. 878n.

4. Anne Davidson Ferry, *Milton's Epic Voice: The Narrator in Paradise Lost* (Cambridge, Mass.: Harvard University Press, 1963), pp. 57-58.

5. Carey and Fowler, eds. *The Poems of John Milton*, p. 919n.

6. Joseph H. Summers, *The Muse's Method: An Introduction to Paradise Lost* (Cambridge, Mass.: Harvard University Press, 1962), p. 106.

7. "The Style of Milton's Epic" (1963); reprinted in *Milton: Modern Essays in Criticism*, ed. Arthur E. Barker (New York: Oxford University Press, A Galaxy Book, 1965), p. 379.

8. Summers, *The Muse's Method*, p. 215.

9. Duncan, *Milton's Earthly Paradise*, p. 262.

List of Works Cited

Allen, Don Cameron. *The Harmonious Vision: Studies in Milton's Poetry*. Baltimore, Md.: The Johns Hopkins Press, 1954.

Babb, Lawrence. *The Moral Cosmos of "Paradise Lost."* East Lansing: Michigan State University, 1970.

Barker, Arthur E.,ed. *Milton: Modern Essays in Criticism*. New York: Oxford University Press, A Galaxy Book, 1965.

– – –. "The Pattern of Milton's 'Nativity Ode.' " In *Milton: Modern Judgements*, edited by Alan Rudrum. London: Macmillan, 1968. Pp. 44-57.

Bate, Walter Jackson. *The Burden of the Past and the English Poet*. Cambridge, Mass.: Harvard University Press, 1970.

Bayley, Peter. *Edmund Spenser: Prince of Poets*. London: Hutchinson University Library, 1971.

Bloom, Harold. *The Anxiety of Influence: A Theory of Poetry*. New York: Oxford University Press, 1973.

Broadbent, John, ed. *John Milton: Odes, Pastorals, Masques*. Cambridge: University Press, 1975.

Brooks, Cleanth, and Hardy, Thomas E. "Essays in Analysis: *Lycidas*." In *Milton's Lycidas: The Tradition and the Poem*, edited by C. A. Patrides. New York: Holt, Rinehart and Winston, 1961. Pp. 136-52.

Carey, John, and Fowler, Alastair, eds. *The Poems of John Milton*. London: Longman Annotated English Poets Series, 1968.

Carrithers, Gale H. "Milton's Ludlow *Mask*: From Chaos to Community." In *Critical Essays on Milton from ELH*. Baltimore, Md.: The John Hopkins Press, 1969: 103-122.

Cheney, Donald. *Spenser's Image of Nature: Wild Man and Shepherd in "The Faerie Queene."* New Haven, Conn.: Yale University Press, 1966.

Cullen, Patrick. "Initiation and Metamorphoses: The Golden-Age Eclogue in Spenser, Milton, and Marvell." *PMLA* 84 (1969): 1559-70.

— — —. *Spenser, Marvell, and Renaissance Pastoral.* Cambridge, Mass.: Harvard University Press, 1970.

Curtius, Ernst R. *European Literature and the Latin Middle Ages.* Translated by Willard R. Trask. London: Routledge & Kegan Paul, 1953.

Daiches, David. *Milton.* London: Hutchinson University Library, 1957.

Drayton, Michael. *The Works of Michael Drayton.* Edited by J. William Hebel. 5 vols. Oxford: University Press, 1932.

Dudley, D. R., ed. *Virgil.* London: Routledge & Kegan Paul, 1969.

Duncan, Joseph E. *Milton's Earthly Paradise: A Historical Study of Eden.* Minneapolis: University of Minnesota Press, 1972.

Eliade, Mircea. *Myths, Dreams, and Mysteries.* Translated by Philip Mairet. New York: Harper & Row, 1960.

Evans, Maurice. *Spenser's Anatomy of Heroism.* Cambridge: University Press, 1970.

Ferry, Anne Davidson. *Milton's Epic Voice: The Narrator in Paradise Lost.* Cambridge, Mass.: Harvard University Press, 1963.

Fish, Stanley E. *Self-Consuming Artifacts: The Experience of Seventeenth-Century Literature.* Berkeley and Los Angeles: University of California Press, 1972.

Frye, Northrop. *Fables of Identity: Studies in Poetic Mythology.* New York: Harcourt Press, 1972.

Hamilton, A. C. *The Structure of Allegory in The Faerie Queene.* Oxford: At the Clarendon Press, 1961.

— — —. "The Argument of Spenser's *Shepheardes Calendar.*" In *Spenser: A Collection of Critical Essays,* edited by Harry Berger. Englewood Cliffs, N.J.: Prentice-Hall, Inc., 1968. Pp. 30-39.

— — —. "Spenser's Pastoral," *English Literary History,* 33 (1966): 518-31.

Harding, Davis P. *The Club of Hercules: Studies in the Classical Background of Paradise Lost.* Urbana: The University of Illinois Press, 1962.

Hardison, O. B., Jr., ed. *English Literary Criticism: The Renais-*

sance. New York: Appleton-Century-Crofts, Goldentree Books, 1963.

Heninger, S. K., Jr. "Sidney and Milton: The Poet as Maker." In *Milton and the Line of Vision*, edited by Joseph A. Wittreich, Jr. Madison: University of Wisconsin Press, 1975. Pp. 57-96.

Hieatt, A. Kent. *Chaucer, Spenser, Milton: Mythopoeic Continuities*. Montreal: McGill-Queen's University Press, 1975.

Hollander, John. "Milton's Renewed Song." In *Milton: Modern Essays in Criticism*, edited by Arthur E. Barker. New York: Oxford University Press, A Galaxy Book, 1965. Pp. 43-57.

Hough, Graham. *A Preface to The Faerie Queene*. London: Gerald Duckworth & Co., 1962.

Hughes, Merritt Y. *Virgil and Spenser*. Berkeley and Los Angeles: University of California Publications in English, vol. 2, no. 3, 1929. Pp. 263-418.

Huizinga, Johan. *Homo Ludens: A Study of the Play-Element in Culture*. London: Routledge & Kegan Paul, 1949.

Johnson, Samuel. *Lives of the English Poets*. 2 vols. New York: E. P. Dutton & Co., Everyman's Library, 1950.

Kermode, Frank. *The Sense of an Ending: Studies in the Theory of Fiction*. New York: Oxford University Press, 1966.

Knott, John R., Jr. *Milton's Pastoral Vision: An Approach to Paradise Lost*. Chicago: University of Chicago Press, 1971.

Lawry, Jon S. " 'Eager Thought': Dialectic in *Lycidas*." In *Milton: Modern Essays in Criticism*, edited by Arthur E. Barker. New York: Oxford University Press, A Galaxy Book, 1965. Pp. 112-24.

Lewis, C. S. *The Allegory of Love: A Study in Medieval Tradition*. London: Oxford University Press, 1938.

– – –. *A Preface to Paradise Lost*. London: Oxford University Press, 1942.

Lyons, Bridget Gellert. *Voices of Melancholy: Studies in the Literary Treatments of Melancholy in Renaissance England*. London: Routledge & Kegan Paul, 1971.

MacCaffrey, Isabel G. "Allegory and Pastoral in *The Shepheardes Calender*." *English Literary History*, 36 (1969): 88-109.

– – –. *"Paradise Lost" as "Myth"*. Cambridge, Mass.: Harvard University Press, 1959.

McKay, Alexander G. *Vergil's Italy*. Greenwich, Conn.: New York Graphic Society, 1970.

Madsen, William G. "Earth the Shadow of Heaven: Typological Symbolism in *Paradise Lost*." In *Milton: Modern Essays in Criticism*, edited by Arthur E. Barker. New York: Oxford University Press, A Galaxy Book, 1965. Pp. 246-63.

Marinelli, Peter V. *Pastoral*. London: Methuen & Co., 1971.

Maynard, Winifred, ed. "The Nativity Ode." In *John Milton: Odes, Pastorals, Masques*, edited by John Broadbent. Cambridge: University Press, 1975. Pp. 6-27.

Mendes, Peter, ed. "Arcades and Comus." In *John Milton: Odes, Pastorals, Masques*, edited by John Broadbent. Cambridge: University Press, 1975. Pp. 87-170.

Miles, Josephine. "The Primary Language of *Lycidas*." In *Milton's Lycidas: The Tradition and the Poem*, edited by C. A. Patrides. New York: Holt, Rinehart and Winston, 1961. Pp. 95-100.

Milton, John. *Complete Poems and Major Prose*. Edited by Merritt Y. Hughes. New York: The Odyssey Press, 1957.

— — —. *The Works of John Milton*. Edited by Frank Allen Patterson. 20 vols. New York: Columbia University Press, 1931-42.

Miskimin, Alice S. *The Renaissance Chaucer*. New Haven, Conn.: Yale University Press, 1975.

Nelson, William. *The Poetry of Edmund Spenser*. New York: Columbia University Press, 1963.

Otis, Brooks. "The Originality of the Aeneid." In *Virgil*, edited by D. R. Dudley. London: Routledge & Kegan Paul, 1969. Pp. 27-66.

Panofsky, Erwin. "*Et in Arcadia Ego*: Poussin and the Elegiac Tradition," In *Meaning in the Visual Arts*. New York: Doubleday & Co., 1955. Pp. 295-320.

Patrides, C. A., ed. *Milton's Lycidas: The Tradition and the Poem*. New York: Holt, Rinehart and Winston, 1961.

Pearce, Donald R. "The Style of Milton's Epic." In *Milton: Modern Essays in Criticism*, edited by Arthur E. Barker.

Perret, Jacques. "The *Georgics*," *Virgil: A Collection of Critical Essays*. Edited by Steele Commager. Englewood Cliffs, N.J.: Prentice-Hall, Inc., 1966. Pp. 28-40.

Poggioli, Renato. *The Oaten Flute: Essays on Pastoral Poetry and the Pastoral Ideal*. Cambridge, Mass.: Harvard University Press, 1975.

Putnam, Michael C. J. *The Poetry of the Aeneid: Four Studies in Imaginative Unity and Design*. Cambridge, Mass.: Harvard University Press, 1965.

— — —. *Virgil's Pastoral Art: Studies in the Eclogues*, Princeton, N.J.: Princeton University Press, 1970.

Puttenham, George. "The Arte of English Poesie." In *English Literary Criticism: The Renaissance*, edited by O. B. Hardison, Jr., New York: Appleton-Century-Crofts, Goldentree Books, 1963.

Riggs, William G. *The Christian Poet in "Paradise Lost."* Berkeley and Los Angeles: University of California Press, 1972.

Roche, Thomas P., Jr. *The Kindly Flame: A Study of the Third and Fourth Books of Spenser's Faerie Queene*. Princeton, N.J.: Princeton University Press, 1965.

Rosenmeyer, Thomas J. *The Green Cabinet: Theocritus and the European Pastoral Lyric*. Berkeley and Los Angeles: University of California Press, 1969.

Rudrum, Alan, ed. *Milton: Modern Judgements*. London: Macmillan, 1968.

Sage, Lorna, ed. "L'Allegro and Il Penseroso." In *John Milton: Odes, Pastorals, Masques*, edited by John Broadbent. Cambridge: University Press. 1965. Pp. 65-86.

Sidney, Philip. "An Apologie for Poetrie." In *English Literary Criticism: The Renaissance*, edited by O. B. Hardison, Jr. New York: Appleton-Century-Crofts, Goldentree Books, 1963.

Smith, Hallett. *Elizabethan Poetry: A Study in Conventions, Meaning, and Expression*. Cambridge, Mass.: Harvard University Press, 1952.

Spenser, Edmund. *The Complete Works of Spenser*. Edited by R. E. Neil Dodge. Boston: Houghton Mifflin Co., Cambridge Edition, 1936.

Steadman, John M. *Milton and the Renaissance Hero*. Oxford: Clarendon Press, 1967.

Stein, Arnold. *Answerable Style: Essays on "Paradise Lost."* Seattle: University of Washington Press, 1953.

Summers, Joseph H. *The Muse's Method: An Introduction to Paradise Lost*. Cambridge, Mass.: Harvard University Press, 1962.

Toliver, Harold E. *Pastoral Forms and Attitudes*. Berkeley and Los Angeles: University of California Press, 1971.

Tuve, Rosemond. "Structural Figures of *L'Allegro* and *Il Penseroso*." In *Milton: Modern Essays in Criticism*, edited by Arthur E. Barker. New York: Oxford University Press, A Galaxy Book, 1965. Pp. 58-76.

Virgil. *Eclogues, Georgics, Aeneid, and Minor Poems*. Translated by H. R. Fairclough. 2 vols. Cambridge, Mass.: Loeb Classical Library, 1934.

Waith, Eugene M. *The Herculean Hero in Marlowe, Chapman, Shakespeare, and Dryden*. New York; Columbia University Press, 1962.

Wallace, John M. "Milton's *Arcades*." In *Milton: Modern Essays in Criticism*, edited by Arthur E. Barker. New York: Oxford University Press, A Galaxy Book, 1965. Pp. 77-87.

Wilkenfeld, Roger B. "The Seat at the Center: An Interpretation of *Comus*." In *Critical Essays from ELH*. Baltimore, Md.: The Johns Hopkins Press, 1969. Pp. 123-50.

Williams, Arnold. *Flower on a Lowly Stalk: The Sixth Book of The Faerie Queene*. East Lansing: Michigan State University Press, 1967.

Williams, Kathleen. *Spenser's World of Glass: A Reading of The Faerie Queene*. Berkeley and Los Angeles: University of California Press, 1966.

— — —. "Milton, Greatest Spenserian." In *Milton and the Line of Vision*, edited by Joseph A. Wittreich, Jr. Madison: University of Wisconsin Press, 1975. Pp. 25-56.

Williams, Raymond. *The Country and the City*. London: Chatto & Windus, 1973.

Williamson, George. "The Education of Adam." In *Milton: Modern Essays in Criticism*, edited by Arthur E. Barker. New York: Oxford University Press, A Galaxy Book, 1965. Pp. 284-307.

Wind, Edgar. *Pagan Mysteries in the Renaissance*. New York: W. W. Norton & Co., 1958.

Wittreich, Joseph A., Jr. *Milton and the Line of Vision*. Madison: University of Wisconsin Press, 1975.

Woodhouse, A. S. P. *The Heavenly Muse: A Preface to Milton*, Edited by Hugh MacCallum. Toronto: University of Toronto Press, 1972.

Index

284